PAUL
TILLICH

Makers of the Modern Theological Mind

Bob E. Patterson, Editor

KARL BARTH by *David L. Mueller*
DIETRICH BONHOEFFER by *Dallas M. Roark*
RUDOLF BULTMANN by *Morris Ashcraft*
CHARLES HARTSHORNE by *Alan Gragg*
WOLFHART PANNENBERG by *Don Olive*
TEILHARD DE CHARDIN by *Doran McCarty*
EMIL BRUNNER by *J. Edward Humphrey*
MARTIN BUBER by *Stephen M. Panko*
SÖREN KIERKEGAARD by *Elmer H. Duncan*
REINHOLD NIEBUHR by *Bob E. Patterson*
H. RICHARD NIEBUHR by *Lonnie D. Kliever*
GERHARD VON RAD by *James L. Crenshaw*
ANDERS NYGREN by *Thor Hall*
FRIEDRICH SCHLEIERMACHER by *C. W. Christian*
HANS KÜNG by *John Kiwiet*
IAN T. RAMSEY by *William B. Williamson*
CARL F. H. HENRY by *Bob E. Patterson*

Makers of the Modern Theological Mind

PAUL TILLICH

John P. Newport

Edited by Bob E. Patterson

Word Books, Publisher, Waco, Texas

PAUL TILLICH
Copyright © 1984 by Word, Incorporated

Library of Congress Cataloging in Publication Data

Newport, John P., 1917–
    Paul Tillich.

    (Makers of the modern theological mind)
    Bibliography: p.
    Includes indexes.
    1. Tillich, Paul, 1886–1965. I. Title. II. Series.
BX4827.T53N48   1984   230′.044′0924   84–13123
ISBN 0–8499–2952–0

Printed in the United States of America

Dedicated
to

ROBERT and RUTH GLAZE

and

HOWARD and MARY D. WALSH

Friends of many years who in
their own distinctive way have sought
to be a bridge between
Christianity and culture

Contents

7

Editor's Preface

Who are the thinkers that have shaped Christian theology in our time? This series tries to answer that question by providing a reliable guide to the ideas of the men who have significantly charted the theological seas of our century. In the current revival of theology, these books will give a new generation the opportunity to be exposed to significant minds. They are not meant, however, to be a substitute for a careful study of the original works of these makers of the modern theological mind.

This series is not for the lazy. Each major theologian is examined carefully and critically—his life, his theological method, his most germinal ideas, his weaknesses as a thinker, his place in the theological spectrum, and his chief contribution to the climate of theology today. The books are written with the assumption that laymen will read them and enter into the theological dialogue that is so necessary to the church as a whole. At the same time they are carefully enough designed to give assurance to a Ph.D. student in theology preparing for his preliminary exams.

Each author in the series is a professional scholar and theologian in his own right. All are specialists on, and in some cases have studied with, the theologians about whom they write. Welcome to the series.

BOB E. PATTERSON, Editor
Baylor University

Preface

The writing of this book has its roots in a particular theological and intellectual odyssey. As a young minister just out of seminary with a doctorate in biblical studies, I became minister of a college church. Soon I realized the importance of relating the biblical faith to contemporary culture. By background and temperament I could not ignore the cultural context in which the Christian message must be communicated. I knew that there must be a way to appropriate that which is valid in modern learning without capitulating to modernity. In my ministry I did not want to force educated people to think that they had to choose between the historic Christian faith and the constructive aspects of modern learning.

To seek help in this faith/culture concern, I left my pastorate to study at the Universities of Edinburgh, Basel, and Zürich. Paul Tillich was the object of discussion, pro and con, in many classes and lectures in these three universities.

Returning to the United States, I discovered that the best resources in the United States for my Ph.D. dissertation research were to be found in New York City at Union Theological Seminary. It was here that I had my first course with Paul Tillich. I studied carefully the detailed syllabus of his system. His German-idealist-existentialist approach was quite different from that to which I had been exposed in Edinburgh, Basel, and Zürich. But I immediately recognized in Tillich a powerfully imaginative theological mind. Despite the difficulty of his thought, I became convinced that Tillich was a person of unique background and immense learning who had much to contribute to those who were seeking to integrate theology and the worlds of art, science, world religions, and philosophy.

In the late 1950s I was awarded a Rockefeller Seatlantic grant to study the relation between religion and culture at Harvard Divinity School. Here I met Tillich again. I saw his ability to communicate with Harvard undergraduates in his popular "Harvard Yard" courses on "Religion and Culture" and "History and the Kingdom of God." In advanced seminars I was impressed with his creative interpretation of the history of theology and philosophy. I came to understand the historical roots of his thought in his seminars on nineteenth-century German Idealism and on the Protestant Reformation. I recognized his appeal to laypersons in his sermons in Boston churches. On several occasions I heard him in dialogue sessions where he pushed so-called secular questions to their theological and philosophical depths. I was impressed with his ability to synthesize.

It was also at Harvard that I realized to what a great extent Tillich's theology was interwoven with his own personal intellectual-spiritual history and his dramatic life experiences. For me, there was much to be learned from Tillich although my approach would have to be both yes and no to his thought and lifestyle.

Tillich's significance for divergent segments of American theological life was recognized by the fact that he became the subject of the Annual Wheaton College (Illinois) Philosophy Conference. In view of my personal acquaintance with Tillich and his thought, I was asked to speak at this conference. The present volume had its inception in material prepared for this conference.

My schedule for writing was interrupted when I became a Visiting Professor of Religious Studies at Rice University in Houston and then accepted the position of Chavanne Professor of Religious Studies there. While teaching at Rice I became aware of the impact that Tillich made at the university and in Houston on the occasion of his visits there in the late 1950s and the early 1960s. My interest in Tillich continued as I conducted two graduate seminars at Rice on his thought. I am indebted to the Rice graduate students who positioned and critiqued Tillich's primary works and representative secondary writings about him. The presence of laypersons in these seminars heightened my awareness of their interest in his theological system.

After returning to Southwestern Baptist Theological Seminary as Provost, I continued my study of Tillich by offering a graduate seminar on his thought. I am indebted to the students in this seminar for insightful critiques of Tillich from a more conservative theological perspective.

Since Tillich's death in 1965, a group of scholars, students, and laypersons have formalized their interest in his thought through the organization of the North American Paul Tillich Society. I have found attendance at the annual meeting of this Society, of which I am currently a Director, to be unusually helpful in seeing Tillich and his work in broad perspective. I am indebted to two leaders in this Society, Robert Scharlemann of the University of Virginia and John Carey of Florida State University. Professor Scharlemann not only encouraged me to finish this volume but furnished me his translation of *Paul Tillich* by Carl Heinz Ratschow and his comprehensive bibliography of Tillich's writings before they were published. John Carey has been helpful in discussions regarding the outline of this study and the approach to be used. John and Jane Dillenberger of the Graduate Theological Union in Berkeley have also been helpful, especially in the area of Tillich's "theology of culture."

Niels Nielsen, Jr., long-time chairman of the Department of Religious Studies at Rice University, undergirded my work on Tillich's thought in many ways. At Southwestern Seminary, Yandall Woodfin, Professor of Philosophy of Religion, spent hours constructively evaluating this manuscript. The library personnel at both Rice and Southwestern Seminary provided every needed assistance.

I am especially indebted to Sharon Gritz, my secretary, and Evelyn Smith, my administrative associate. A scholar in her own right, Sharon Gritz has helped in research and typing over a period of four years. I am also indebted to President Russell Dilday of Southwestern Seminary for the constancy of his friendship and encouragement.

If there is any one person who has made this volume possible, it is my wife, Eddie Belle. She, as always, is the one who has helped me the most.

Introduction

A. Purpose and Approach

This is a book for the pastor, theological student, and interested layperson. It will seek to set forth in clear, intelligible form the basic purpose, idea, method, and key concepts of Paul Tillich's theological writings. The life of Tillich will be described in a way designed to provide a background for understanding his thought. His thought will be evaluated in terms of representative criticisms, strengths, and contributions.

There is a large amount of material now available on Paul Tillich in both English and German. For the purposes of this book the emphasis will be on the materials in English or available in English translations.

To achieve an understanding of Tillich, it is important to practice what Kenan Osborne calls willful suspension of disbelief. By this he means that a person must first seek to approach Tillich's theology in an open, willing-to-learn attitude. In other words, a person must first follow Tillich's system as a working model. This approach obviously does not mean that the author will forego criticisms or necessarily fully endorse Tillich's approach.[1]

B. Continuing Interest in Tillich's Life and Thought

There are numerous reasons for the continuing interest in the life and work of Paul Tillich.

1. The revival of popular interest in the life of Paul Tillich. This revival was occasioned by the publication of three Tillich-related biographies within a short period of time in the 1970s. These biographies are *Paulus* by Rollo May,[2] *From Time to Time* by Hannah Tillich,[3] and *Paul Tillich: His Life and Thought* by Wilhelm and Marion Pauck.[4] As a result of the wide circulation of these books, a "Tillich as Person" controversy has arisen which seeks to assess the relevance of his life to his thought.[5]

2. There has also been a renewed scholarly interest in Paul Tillich's thought. A German Paulus Tillich-*Gesellschaft* (1959), a North American Paul Tillich Society (1975), and a French Paul Tillich Association (1978) have been founded to encourage creative scholarship commensurate with Tillich's wide range of interests.[6]

Tillich archives have been established in Germany (University of Marburg) and in the United States (Harvard Divinity School). The massive German edition of his works (*Gesammelte Werke*) has now reached twenty volumes (fourteen main volumes and six supplementary volumes).[7]

The Council on the Study of Religion published in 1977 *A Directory of Systematic Theologians in North America.* Included in this book is a study conducted by the editor, Thor Hall. This study incorporates the response of 554 theologians to a question concerning their major mentor (the person with whom they have affinity of thought and from whom they have drawn significant insights). Tillich ranked in first place as the major influence upon America's theologians.[8]

The study by Thor Hall also sought to identify the books most often referred to as sources for teaching by America's theologians. The study found Tillich's three-volume *Systematic Theology* as the most widely used textbook among North American systematic theologians.[9]

In the matter of doctoral dissertations, it would also appear that no other religious thinker (on the basis of current statistics) has been discussed as much as Paul Tillich. This includes American, British, and German dissertations.[10]

3. The world-wide interest in Socialism and Marxism has revived the study of Tillich's rather extensive analysis and assessment of Marxism made in the 1920s. His writings on Protestantism and Marxism are some of the most elaborate and systematic available.[11]

The recent translation of Tillich's *Socialist Decision* reveals that Tillich foreshadowed in some aspects of his thought the "theology of hope" theologians such as Jürgen Moltmann and Wolfhart Pannenberg.

4. Interest in Tillich continues because there is a renewed concern in the United States for making the Christian faith meaningful for modern readers, especially young people. Despite objections to many of his methods, people continue to study Tillich because he sought to show how the Christian message meets people's perennial problems.

In the post-neoorthodox period, there is a renewed interest in *Christian humanism*. In keeping with Tillich's Christian humanism is his attempt to relate philosophical eros to Christian agape. In fact, a number of theologians and art critics, such as David Tracy, Langdon Gilkey, and Nathan Scott, continue to find validity in Tillich's method of correlation which believes that philosophy and culture furnish the questions, and Christian theology provides the answers.[12]

5. In the nineteenth century there was an emphasis on the correlation between philosophy (ontology) and the Christian faith. This emphasis has been revived by the affirmation that the Christian faith cannot finally avoid a philosophical or ontological framework. Such developments have stimulated interest in Tillich's ontological approach to theology. Closely related to this renewal of interest in ontology is a growing appreciation for Tillich's doctrine of mystical participation in ontological reality through Christ.

Part One

Paul Tillich's Life and Perspective

I. Paul Tillich: Life of an Identifying and Participating Philosophical Theologian

Introduction

Wilhelm Pauck suggests that there are two kinds of thinkers: autobiographical and impersonal or objective. Paul, Augustine, Luther and Tillich are seen as autobiographical thinkers while Thomas Aquinas is seen as one of the more impersonal thinkers.

Paul Tillich is an involved, existential and empathetic philosophical theologian. His thought tends to be an immediate expression of his own complex personal pilgrimage. Tillich identified with the problems of his generation in an extremely personal way. He sought to work out the problems of his generation as his destiny. There is a unity of Tillich's thought and his life and destiny. It can readily be seen, therefore, that some knowledge of Tillich's life is necessary to understand his thought.

Tillich himself spells out the importance of his life for his thought in major autobiographical essays. The first is entitled *On the Boundary*. Others constitute introductions to *The Interpretation of History*, *The Protestant Era*, and *My Search for Absolutes*. Another is found in the "Autobiographical Reflections" section of the 1952 volume on *The Theology of Paul Tillich* edited by Kegley and Bretall.[1]

For the purposes of this study, Tillich's life can be divided into five periods.

A. *Life before World War I (1886–1914)*

The early period of Tillich's life, a time when he was steeped in nineteenth-century German culture, can be further divided into the period of
his childhood and early youth (1886–1904) and the period of his university
and early professional years (1904–1918).

1. *Childhood and early youth (1886–1904)*. On the surface the essential
facts of these early years of Tillich's life appear as uneventful. He was
born on 20 August 1886 in the small village of Starzeddel. Today a part
of Poland, in 1886 it was in the province of Brandenburg in eastern Germany. His father was the pastor of the Evangelical Church of Prussia in
the village. When Tillich was five years of age, in 1891, his father became
superintendent of the diocese of Schönfleiss-Neumark in the same province
of Brandenburg. As Tillich's home during his childhood years, this town
of Schönfleiss with its medieval walls made deep impressions on him. During
these early years, at the age of twelve, Tillich went to near-by Königsburg
for two years to attend a *Gymnasium,* an academic high school. In 1898
Tillich's father was called to a church in Berlin and later took over an
important administrative post within the Prussian territorial church.[2] The
death of his mother in 1903 made a deep impact on Tillich's life. He
attended a Gymnasium in Berlin until he was graduated in 1904.

In Tillich's autobiographical writings he describes the joys and tensions
of his early life. For example, he had a deep appreciation for his father
who was a leading Lutheran pastor. From his father he gained security
and a love of Greek philosophy. His father also contributed meditative
influences with an emphasis on soberness, duty and authority. These were
characteristics of the eastern or Prussian area of Germany.

Tillich rested secure in the love of his mother during his early years.
She came from the Rhineland, in western Germany, with its lively "democratic" and more progressive and sensuous perspectives. According to Rollo
May, Frau Tillich's premature death at the age of forty-three when Paulus
was seventeen deepened Tillich's identity crisis.[3]

In later life Tillich was to be torn between the authoritarianism and
conservatism of his patriarchal father and the more open and Dionysian
influences of his mother. Tillich confesses that his lifelong struggle against
traditional authority was rooted to some extent in his struggle with his
patriarchal father.

Though he played with the children of the common school, his father's
position and contacts and Tillich's own transfer to the Gymnasium set
him apart from the other children of the town.[4] He was also set apart
because he was stimulated quite early by his philosophically interested
father to an intense interest in philosophical books and a ceaseless occupa-
tion with "ultimate questions."[5] His unique status was further augmented

by his early study of Latin and Greek. In his studies at a second Gymnasium in Berlin he spent much time in the study of the language, culture, and early philosophy of the Greeks. By the time he entered the University of Berlin, Tillich had a good knowledge of the history of philosophy and a basic acquaintance with Kant and Fichte.[6] He was so unique in his interest in philosophical problems that he was later to be called the "unconditioned" by his fraternity brothers.[7]

During his childhood years Tillich developed a strong feeling for nature and history. He loved the landscapes and the smells and life associated with farming. Tillich also loved the Baltic Sea where his family spent annual vacations. The small medieval towns with their walls, Gothic churches and old houses (which were characteristic of the villages where Tillich lived as a boy) gave him a feeling for history and a sense of participation in the struggles of the past.[8] Later, when his family moved to Berlin, Tillich also developed a love for the life of the great city with its dynamism and extensive possibilities for intellectual and cultural life.[9]

2. *University and early professional years (1904–1914)*. In the German university system of the early twentieth century, a typical program of study for an evangelical pastoral-academic career involved study at several universities. In Tillich's time theological education in Germany was determined by the state universities. After satisfying the state requirements, the candidates were examined by the church. The first years of the academic program were devoted to biblical exegesis and historical studies. Tillich had admirable preparation in Latin and Greek. He later studied Hebrew at Halle. The middle period of the theological studies program concentrated on systematic theology, philosophy of religion and ethics. The last period (usually the fourth year) emphasized practical theology including homiletics, religious education and pastoral ministry. In a letter to Thomas Mann, Tillich described his academic courses as "typical." [10]

Tillich matriculated at Berlin University in the fall of 1904. Then he studied a semester at Tübingen and later four semesters at Halle. At Halle he became a member and presiding officer at the Wingolf fraternity (a Christian, non-dueling organization). Later Tillich was to study at Breslau. In the fall of 1907 he returned to Berlin to prepare for his theological examinations. He passed his first examination in the winter of 1909 before the Berlin-Brandenburg consistory, and his second examination in 1912.

In August, 1912, Tillich was ordained in the Evangelical Church of the Prussian Union. This was a church containing both Lutherans and Calvinists. On the academic side, Tillich received the Ph.D. degree from the University of Breslau in 1910. In 1911 he received his licentiate in theology degree from Halle. This was the highest degree awarded in theology at that time.

Following the conclusion of his theological studies in 1912, Tillich served

briefly as assistant pastor in parishes of the Old Prussian United Church.[11]
During these days the unrest in German society and his experiences in
ministry in the working section of Berlin revealed to him the alienation
of the industrial workers' needs. He knew personally the shock of the
rural persons' migration to the city.[12]

Tillich's personal life during this period involved his first serious romance. The young woman was Grethi Wever. The courtship took place at
Butterfelde where Grethi's father had a large estate. The couple was married
in 1914.

Perhaps the outstanding influence on Tillich during these years was
that of the Wingolf Society, a famous Christian student fellowship at Halle.
He became president. His understanding of the nature and possibilities
of the church was influenced by his experiences in Wingolf. In this fraternity
he learned the importance of membership in a voluntary Christian fellowship
with purpose. He further saw the need for a group to have confessional
creeds upon which it might establish its identity and actions. Tillich honored
the traditions of the society and argued for the orthodox side in an attempt
to sustain its Christian principles and high standards concerning sex.

Even though the Wingolf society was a Christian fellowship and a non-
dueling fraternity, it emphasized martial symbolism and dress and the aca-
demic-Lutheran monarchism of nineteenth-century Germany. The friends
he made in the Wingolf Society provided fellowship and comradeship for
Tillich all of his life.[13]

At Halle, Tillich came under the influence of the young teacher, Fritz
Medicus, who specialized in the philosophy of German Idealists. Medicus
soon recognized Tillich's philosophical gifts and encouraged Tillich to concentrate on the work of the later Friedrich Wilhelm Joseph von Schelling
(1775–1854) and his so-called "positive philosophy." As we shall see,
Tillich derived from Schelling many of the themes of his theology, such
as "kairos," and the "demonic." Tillich saw in Schelling the basis for a
new philosophical formulation for the Christian faith. He was also influenced
by Schelling's concern for freedom and cultural creativity. Although in
later years other authors enriched Tillich's ideas, his basic formulation
which became determinative for his career was drawn from Schelling. During
the period from 1909–1912, when Tillich was an assistant pastor and
student, he wrote two dissertations on Schelling.

Upon arriving at Halle, Tillich found the faculty divided between the
pietists, who emphasized revelation, orthodoxy and traditional exegesis,
and the liberals. The liberals had adopted the historical-critical method.
This method opened Tillich's thought to skepticism concerning the literal-
ness of the historical claims of traditional Christianity. And yet he found
the traditional orthodox picture of theological anthropology more persuasive
than liberal optimism.[14]

Tillich has expressed deep gratitude for what he owes to Martin Kähler, a professor of systematic theology whose lectures and seminars Tillich attended at the University of Halle. Kähler helped Tillich work out a synthesis of theological options. Kähler combined a sympathetic appreciation of the Protestant Reformers, especially Luther, with an openness to the humanism of the German literary and philosophical classics.

Tillich also learned from Kähler a theology of mediation, which sought to mediate between philosophy and theology, the secular and the sacred, and between existential questions and theological answers.[15] Inspired by Kähler, Tillich's time as vicar and assistant pastor in Berlin was occupied with the formulation of a new kind of apologetics. In 1913, Tillich and his friend Richard Wegener completed a manuscript called "Church Apologetics." They announced evening lectures in Berlin called "Evenings for Reason" where they sought to build bridges from the truth of faith to the world of the secular citizen of the large cities.[16]

It was Kähler who suggested to Tillich that the Christian faith is not centered in the Jesus of history, but in Jesus as he is proclaimed and believed to be the Christ, that is, the Messiah and the Redeemer.[17] In other words, the picture we have of Christ must depend on the picture imprinted on his disciples. The Bible carries this picture which was imprinted on his disciples and the church maintains this picture of Christ. Kähler claimed to have received much of his insight on this idea from Martin Luther. For Tillich this idea caused the Bible to come alive.

B. World War I (1914–1918)

1. *External events of 1914–1918.* The external events related to Tillich's life during the war period can be stated briefly. But, as we shall see, these events were to have far-reaching influence on his future life and thought.

Like many of his friends, Tillich was caught up in the nationalistic fervor of World War I. He volunteered for service as a chaplain in the German army in September of 1914 and served through the end of 1918. His motives for enlisting in the army as a chaplain were romantic, religious, and nationalistic. In early childhood he had relived the Prussian War of 1870–71 which took place fifteen years before his birth. He had enthusiasm for uniforms, parades, maneuvers, and this history of battles.[18] His readiness to participate in the next war was inbred. When World War I began, he was eager in a time of crisis to aid his "fatherland."

In the first few months of the war, Tillich went to the Western Front and conducted services and performed his other chaplain's duties under fire. By December, 1914, he was given the first of two Iron Crosses for valor. For a military chaplain this was something special. It revealed that he had identified with the men in battle at the front line.

Tillich's original enthusiasm for the war was evident in his early reports to his superiors. By 1915, however, his sermons and letters indicated that he was losing enthusiasm for the war. In early 1915 he was not closely related to external fighting on the front. It was a time of boredom.

In October of 1915 the situation changed. For the next six months Tillich's division was in the trenches at the heart of battle. These were difficult and dangerous months for Tillich. He was close to front-line action. His duties involved mass burials (he reported that he had become a grave digger), comfort for the dying and encouragement for the men through sermons. By December of 1915 Tillich was discouraged and had adopted an air of resignation about the possibility of peace.[19]

The early months of 1916 were relatively uneventful. Fighting was interposed with recreational periods and time for study.[20] However, in May of 1916, there was a terrible battle at Verdun. Tillich suffered intensely as his friends and colleagues were killed.[21] Horror replaced his original enthusiasm. The constant presence of death revealed life's abyss.[22] He tended to preach about death and heaven during this period. In the midst of such agonies Tillich suffered a nervous breakdown. Fortunately he recovered quickly,[23] and a visit to the University of Halle for a lecture was allowed by the military.

By October of 1916 Tillich was transferred to the Seventh Division. Soon he was close to the front again. After a particularly difficult period he collapsed and was sent to a hospital [24] where he gradually recovered. He was later to see this experience of illness as a turning point in his life.

The winter of 1917 was a time of starvation in Germany and loneliness on the battlefield. In April of 1917 the United States entered the war which made the outlook for peace more bleak than ever. By August of 1917 Tillich was provided with an assistant and had more time for intellectual work.[25]

In April of 1918 Tillich suffered a third collapse. As a result, in May he asked to be relieved of army service. His request was rejected. Returning to the front, Tillich had a change of mood. He experienced joy as his division enjoyed some successes.[26] For his valor Tillich was rewarded a second Iron Cross (first class) in June of 1918.

In August of 1918 Tillich was assigned as a chaplain for a military base in the Berlin area. During this time (August to December) the army collapsed, and the Kaiser was forced to abdicate. On 9 November 1918, the war came to an end. Germany had lost more than 1,750,000 men. Four million Germans were wounded, and over a million were imprisoned or missing. Tillich was in Berlin while a revolution and civil war were taking place. There was an uprising of workers and shooting in the streets.[27]

2. *Underlying significance of the external events of 1914–1918*. But what of the underlying religious, philosophical, psychological, and political impli-

cations of the events in Tillich's experience during this period of 1914–1918?

For Tillich, the war marked the breakdown of an old order and the end of an historical epoch. According to Tillich, the building of the nineteenth century had been destroyed, and it was impossible to bring it back. There must be change and a new building.[28] In a vision which Tillich had on a frightful night on the battlefield of Verdun, he saw the end of feudalistic and militaristic monarchies and the end of an era of Protestant-bourgeois civilization.[29]

During the war Tillich had become increasingly disturbed by the role of the political-ideological-religious establishment in sending millions of soldiers to their premature and terrible death.[30] His sermons began to lose their nationalistic fervor and their enthusiasm for war.[31] Moreover, with the breakdown of the old orders there came the collapse of Tillich's belief in the traditional conception of God. Philosophically his old conception of God was dead, even if this change was not announced in his sermons to the troops.

Tillich's conception of God was closely related to his essentialist or idealist philosophy. The war modified his idealist view and threw him into the existence of the twentieth century.[32] In the middle of a terrible battle Tillich had what he called a personal "kairos." The whole structure of classical idealism under which the war had taken place was shattered.[33] During this experience Tillich reported that he became an existentialist. He turned from pure abstraction to a realization of the importance of encounters in living contexts. The war, for example, brought to Tillich the experience of the abyss of existence.

It was also during the war that Tillich began to crystallize his view that objective religion should be erected on an experimental basis. During this period he read Rudolf Otto's *The Idea of the Holy* and was impressed with Otto's experience of the numinous or holy as a means for conveying a new depth or revelation of being. Later Tillich was to make much of the concept of "depth of being" for he believed that behind and beyond rational doubt lies the realm of experience and the possibility of being grasped by the ultimate.[34]

A development in Tillich's personal family life also contributed to the breakdown of old loyalties and absolutes. He had come to his marriage to Grethi Wever in 1914 at the age of twenty-seven, true to the vows of chastity which he had taken in the Wingolf fraternity. His standards were high. He soon found that Grethi scoffed at the idea of monogamy and ridiculed his wish to be faithful only to her. During the war she became attracted to Tillich's friend, Richard Wegener, with whom she had an affair.[35] Tillich's marriage deteriorated increasingly through the unfaithfulness of his wife.

It should be noted at this point that Tillich continued to reaffirm life and faith despite his doubts about the traditional concepts of God. Faith, as the state of being ultimately concerned, did not have to imply that one did not have doubts about traditional views of God.

It was the German philosopher, Friedrich Nietzsche, who helped Tillich live through the horrors of the war. During the war death was dominant and there did not seem to be any empirical or provable hope. In the French woods, surrounded by death, Tillich found in Nietzsche's writings an exaltation of life that revived him and gave him "ecstatic experience." He found in Nietzsche the possibility of life's being born anew or being affirmed infinitely.[36]

Nietzsche reminded Tillich of the battle for the creative and affirming life which Martin Luther declared over against that which he saw as a stifling and medieval type of Christianity. He saw in Nietzsche a needed protest against a bourgeois religious, political, and social perspective.[37]

It is true that Tillich became addicted to life's vivid joys while on leave, but he never embraced Nietzsche's normlessness.[38] Furthermore, Tillich did not accept all of Nietzsche's extreme criticisms of Christianity and his view of eternal return or his superman concepts. Elements of Nietzsche's philosophy of life and views of will to power, however, were to remain in Tillich's thought.[39]

Another important aspect of Tillich's wartime experience was his discovery of painting. His Lutheran heritage had evidently not stressed the visual arts. In earlier years he had known more exposure to literature, poetry, architecture, and music.

Tillich's passion for painting began in an existential way. During the war he found that he could escape the destruction, horror, and ugliness of battle through the visual arts. On leave he haunted art museums. He delighted in paintings that appeared on pieces of military mail deliveries. On the army post he read art books.

This attachment to visual arts developed, deepened, and endured in Tillich's experience. His interest moved from a primitive escapism into a study of art history. It was during the war, on his last furlough, that Tillich had an experience which he described as revelation. It happened as he stood before a Botticelli painting in a Berlin museum. In the presence of this painting Tillich felt that he was grasped by the reality of the absolute or the holy.

Tillich was later to develop a special appreciation for Expressionist painting. He believed that the Expressionists sought, in their mystical religious manner, to disclose the transcendental reality which is not just external. It was style, he was later to state, not subject matter that revealed transcendent reality. Tillich called these experiences with painting "breakthroughs." This idea of breakthrough was later to dominate his idea of revelation.[40]

The "breakthrough" approach which came from his experience of painting was used by Tillich in gaining insights in areas other than painting. First, there was a vital impulse or ecstatic experience and then a historical orientation. Finally, there came an interpretation and a set of concepts. This sequence shows the importance for Tillich of experience in determining concepts. This existentialist emphasis causes his work to have problems in terms of conceptual precision.[41]

It was Tillich's experience in the war that aroused in him a new political interest. As he thought of all that happened he saw that the war was the inevitable consequence of social developments. He became angered at the society that had permitted such a conflict to happen.[42]

During the war Tillich came into personal contact with the proletariat. This experience was not easily available in pre-war Germany for a young man with Tillich's background. By talking to the troops he discovered that the nation was split into classes and that the industrial workers saw the church as an ally of the ruling groups.[43] He also saw the contrast between the gains of war profiteers and the losses of the masses of people. It was during the war that Tillich began to think about the exploitation of the common man by the landed aristocracy, the army and the church.[44]

It was also during the war that Tillich saw the dangers of nationalism and its implications for power politics. He never thought that one could get along in the world without power.[45] This concern with power showed him the necessity of new experiments in politics such as religious socialism.

In the last part of the war period he gained insights from Karl Marx which helped him understand the war politically. Undoubtedly he was keenly aware of the Russian revolution of October, 1917.[46] This initial encounter with Marx was to continue as a life-long dialogue.[47]

Perhaps Tillich sublimated some of the guilt feelings which he had about surviving the worst battles of the war with an attempt to participate in social and democratic action in the new German republic. In any case, he emerged from World War I alienated from his conservative past, with new perspectives and new purposes.

C. German Universities Era (1919–1933)

1. *Berlin University (1919–1924)*. In the spring of 1919 Tillich became a *Privatdozent* or free-lance instructor at the University of Berlin. Since there was no set salary, the teacher received the fees paid by the students. This was supposed to be a period when a young teacher would become established by writing articles and books and then be called to a higher position. To help him, Tillich's father arranged for Bishop Händler to appoint Tillich as one of his vicars. In reality this was a token position but it did help Tillich financially. When this appointment ran out, Hugo Simons, a banker, helped to support Tillich for a year. Tillich also rented out a room in his apartment to help pay expenses.

Tillich's first course at Berlin University was on "Christianity and the Present Social Problems." His first public lecture was "On the Idea of a Theology of Culture" and was delivered before the Kant Society of Berlin. It was well received.

Tillich conducted a question and answer period at the close of his lectures. This was an innovation and brought a favorable response from the students. He also developed a plan to invite the students to his apartment for social evenings. This type of hospitality was unusual in German university circles.

Upon being released from the army, Tillich became involved, at least indirectly, in political affairs. As early as December, 1918, he signed a statement supporting separation of church and state. He saw this move as an opportunity to renew the church. During the war he realized that the power of the old Prussian church was resented by the majority of the people. Tillich's view on church and state was in opposition to the views of his father and most of the leadership of the German church. This attempt at separation of church and state was ultimately defeated, and the state church retained its privileges.

In 1919, Tillich gave a lecture to the Independent Social Democrats, a group to the left of the ruling Social Democrats. The Evangelical consistory which ordained him sent a formal inquiry about the lecture which was in reality a protest against the lecture. Tillich's reply to the church leaders is his first formal statement urging the church to be sympathetic with socialism.

In 1920 Tillich participated in the foundation of the "Kairos Circle." This group included both Christians and non-Christians of intellectual bent. It had as members men who were later to become well known in the United States such as Alexander Rüstow, Adolf Löwe, and Eduard Heimann. This group published a journal called "Pages for Religious Socialism." In 1923, a lengthy essay by Tillich entitled "Basic Principles of Religious Socialism" appeared in the journal of the Kairos Circle.[48] In the same year he published a thoroughgoing criticism of Karl Barth's theological position.[49]

By the spring of 1921 Tillich was giving formal classroom lectures on the Expressionists. He featured the work of the painter Franz Marc whose work depicted animals. For Tillich, these paintings represented a breakthrough in their disregard and even disparagement of form. The work of Marc gave a courageous revelation of a disrupted society as well as a presentation of beauty and depth.

Tillich's personal life during the period from 1919–1924 has been described as a period of "creative chaos." As mentioned earlier, his wife, Grethi Wever, had an affair with Tillich's friend, Richard Wegener, while Tillich was away at war. On 19 June 1919, Grethi gave birth to Wegener's child, Wolf, to whom Tillich gave his name. Tillich's own child by Grethi had died in infancy. Grethi left Tillich later in 1919, but Wegener refused to marry her. Tillich then arranged for a divorce which would neither ruin Wegener's career nor give Tillich the burden of the support of the child. The divorce was granted in February, 1921, on the grounds of Grethi's desertion. Tillich was not to see Grethi again until 1948.[50]

Tillich was influenced by and became a part of the Berlin Bohemianism which disregarded traditional conventions. The Weimar Republic of post-war Germany was filled with decadence and exuberance. The culture was self-consciously Freudian. The watchwords were emancipation, liberalism and artistic flair.[51] Tillich was caught between the conservative Christian tradition of his earlier life and the radical new views of the Weimar era. The break-up of his marriage appears to have turned him toward Bohemianism.

The life of Tillich during this period is only understandable in the light of the times and his own experience since 1914. He attended revolutionary theater. He enjoyed the company of a number of women whom he met at masked balls, bars, and cafes. He claimed that the experience of the erotic, either actual or sublimated, stimulated his creativity. But he was beset by guilt and gossip. It was suggested that he should resign from the Wingolf fraternity and leave the field of theology.

Tillich was plunged into depression by the loss of his older sister Johanna who died in childbirth in 1920. To help him recover, Tillich's younger sister, Elizabeth, urged him to attend a Mardi Gras masked ball. It was at this ball that he met a woman ten years his junior named Hannah Werner. In the midst of a tempestuous romance which followed their meeting Hannah confessed that she was already engaged to an art teacher and felt obligated to marry him.

In 1920, Hannah married Albert Gottschow. But within a year Hannah returned to Berlin to a relationship with Tillich despite the fact that she was pregnant with Albert's child. She left Berlin to give birth to the boy. Soon Hannah returned to Berlin to resume the relationship with Tillich. In Berlin she placed the child in a nursing home. It was only after the child died, probably because of neglect at the nursing home, that Albert gave Hannah a divorce in 1923. Hannah married Tillich on 22 March 1924. She accused Tillich of leaving her on the night of their marriage to carouse with another woman in the company of Richard Wegener. (It is ironic that Wegener had seduced Tillich's first wife during Tillich's absence in the war.) This was the beginning of a marriage that never worked well, although it never failed entirely.[52]

2. *University of Marburg (1924–1925)*. In the spring of 1924, shortly after his second marriage, Tillich accepted a position as associate professor of theology at the University of Marburg. The university was located in the provincial university town of Marburg which was sixty miles north of

Frankfurt. Tillich and his wife Hannah did not want to leave the city life of Berlin. The possibilities of an advanced position at Berlin University, however, were quite limited for a young man. It was also pointed out that he was to succeed the revered Rudolf Otto at Marburg. Furthermore, Marburg, founded in 1527 by Philip Hesse, was the first Protestant university in Germany.

Tillich found immediately that the theological faculty at Marburg was dominated by neoorthodoxy. There was a general disregard for Tillich's interest in the relationship of religion and culture. The chief interest was in Karl Barth. Both Rudolph Bultmann and Martin Heidegger were teaching at Marburg. Tillich was soon to have lively dialogue with Heidegger through the medium of the students who attended the lectures of both professors.[53]

The first lectures given by Tillich were on the subjects of philosophy of religion and the Protestant mystics. In his third and last semester at Marburg Tillich began work on his *Systematic Theology*.[54] By this time he had thirty students in his class and was being more widely accepted.

A delayed honeymoon trip to Italy in September of 1924 caused the Tillichs to have even more dissatisfaction with the provincialism and lack of social opportunities in Marburg. They did enjoy the countryside near Marburg and Tillich treasured his close fellowship with Rudolf Otto. They felt, however, that they were marking time until a new opportunity would be offered. The publication of Tillich's book, *The Religious Situation*, in 1925 was his first genuine publication success. This book made his name known all over Germany and helped prepare the way for his next opportunity at Dresden.[55]

3. *Dresden Institute of Technology (1925–1929).* Tillich's love of the culture, stimulation, and openness of a large city had developed during his years in Berlin. Dresden was a beautiful city and had a splendid reputation for the arts and music. Although the Dresden Institute of Technology was not one of the major German universities, Tillich accepted an offer of a full professorship in a new department of humanities with a substantial salary.

Richard Kroner, a distinguished philosopher, recommended Tillich for the position in Dresden. Tillich was to teach in the area of religion and the arts and religion and history. Soon he attracted large classes and many adult auditors. Some of Tillich's Dresden students were later to edit and translate his works and establish the Tillich archive in Germany.

As already indicated, Tillich was becoming well known in Germany. In 1925 he was given an honorary doctorate of theology by the University of Halle. In 1926 he edited a two-volume work, *Kairos*, which included two of his own essays. In that same year Tillich delivered and published a lecture on the subject of "The Demonic." He considered this emphasis on the irrational potential in God as one of his few original ideas.

In terms of family life, 1926 was a notable year for the Tillichs. A daughter, named Erdmuthe, was born to Hannah and Paul. Socially, the Tillichs made friends among the prominent society leaders and professional people of Dresden such as psychoanalysts and architects. At parties in the home of the Kroners, Tillich met some prominent artists including well-known dancers. He soon wrote an essay on "Dance and Religion" and continued his interest in the visual arts.

Criticisms of his lack of theological emphasis by Kroner and others and his own fear that he might drift away from theology influenced Tillich to accept an adjunct professorship of systematic theology at the University of Leipzig. From 1927 to 1929 he lectured at Leipzig every two weeks during school terms.[56]

In the spring of 1928 Tillich joined eighty other religious socialists for a three-day conference near Heidelberg. This was an important conference which helped him to crystallize his understanding of the theoretical foundations of socialism.[57] It was also during this period at a conference in Geneva, Switzerland, in 1928, that Tillich engaged in dialogue with the well-known philosopher and sociologist, Max Scheler. Later Tillich was to assume the chair of philosophy at the University of Frankfurt to which Scheler had been appointed before his sudden death.[58]

4. *University of Frankfurt (1929–1933).* Paul Tillich's dream of becoming a full professor of a fully accredited German university was fulfilled in 1929 when he was invited to the University of Frankfurt. This was a modern university different from the traditional Prussian university. It was in part privately financed, and its faculty was largely Jewish. In fact, there was no theological faculty and Tillich was the only Christian scholar on the teaching staff. He was called "Paul among the Jews" in this liberal school. Some of Tillich's Frankfurt colleagues were later to become well-known in the United States. His fellow professors included Karl Mannheim, Karl Reinhardt, Erich Fromm, Herbert Marcuse, Max Horkheim, Kurt Goldstein, and Adhimar Gelfe.

In the early years at Frankfurt Tillich was fulfilling his dreams. He lectured on religion and culture, the social situation, religious experience, and the essence of religion. He also taught social education, history of philosophy, and philosophy of religion. Here he more fully developed his theology of culture. During these years Tillich became more widely known in Germany. He spoke at art exhibits, literary festivals, and architectural meetings. Tillich was extremely popular with both students and faculty colleagues. His appreciation of the opportunities at Frankfurt led him to turn down a professorship in theology at the University of Halle in 1930.[59]

On the political side, Tillich reluctantly joined the Social Democratic party in 1929. Although he was never in complete agreement with the party, he saw the Social Democratic party as something to ward off the

growing threats of the National Socialism of the Nazis. Tillich was a key
person in initiating a new independent socialist journal called "New Pages
for Socialism." The first issue in January, 1930, contained a lead article
by Tillich on "Socialism." [60] The magazine was published monthly until
the Nazis prohibited its publication in June, 1933. Tillich was primarily
a theorist of socialism rather than an active political participant.[61]

As early as 1932, Tillich was opposing Nazism in print on theological
grounds. In that year he published "Ten Theses on the Church and the
Third Reich." Hitler himself was sent a copy of this essay which was
contained in a book entitled *The Church and the Third Reich*. In this essay
Tillich stated that the justifying of the Nazi mythology of blood and race
was a retreat to paganism and a denial of God and humanity. Protestantism
must stand against the heathenism of the swastika and for the cross.[62]

In 1932, Tillich was appointed Dean of the philosophical faculty at
Frankfurt. In that same year he helped Max Horkheimer found the Institute
of Social Research. This so-called "Frankfurt School" became famous and
later moved to New York City.[63] The institute was founded to develop a
critical theory of society. Its members were mostly leftist-Hegelian or humanist-Marxist. At a later date this group was to influence Tillich in his move
from a Marxist-related social philosophy to a more psychological or Freudian
approach. Tillich's writings in the United States would utilize Freudian
insights more and more while playing down the Marxist elements.[64]

Tillich began writing his most important political book, *The Socialist
Decision*, during the summer of 1932 in Switzerland. Completing the book
at the home of friends in Potsdam, Tillich had it published early in 1933.[65]
This book was later to be used as evidence against him for his removal
as professor at Frankfurt. It was also to be used during World War II to
bolster the courage of those who opposed Hitler.[66] *The Socialist Decision*
had a political program which Tillich's later volume on abstract political
philosophy, *Love, Power and Justice*, lacked.[67]

Beyond the local level, 1932 found Tillich relatively unknown in the
wider leadership of the Nazis. The situation changed in July, 1932, when
he made a public speech against storm troopers and Nazi students who
rioted at the University of Frankfurt and beat up left-wing and Jewish
students. Tillich demanded that the Nazi students be expelled. He also
heard Hitler speak and was disgusted by his speech and physical manner-
isms.

Tillich's actions against the Nazi students and his writings were remembered when Hitler became chancellor on 30 January 1933. By 24 March
1933, Hitler was given dictatorial powers. Tillich's book, *The Socialist Decision*, was banned, and the journal for which he wrote was closed down.
The University of Frankfurt was denounced as an anti-German and pro-
Jewish school. On 13 April 1933, Tillich's name appeared on the first

list of professors to be dismissed.[68] Of the twelve suspended at Frankfurt
on April 13, one was Tillich and the other eleven were Jewish.[69] Within
a year a total of 1,684 scholars were removed from German university
circles.[70] On 10 May 1933, Tillich saw the Nazi book-burning celebration
on Frankfurt square in which his own book was burned. The death of
President Hindenburg in August, 1934, gave Hitler the opportunity to
assume the offices of both president and chancellor and gave the Nazis
complete power.[71]

Although he was without a job, Tillich wanted to remain in Germany
to influence the political situation. Traveling throughout the country to
confer with friends, he even visited a high official of the Nazi ministry of
education in Berlin. The advice of all concerned was that Tillich should
go into exile. By October, 1933, the Gestapo members were following him
in the city of Dresden. Tillich realized that his identification with prophetic
principles could lead either to his death or his exile.

Fortunately for Tillich, a meeting was held in May, 1933, at Columbia
University in New York City concerning help for creative and distinguished
German intellectuals who had been purged. Henry Sloane Coffin, president
of Union Theological Seminary in New York City, attended the meeting
at Columbia and became interested in Tillich. Reinhold Niebuhr of the
Union Theological Seminary faculty took the leadership in facilitating a
plan to bring Tillich to Union Seminary. Each member of the Union Seminary faculty voted to give five percent of his or her salary to furnish a
salary for him for the first year.[72] A telegram was sent to Tillich in Germany
on 1 July 1933. After visiting friends and relatives, including Tillich's
aging father, the Tillichs left Hamburg, Germany, by ship for the United
States at the end of October. On 4 November 1933, Tillich, now forty-
seven, landed in New York City to begin a new life in a strange land.[73]

D. *New York Period (1933–1955)*

It should be helpful to group the events of the 1933–1955 New York
period of Tillich's life around the following outline: Pre-World War II
period (1933–1939), World War II period (1939–1945) and Post-World
War II period (1945–1955).

1. *The pre-World War II period (1933–1939).* The Tillichs received a
warm welcome from Union Seminary professors and from some of the
Columbia University teachers whom they had known when they reached
New York City on 4 November 1933. From November, 1933, until early
1934 Tillich gave himself to an intense study of the English language
and an exploration of New York City itself. Always in love with the great
city of Berlin, he found New York City equally stimulating. The Tillichs
were especially enamored by the Museum of Modern Art.[74] For Tillich,

New York City was important for the development of the critical side of his intellectual and artistic life and as a place to gain firsthand knowledge of political and social movements.[75]

Tillich received an official letter on 20 December 1933, from the Nazi Minister of Culture, depriving him of his professorial post and academic standing in Germany. As was indicated earlier, Tillich prized his full German professorship highly along with its generous pension. Tillich officially protested his dismissal in a long and carefully worded letter. In a return letter dated 15 June 1934, the Nazi Ministry of Culture refused to sustain Tillich's protest. Moreover as indicated above, Tillich had a tenuous teaching situation. Now he found himself without an assured permanent position either in Germany or America.

January, 1934, found Tillich making his first speech in English in America. As one who heard him lecture in the late 1940s, the author can verify that Tillich had great difficulty in mastering the American pronunciation and idioms. Horace Friess and John Hermann Randall, Jr., did their best to help Tillich with his language barriers in his Columbia University seminar.[76]

Fortunately for Tillich (and the other members of the group), as early as 1934 he was invited into membership of an exclusive theological discussion group which met either at Yale University or in Washington, D.C., led semiannually. Its limited membership of thirty placed Tillich in the midst of the most active academic theologians in the United States.[77] Among the members of the theological discussion group were the Niebuhr brothers, Roland Bainton, George Thomas, John Mackay, and Henry Van Dusen. Tillich wrote the lead article entitled "The World Situation" for a collection of essays by the members of this theological discussion group. In this article Tillich called for an order that would avoid "totalitarian absolutism" and "liberal individualism." Human dignity must be protected.[78]

In November, 1934, Tillich's final break with his lifelong friend, Emanuel Hirsch, symbolized his final break with the German Nazis and their sympathizers.[79] In 1934 and 1935 Tillich carried on an open and public disagreement with Hirsch over the relation of Christianity to the Nazis. This debate took place as a result of two Hirsch books, *The Present Cultural Situation in Philosophical and Theological Perspective* and *Christian Freedom and Political Obligation.* Tillich accused Hirsch of giving up his role as a Protestant theologian in his endorsement of the Nazi movement. For Tillich, an event such as the Nazi movement is a "Kairos" or divinely ordained event only if it shows a fresh realization of the original revelation which is the cross of Christ and the gospel of the coming kingdom of God. Tillich also criticized Hirsch for supporting racial hatred against the Jews. It is noteworthy that Professor Hirsch was driven out of Frankfurt University by the victorious Allies in 1945 even as Tillich was driven out of the same university by the Nazis in 1933.[80]

From the moment that Tillich reached New York City his Union Seminary apartment became the place where German (mostly Jewish) refugees came for help and counsel. There were long evenings of discussion. People who later became prominent in American academic and cultural life such as Eduard Heiman, Adolf Löwe, Theodor Adorno and Kurt Goldstein were among those who found help from Tillich.[81]

The need to help the emigrés was so great in the depression days that an organization called "Self-help for Emigrés from Central Europe" was organized in 1936. Tillich was the chairman and chief force in this organization for fifteen years.[82] Many people never forgot Tillich's patience and encouragement and practical help.

Tillich's devotion to others is even more remarkable because he did not as yet have a secure place in America's academic world. Not only did he have language difficulties, but there were other problems. Was he a philosopher or a theologian? Was he too secular for a theological seminary? Was he practical enough to train prospective ministers? The Columbia University philosophy department was glad to have Tillich as an adjunct professor, but his romantic German idealism was not in vogue in American philosophical circles and at Columbia at that time.[83] Tillich visited the University of Chicago in 1935 in view of a possible position there but he did not find himself congenial in thought with Chicago professors Henry Weiman and Dean Shirley Case.[84]

Tillich had to begin all over again as *Privatdozent,* or Visiting Lecturer, at Union Seminary. It was four years before he was given tenure at Union. He was reappointed on a yearly basis. It was another three years, at age fifty-four, before he was made a full professor.[85] For a number of years Tillich's income did not exceed $3,500 a year. Hannah rented out one of their rooms to help buy clothes and theater tickets. She also reports in her book *From Time to Time* that during those days Tillich had a lady friend who lived across the street from Union. This situation created intense friction in their home.[86]

Gradually Tillich developed required courses at Union such as "Church History from the Reformation to Modern Times" given in conjunction with John T. McNeill. He also introduced seminars on Luther, Calvin and his own systematic theology. Tillich's joint Columbia University philosophy seminar with John Herman Randall reached two hundred in size during some semesters. For over twenty years Tillich also conducted a seminar and other courses at New York's New School for Social Research.

Tillich's introduction of philosophical theology into the Union Seminary curriculum eventually resulted in a department in this discipline. His long-standing German friend, Richard Kroner, joined Tillich at Union. The third member of the philosophical theology department was the young and brilliant David Roberts. Roberts' course on the history of philosophy prepared students for the more complex courses offered by Tillich and Kroner.

David Roberts' early death in 1955 was a great personal loss to Tillich. The author of this book found Roberts especially helpful as a teacher who helped persons understand Tillich's thought during days of study in New York City.

Despite limited resources and lack of firm academic security, Tillich's inquisitive and restless mind led him to take every opportunity to see more of America. In March of 1935 Tillich made his first visit to the Southern United States as a participant in the University of Chicago social ethics seminar field trip. He was fascinated by the black people in the South. He saw the Tennessee TVA project as a socialistic gain in America.[87] In fact, he addressed a mass meeting of Norris Dam workers on religious socialism.[88]

Not long after Tillich returned to New York City, on 7 June 1935, his son, René Stefan, was born. Reinhold Niebuhr baptized René in Lampon Chapel at Union Seminary shortly after his birth.[89]

Although Tillich was taking every opportunity to explore the United States, his heart and mind were always in close touch with the European scene. He had his first chance to return to Europe in the spring and summer of 1936. This trip was to prepare for the 1937 Oxford Ecumenical Conference in which he was to participate. We know a great deal about this particular trip because Tillich kept a detailed travel diary. In 1970 this diary was published by Harper and Row under the title, *My Travel Diary— 1936, Between Two Worlds*.[90]

From his travel diary and other sources we learn that Tillich visited with friends in England, Holland, Belgium, Luxemborg, France, Switzerland and Italy. The diary gives an intimate view of both his character and cultural interests. It also gives no hint that Tillich wanted to return to Germany. Tillich saw Hitler as an implacable enemy. Tillich even talks in his diary of the possibility of a coup versus Hitler or an assassination attempt on the life of Hitler.[91] Tillich had his last talk by telephone with his aging father while he was in a country near Germany. In lectures in England Tillich sought to reveal the causes of National Socialism. He also attempted to warn the English that they should defend themselves from Hitler before it was too late.[92] Tillich made a strong impression in England and was offered a position at the University of Manchester which he declined.

In London, Tillich conducted conferences seeking to inaugurate a new type of religious order which would involve religious, socialist and monastic features. This new order was to serve as a resource of renewal for the decaying institutional churches in Europe.[93]

For people concerned with the work of Carl Jung, it is interesting to note that Tillich attended the famous Jungian Eranos meeting in Switzerland in the summer of 1936. Tillich was disappointed in what he called a Jungian unpolitical mysticism which was being emphasized at this meeting.[94]

Upon returning from Europe in 1936 Tillich often commented on the tragic and demonic elements in history. He felt that war in Europe was inevitable. For Tillich, the present task was to start preparing for the right kind of reconstruction in Europe after the war.[95]

Tillich's poetic and very personal autobiographical essay, *On the Boundary*, was also released in its first American version in 1936. It was published as the first chapter of a book entitled *The Interpretation of History*.

It has already been mentioned that despite Tillich's growing popularity he had not been given tenure at Union. Students were petitioning for him to have a more permanent position. Tillich himself emphasized what he felt was his unique role at Union in blending systematic theology, philosophy and history. Conservative members of the Union faculty were concerned that he was not sufficiently biblical. Was he a philosopher or a theologian? Finally, the first chair in philosophical theology in the United States was created for Tillich at Union Seminary. On 9 March 1937, Tillich was appointed as Associate Professor of Philosophical Theology with a three-year contract. Conservative faculty members held off his promotion to a full professorship for another three years.

On 30 July 1937 Tillich's father died in Germany at the age of eighty. Despite the discussion in earlier sections about negative factors related to his father, Tillich had kept up communication with him. In turn Tillich's father had followed his son's career with admiration and interest.

In July of 1937 Tillich went back to Europe to participate in the Oxford Conference on Life and Work. He was convinced that his major contribution to this ecumenical meeting was his emphasis that God often speaks more clearly through men concerned for social justice who were enemies of the church than through those who spoke in the name of the church but exerted no social responsibility.[96] Tillich also emphasized that so-called idealism has its roots in the social and economic security of the upper classes.[97] This conference was Tillich's first and last official engagement with the ecumenical movement and the later-to-be-organized World Council of Churches. He was never actively and publicly identified with the practical life and local programs of the churches. He saw himself as a philosopher-theologian and not as a strong churchman as far as active involvement.

Because Tillich was an emigré who had not yet obtained American citizenship, during his first five years in the United States he had refused to speak in public about international politics.[98] He broke this silence on 21 November 1938, when he spoke at a Protestant rally in Madison Square Garden on German anti-Semitism. His appeal to the Christians was based on the common prophetic heritage which Christians have with the Jews. He saw the Nazis' attack on Judaism as an attack on the God of Christianity. Furthermore, Tillich stated that German Americans should oppose Nazism for the sake of the true or classic Germany which was being destroyed by the Nazis. By this time Tillich saw that no compromise was possible with Nazism and so he called for a life-and-death struggle against it.[99]

Despite Tillich's concern with the European scene he continued to grow in stature among American intellectuals. In 1939, he was elected to the famous Philosophy Club. Organized in 1900, the Philosophy Club was limited to twenty-five philosophers on the Eastern seaboard. Membership was by invitation and included the great names of American philosophy. The meetings which were scheduled each month from October through May involved a rigorous exchange of ideas.

Tillich learned much about American philosophical thought at these meetings which he attended regularly from 1939 until he went to Chicago in 1962. At that time he became an emeritus member. The Philosophy Club also gave an opportunity for the American philosophers to become acquainted with Tillich's thought. Although some analysts and pragmatists had reservations about certain facets of Tillich's thought, he gained the intellectual respect of all of the members of the Club. The Philosophy Club, along with the theological discussion group already mentioned and his lectures and writings, gave Tillich a prominent place among American intellectuals during his first six years in the United States.[100]

2. *The World War II period (1939–1945).* World War II was ignited by Hitler's invasion of Poland in September, 1939.[101] Although Tillich had anticipated this war and urged preparation for it, he became quite depressed about the war and would walk on Riverside Drive or work late at night to overcome his discouragement.[102]

In his work with German immigrants Tillich urged them to identify with their new country of America as soon as possible. With the help of Henry Sloane Coffin, President of Union Seminary, and others, Tillich hastened his own citizenship process and became a United States citizen on 4 March 1940 at the age of fifty-three.[103] Although Tillich could never change his roots and formative training, he did renounce certain German characteristics that seemed to be provincial in light of his new identification with the United States.[104]

It was also appropriate that in 1940 Tillich should be given the rank of full professor at Union Seminary with the security and larger salary related to this promotion. As we have noted, one of Tillich's most difficult problems had been the adjustment to the loss of his full professorship and government retirement security at the University of Frankfurt in 1933. Tillich's formal installation as Professor of Philosophical Theology at Union Theological Seminary took place in September of 1940 when he gave his inaugural lecture on "Philosophy and Theology."

It seems as if 1940 was a turning point in the career of Paul Tillich. Yale University awarded him an honorary doctorate of divinity on 19 June 1940. This was the first of many American honorary doctorates. In the

1940s Tillich's joint seminar with John Hermann Randall, Jr., at Columbia University on "The Cognitive and Religious Use of Myth and Symbol" grew in attendance and acclaim. More than one hundred graduate students crowded the seminar. In this same year of 1940 Tillich became active in the New York Psychology Group which met monthly. Among the members were Rollo May, Seward Hiltner, David Roberts, Erich Fromm and Ruth Benedict.

In the years 1941–43 Tillich was able to express many of his views because of his position as chairman of the editorial board of the *Protestant Digest* (later changed to *The Protestant*). Tillich's thesis that vital religion criticizes absolute pretensions of religious communities but at the same time affirms the need for religious communities and religious symbols received a wide hearing. His dialectical approach affirmed that in politics there is no absolute Christian answer but rather a continual Christian pursuit of relevant and helpful penultimate answers.[105]

As already indicated, Tillich wanted to help as a new American citizen in the war effort. One way he helped was by preparing a series of politico-religious talks which were broadcast to the German people every week from early 1942 to May 1944.[106] Tillich prepared 109 talks of approximately 1500 words each. Not even his closest friends knew of this work for the government.[107] In these remarkable speeches Tillich held out hope for a new beginning in Germany once Hitler was defeated.[108] He stressed the urgency for the Protestant churches in Germany to resist Nazism, affirm the rights of man and remember the Nazi burning of books. He urged the German people to throw off the yoke of Hitler and be prepared to pay the cost of building a new order. Toward the end of the war he begged the German people to surrender and sue for peace before the entire country was destroyed. Tillich hoped for a new *kairos* or renewal of justice for the world.

In 1944 and 1945 Tillich made one of his last major political efforts in regard to postwar Germany. He became chairman of the Council for a Democratic Germany. This Council was composed of a group of anti-Nazi German refugees who published "a program for a Democratic Germany" in May 1944. Many prominent Americans, among them Reinhold Niebuhr, Norman Cousins, John Dewey and Dorothy Thompson, supported the statement. The statement issued by the Council called for a disarmed Germany, but the Council was against an economic and political dismemberment of Germany. The economic power of Germany was to be conserved and integrated with the rest of Europe. The Germans themselves were to expurge Nazism. Healthy elements in Germany were to be nurtured.[109]

Tillich and others were temporarily blacklisted by United States military leaders for their opposition to an extreme punishment for Germany. Tillich was also criticized for not planning to return permanently to Germany.[110]

With the imposition of Allied military rule (over Germany) and the return of monopoly capitalism in Germany, Tillich's dream of a liberating religious socialism in Germany was shattered.[111]

On several occasions during these war years Eleanor Roosevelt invited Tillich to Hyde Park. This friendship eventually led to a dinner at the White House in the company of President and Mrs. Roosevelt, Vice President Henry Wallace and others.[112] At the dinner table Tillich made a brief prepared statement to the President on the reconstruction of Germany. President Roosevelt replied that the Germans had fooled the Allies in 1918 but that this time the United States was in charge. In other words, Roosevelt rebuffed Tillich's idea of moderation in relationship to the treatment of Germany.[113] President Roosevelt told the German professors present at the dinner that one thing they could do was to write textbooks for the conquered Germany. Tillich concluded later that Roosevelt rejected his idea because he was influenced by Stalin to take a hard line against the Germans.

Experiences like the one with President Roosevelt and Tillich's being temporarily blacklisted by the United States army depressed him greatly and in general frightened him regarding the political scene. Tillich also came to believe that he had a somewhat limited grasp of American political problems and the American political mentality. Consequently, he turned to other than political activities.

It was at this time that Tillich resolved to put more emphasis on writing. But where would he write? For years he had visited California, Massachusetts, Tennessee and Maine. Finally, in 1945, he decided to buy a vacation home in East Hampton, Long Island. The home was located a hundred miles from New York City on the eastern end of Long Island near old farms and hamlets. East Hampton also had a rich and artistic summer colony which appealed to Tillich.

The East Hampton home was near the sea, and over a period of years the old house was renovated. Tillich was especially fond of the trees which he planted around the house. Friends such as Rollo May commented on Tillich's love of the great waves which would crash against the sea wall near his home. These scenes surely reminded Tillich of his beloved Baltic Sea where he spent vacations as a boy in Prussia. It was here in East Hampton that he wrote many of his later books and most of his *Systematic Theology*. It was also here that he first heard the news that the Allies had broken into Germany and that the war in Europe was drawing to a close.[114]

In Hannah Tillich's book, *From Time to Time*, the last chapter is devoted to the story of the Tillichs' life at East Hampton. Obviously, East Hampton was an important stabilizing factor for the entire family.[115]

3. *The post-World War II period (1946–1955)*. When World War II

ended, fifty million people were dead. From cultural, spiritual, economic and political perspectives, the European world, especially Germany, was a disaster area. Tillich's beloved native provinces in Eastern Germany were occupied by the Russians and were to become a part of Poland.[116] The war's end did not bring one Germany, but a Germany controlled by two antagonistic powers. Tillich's hope for *"kairos"* or a moment of rebirth for Europe did not arrive on schedule.[117]

Tillich's first order of business after the war was to reestablish communications with his family and friends in Germany. Soon letters began arriving and they never stopped. At first, Tillich thought that many of his friends would resent the fact that he had emigrated to the United States. Instead, they reached out to Tillich in letters of good will. He replied to all of the letters either in a personal way or by circular letters. Tillich and many others also sent food and clothing to Germany. Tillich's sister, Elisabeth, and her husband were safe in Berlin. Their daughter Heidi also returned to Berlin where she became the wife of the mayor, Klaus Schutz. As early as 1946, the University of Halle reinstated Tillich's title and academic honors.

As an "involved" person, Tillich was not to be satisfied until he could see the suffering and devastation and actual conditions in Germany for himself. This visit was not easy to arrange since several military groups occupied Germany. The United States military had to approve, and an invitation from a German university was necessary for a professor to visit Germany.

Both the universities of Marburg and Frankfurt invited Tillich. Once again Henry Van Dusen of Union offered practical help by raising the money for Tillich's trip. He sailed on 8 May 1948 and returned to New York on September 10. It was his first return to Germany in fifteen years.[118]

From information gained from letters and his comments on his visit, it is clear that Tillich did not like the social-cultural directions of German Christianity. It was a time of totalitarian tendencies with little cultural creativity.[119] Tillich did his best to help. He gave nineteen different lectures during his visit in the summer of 1948. Tillich stopped in Paris to visit the Louvre once again. In Geneva he saw Adolf Keller of ecumenical fame. In Basel he had a jovial visit with Karl Barth. But Tillich was not prepared for the terrible destruction and the ill-clad people he saw in Frankfurt and in other places in Germany. There were few men of middle age and the few left were indifferent.

Tillich left Frankfurt to lecture both formally and informally in Marburg. It was here that he was reunited with his sister, Elizabeth. But as a representative of a conquering nation, he had to be careful in the giving of gifts and in the choice of his topics.

The problem of dealing with German guilt was a delicate subject. He met with Emanuel Hirsch on the 1948 trip. By this time Tillich had decided to deal with all, even those who had been pro-Hitler, like Hirsch and Heidegger, with outgoing love and patience. The almost blind Hirsch still affirmed that he thought Hitler had been sent to create a unified German nation.

Tillich's most moving and memorable stop during his 1948 European trip was in his beloved Berlin. Although Berlin was physically devastated, Tillich found human warmth and an unanticipated receptivity for his lectures and for him personally in Berlin. He was reunited with former students and friends. Even his first wife, Grethi, came to visit him. He and his sister revisited their former home and Tillich's old school which were still standing. Large crowds came to his lectures on "Christology and the World." He even had an opportunity to speak in East Berlin. He appeared to these impoverished and defeated Germans not only as a friend of their past but as a symbol of stability and hope for the future. Since Tillich was one who lived "on the boundary," and Berlin was a boundary or bridge city between the East and the West, he was in his element in Berlin. All types and levels of persons came to hear him, and his ideas were received with enthusiasm and appreciation.[120]

Several universities such as Marburg, Frankfurt, Hamburg and the newly established Free University of Berlin set plans in motion to bring Tillich back to Germany. He felt a strong sense of responsibility for the postwar spiritual and intellectual development of Germany and so considered these invitations at length. But his decision was to return to America. Later a plan was worked out so that after 1951 he would teach alternate summer sessions in Hamburg and Berlin.

In the Fall of 1948 Tillich returned to the United States. Despite his enthusiastic reception in Germany he described the situation there in pessimistic terms in light of a divided Germany and the discouraged people. His decision to continue his work in the United States was confirmed by developments beginning in 1948. As we have indicated, his recognition had developed slowly as he worked on the language barrier and concentrated on the peculiar American cultural and social problems. But his books and lecture tours were bearing more fruit. Union Seminary's location in New York City made it a bridge between the United States and Europe. Tillich began to receive invitations from Switzerland, Holland, Denmark, England and Scotland, as well as more and more significant opportunities in the United States. He called this period "harvest time." The intellectual climate created by the war had made people more open to Tillich's realistic themes. He also communicated more clearly and was learning how to relate to American thinking.

As will be recalled, Tillich wrote a number of books during his fourteen years of teaching in Germany. Several of these books were translated and brought into print beginning in 1948. The first was *The Protestant Era.* This was a collection from twenty years of his German writings. James Luther Adams of the Federated Theological Faculty of the University of Chicago was the translator and editor. The translation of Tillich's German works was difficult but the publication of these essays by the University of Chicago Press in 1948 brought Tillich even wider recognition.

The essays in *The Protestant Era* dealt with religion and culture. An emphasis was placed on the need for a spiritual reformation to offset the dehumanization and despair and meaninglessness brought on by industrial technology. The Protestant Principle and Religious Socialism were also given emphasis in *The Protestant Era.*

It was also in 1948 that the first volume of Tillich's sermons, *The Shaking of the Foundations,* was published. This volume and two other subsequent books of sermons were widely read and were helpful to many people. In Germany, especially at Frankfurt, Tillich had led a secular life and did not attend church. He had preached seldom since 1919. Upon joining the Union Seminary faculty in 1933 President Coffin suggested that chapel attendance was edifying for the faculty. From that time on Tillich seldom missed chapel and preached there at least once a year. Even after he left New York City, he returned to preach at the Union chapel. He sent out notifications of the event and then held an after-sermon party in his apartment or in the apartments of friends.[121]

Tillich's sermonic style was very appealing to intellectuals—both theologians and laymen. To communicate more effectively, Tillich coined new language for traditional religious terms. Sin became separation, or estrangement, and God was called the Ground of Being. Christ was related to New Being and the Holy Spirit to Spiritual Presence. In his sermons, Tillich always used and stayed with the biblical text and always seemed to be preaching to himself.

In 1951 Tillich went abroad. During this trip he received a Doctor of Divinity degree from the University of Glasgow in Scotland. He then lectured at the Institute of Politics at the Free University of Berlin on "The Political Meaning of Utopia." In June and early July he visited other leading centers of Germany.

In mid-July of 1951 Tillich returned to East Hampton to begin work on material related to one of the great honors which had come to him—the opportunity to deliver the famous Gifford Lectures. Once again President Van Dusen of Union Seminary was an important person in this arrangement. Van Dusen had noticed the distractions which were keeping Tillich from finishing his *Systematic Theology.* He recommended to the University of Aberdeen in Scotland that Tillich be asked to give the Gifford Lectures in 1953 and 1954. He was to use materials to be included in Volumes II and III of the *Systematic Theology* as the basis of the lectures. Furthermore,

Van Dusen and the Union officers granted him the Fall of 1951 to work on the lectures.

Tillich interrupted his sabbatical to give the Richard Lectures at Union Seminary in Richmond, Virginia, in the Fall of 1951. The lectures were published in 1955 under the title, *Biblical Religion and the Search for Ultimate Reality.* In these lectures Tillich defends his own roots in the biblical religion and states that every theologian utilizes or implies a philosophical position when he uses biblical language.

Volume I of Tillich's long anticipated *Systematic Theology* also appeared in 1951. This volume contained the Introduction to the System, sections on Reason and Revelation, and Being and God. In New York City, students crowded the Union Seminary bookstore for Tillich's autograph. The book brought forth praise from men like H. R. Niebuhr. On the other hand, some said it was too difficult and abstract. The book states Tillich's epistemology, or theory of knowledge, and some think it is the most difficult part of the system for non-specialists in theology. Henry Sloane Coffin, President-Emeritus of Union Seminary, is reported to have said that Volume I confirmed his suspicion that Tillich was not a Christian thinker, but a Greek mystic who held the heretical views of Plotinian dualism, Hegel, and Schelling.[122]

Tillich had made notes for his *Systematic Theology* before World War I. In 1924, in Marburg, he had planned its creation and even announced its publication for 1927. The *Systematic Theology* was the driving passion of his life. After reaching the United States he had given courses on the three parts of his theological system at Union Seminary from 1934 through 1951.

To help get Tillich's System into print, his assistant, John Dillenburger, wrote down everything Tillich said on his System in his lectures and had the material typed. This manuscript became Tillich's first draft of Volume I. A number of other people helped Tillich write and rewrite Volume I until it was finally published in 1951.

In May of 1952, Tillich returned to England to give the Firth Lectures at the University of Nottingham on "Love, Power and Justice." He also lectured on "Man in Late Industrial Society" to a British audience which included the Queen Mother Elizabeth and Princess Margaret.

A significant recognition for Tillich came with the publication in 1952 of *The Theology of Paul Tillich*, edited by Charles Kegley and Robert Bretall. For this volume Tillich wrote an autobiographical essay. Since Volumes II and III of the *Systematic Theology* were not yet in print many considered this book as preparatory and inadequate. However, some of the essays in the book are quite definitive.

One of Tillich's best-selling books, *The Courage to Be*, was also published in 1952. In this book Tillich emphasized that the chief characteristics of the twentieth century are anxiety and meaninglessness. Although neurotic anxiety is often curable, existential anxiety cannot be escaped and, therefore, must be faced with "the courage to be." This courage includes the audacity to be part of society, to be one's self and, finally, the boldness to let one's self be upheld by the creative power of being in which every person participates.

In the light of his emphases in *The Courage to Be*, some critics accused Tillich of being more of a Greek philosopher than a biblical theologian. On the other hand, this book enlarged Tillich's influence with psychologists and psychoanalysts and in nonacademic circles. He was given the title of "therapeutic theologian." [123]

The year 1953 was to be important for Tillich. He left New York for Europe on June 20 and was not to return until mid-December. His son René was to accompany him on the first part of this trip. The first four months were spent in Germany, Switzerland and Denmark lecturing and sight-seeing. One important lecture series was in Berlin on "The Jewish Question: A German and a Christian Problem." In these lectures he faced the problem of German guilt directly and openly even though he knew most Germans did not want to face it. The response was guarded and some Germans disagreed. These lectures are, however, some of Tillich's most profound statements and will be discussed when we deal with his perspective on the Jews. [124]

By November, 1953, Tillich arrived at the University of Aberdeen in Scotland to give the first half of the Gifford Lectures in November and early December. In 1957 these lectures were published as *Existence and the Christ*, which is Volume II of the *Systematic Theology*. The weather was cold in Aberdeen and the average attendance at the lectures was less than twenty.

Another monumental year in the career of Paul Tillich was 1954. He was receiving considerable acclaim for Volume I of *Systematic Theology*. For example, T. S. Eliot wrote to Tillich in March, 1954, that he had read Volume I of *Systematic Theology* twice and that it had a fertilizing effect on his mind. Harvard University gave Tillich a Doctor of Letters degree in 1954. In April of 1954, a full year before his retirement at Union, his appointment to Harvard was announced. A large number of congratulatory messages were received from both Europe and America.

In May of 1954 Tillich left for another European trip which would extend until December of 1954. For the first part of this trip his daughter, Erdmuthe Farris, accompanied him. From May until October Tillich again lectured and traveled widely in Europe. A highlight of the trip occurred on September 26 in Stuttgart, Germany. Here he delivered a lecture commemorating the centennial of Schelling's death in 1854. As will be recalled, this lecture would represent for Tillich a return to his intellectual beginnings.

In October, 1954, Tillich reached Aberdeen, Scotland. During the months of October and November, he delivered the second in his series of Gifford Lectures. The subject was "Life and the Spirit." This was the first part of Volume III of the *Systematic Theology* which was not to be published until 1963. In contrast to 1953, the weather was good in Aberdeen and the audience was larger and more enthusiastic. Tillich expressed gratitude for the opportunity which the Gifford Lectures gave him to concentrate on his main life's work which was to write the *Systematic Theology*.

The year 1954 saw the publication of *Love, Power and Justice*. Before the book was finished, he had lectured on the subject in Nottingham, England, Princeton and at Union Seminary in Virginia. In *Love, Power and Justice* Tillich seeks to show that love and power have to be understood together if sensitive people are not to abandon politics to the cynics. These lectures reveal Tillich as a faithful realist rather than as a cynic or a perfectionist.[125]

The year 1955 constituted a significant period for Tillich since it was the year of his retirement from Union Seminary. His second volume of sermons, *The New Being*, was also published in 1955. In May of that same year, Tillich gave a farewell speech to the New York Christian Action Group. He had been a member of this group since the 1930s. In this address he outlined how he and most of the group had adopted a pragmatic, gradualist attitude toward most of the political questions of the day.[126] Tillich also gave the commencement sermon at Union in the Spring of 1955.

In Tillich's farewell address to the Union Seminary board of directors, he affirmed that Union would always remain his "home" no matter where he went. With a greatness of spirit and affection that should not be thought deceptive he was to repeat this same statement seven years later in his farewell address at Harvard. After more than twenty years at Union Seminary in New York, the Tillichs had deep roots and many friends. It was not surprising that they were involved in a constant round of farewell parties which stretched out into the summer of 1955. A negative note was the loss during the school year of his young colleague in Philosophical Theology, David Roberts.[127] Union Seminary and Paul Tillich would always be closely associated in the minds and hearts of literally thousands of students and visitors who were influenced by his life and teaching during these momentous twenty-three years.

E. *Harvard (1955–1962)*

In the fall of 1955, at age sixty-nine, Tillich began his seven-year tenure as University Professor and member of the Divinity School faculty at Harvard University. As University Professor, he joined a select group of five or six distinguished and productive scholars who had the freedom to teach in interdisciplinary areas. These professors were appointed by the President of the University and were responsible only to him. President Nathan Pusey, a devoutly religious man, was determined to rebuild the Harvard Divinity School. Tillich was a "star" who would help Pusey in his Divinity School revitalization program.[128]

Both Paul and Hannah Tillich were highly pleased with the new appointment at Harvard. The handsome salary was nearly double his Union Seminary salary. Hannah states that they were both glad to be back on a university campus with its more open atmosphere. Hannah was also glad to get Tillich away from a lady friend and from German emigrés in New York City. She stated that the move was good for their marriage. In fact, the Tillichs entered into a new secret marriage pact. Paul gave Hannah a heavy gold ring as a symbol of this revitalized relationship.[129]

Tillich's large office in Widener library with a view of the Harvard campus symbolized for him a new-found freedom. As a University Professor he was in contact with a number of departments and faculties. He gave lectures in the Medical School on God, in the Business School on the theology of business, and in the Department of Social Relations on conformism. He spoke at the Fogg Art Museum on modern religious art and at the Massachusetts Institute of Technology on "Science and Man's View of Himself." As a "Boundary Line" theologian, Tillich maintained close ties with the Harvard Divinity School where he lectured and attended faculty meetings.

In his New York years Tillich had lectured primarily to professional and graduate students (Union Seminary and Columbia University). At Harvard he was to lecture to large crowds of undergraduates. His four-semester undergraduate courses on "Self-Interpretation of Western Man" were so popular that students came an hour early to get seats. Other highly attended undergraduate courses were on Philosophy of Religion and Religion and Culture.

In addition to his undergraduate courses, Tillich taught professional and graduate courses. The author was involved in advanced classes on German Classical Philosophy and the Theology of the Reformers. Tillich especially enjoyed a Graduate Colloquium for doctoral candidates which met in his apartment. A student would present the key ideas of his or her dissertation, and Tillich would respond. Harvey Cox reports that almost one-half of the students in the colloquium were from nontheological graduate departments.

On a number of occasions Tillich was to state that Harvard made him famous. The Harvard publicity machine ground out many stories on him. In turn, Tillich received hundreds of invitations to speak. He estimated that he turned down 90 percent of his invitations. In the first few years at Harvard he lectured away from the campus nearly every weekend. His itinerary included Boston, New York, Chicago, Los Angeles and points in between. Former students and German friends would usually act as his host. Tillich held the attention of students as did no other theologian in the United States. He had the great gift of making ancient ideas relevant to the twentieth century. On at least two occasions at the University of California at Berkeley, for example, he drew from 3,500 to 7,000 students for lectures.

Tillich's fame extended far beyond the borders of the United States. The German press was flooded with articles about him. It has been pointed out that from 1948 to 1955 he had lectured repeatedly in German universities. In 1956, on his seventieth birthday, the University of Berlin honored him with a Doctor of Philosophy degree. He stated that this honorary degree meant more to him than any other honorary degree he had received. Since he was a small boy, Berlin had been a symbol to him of all his yearnings and fulfillment. In the same year, 1956, Tillich was given the Goethe Medal of Frankfurt and the Great Order of Merit of the West German Republic.[130]

From his student days Tillich was devoted to the Greek language, philosophy and culture. In 1956 he was to have a dream fulfilled and travel to Greece. The sights of Greece overwhelmed him. After seeing the Parthenon he stated that the pagan Greek gods were real as creative forces. As Tillich toured Greece, he was deeply impressed with the unity of nature and landscape with the surrounding culture and architecture.

The year 1957 was to be known as the year of publication for Tillich. The first book to appear was *Dynamics of Faith*, a popular summary of some of his basic theological views which had often been emphasized in earlier writings. This was followed by the publication of, Volume II of the *Systematic Theology*. This volume contained part three of Tillich's system entitled "Existence and the Christ." It also contained the first part of the Gifford Lectures which Tillich delivered at Aberdeen, Scotland in 1953.[131]

The summer of 1958 found Tillich back in Europe. While in Switzerland he visited Karl Barth. Eberhard Busch, in his biography of Karl Barth, gives details of the visit. Barth commented that "Tillich is a charming man but his theology is impossible." Barth went on to say, "Oh dear, I have undertaken to hold a seminar on him for a whole winter." It is true that Barth spent the winter term of 1958–59 at Basel diagnosing Tillich's method of correlation. In the summer term of 1959 Barth had a seminar on his own view based on his new book on Anselm in order to contrast it with Tillich's view. One of Barth's problems in getting along with Tillich was that, according to Barth, Tillich thinks that "I have been asleep since 1920." [132]

Barth's negative opinion of Tillich did not prevent Tillich from becoming more and more popular in Germany. In 1958 plans were set in motion in Germany to publish Tillich's Collected Works. Tillich was consulted on what was important enough to be collected. Instead of an originally projected six volumes, the Collected Works were expanded to fourteen volumes which included an index and a complete bibliography. The first volume was published in 1959 and the last in 1975. By 1983, six supplementary volumes had been published.

In 1958 Tillich was awarded the Hanseatic Goethe Prize. This coveted prize was awarded annually to the person whose life work contributes to understanding among nations. Tillich attended the elaborate award ceremony in Hamburg City Hall.

The year following, the Circle of Friends of Paul Tillich was established in Germany under the leadership of Carl Heinz Ratschow, Professor at Marburg. This organization is now known as the German Paul Tillich-*Gesellschaft*. Its present headquarters is at Marburg. It meets annually and has grown to a membership of over two hundred. The membership of this group supports the German archive of Tillich's work in Marburg.[133]

That same year a Festschrift honoring Tillich entitled *Religion and Culture* was released in the United States. The volume contains articles by twenty-four of Tillich's contemporaries representing diverse disciplines.

Some of Tillich's finest essays were published in a volume entitled *Theology of Culture* in 1959. The book was edited by Robert Kimball, Tillich's literary executor. After reading these essays, Reinhold Niebuhr commented that Tillich was the most creative man in philosophy of religion in our time.

Perhaps the apex of popular recognition in the United States is to be featured as the cover personality of *Time* magazine. That recognition came to Tillich on 16 March 1959. Tillich sat for days for the artist who painted the cover picture and gave considerable time to interviews with *Time* writers. He was well-pleased with the cover story.

In perspective, many people such as Mircea Eliade, see Tillich's visit to Japan in 1960 as one of the most important events in his later life.[134] Tillich himself said that the visit had widened his horizons as much as his transplantation to America had done twenty-seven years earlier. This visit is delightfully described by both Paul and Hannah in Hannah's book entitled *From Place to Place*.

The Japan visit was under the auspices of the International Exchange Committee. This committee, composed of distinguished Japanese leaders, arranged an almost ideal program of lectures, sightseeing and discussions. They furnished Tillich with an interpreter, secretary and guide.[135] He had an opportunity to explore Shintoism, Buddhism (especially Zen and Jodo Shinshu), Japanese Christianity, Confucianism and the New Religions.[136] The Japanese people, with their patience and politeness, captivated Tillich.

The schedule concentrated on Tokyo and Kyoto with side visits to important shrines and a mountain resort. Tillich lectured in ten universities and preached in several churches.[137] His lectures emphasized religion and culture, philosophy of religion, religious socialism and the spiritual foundation of democracy. Tillich came to Japan to learn, but he was also quite candid and straightforward in some of his lectures and evaluations. He told the Japanese people that democracy was dependent upon the principle of individuality. He further stated that he did not find that principle emphasized in Buddhism and Islam. Tillich stated that he realized the fragility of democracy, but he saw democracy as the best way to protect creativity and individuality.[138]

Tillich's descriptions of his Japanese visit leave the distinct impression that the most stimulating part of his visit was the opportunity to have discussions with Shinto and Buddhist leaders and visit and enjoy their shrines, rituals and art treasures. An especially memorable discussion took place with the Zen Master, Hisamatsu, whom Tillich had known at Harvard. After a visit to a seven-hundred-year-old Zen rock garden, they discussed for over an hour the questions of whether the rock garden and the universe are identical (Buddhist position) or nonidentical but united by participation (Tillich's position).

Tillich also had lengthy discussions with Japanese Christian leaders. He admired the courage of the Christians and noted their widespread influence despite the fact that Christians make up less than one per cent of the Japanese population. He sounded a familiar theme in speaking to the Christian leaders. The Christian faith should present itself as a message over against all religions, Christianity included. Furthermore, Christianity should seek to express the "Christian event" in concepts which can be received by a highly civilized nation in its own language.[139]

Despite bad weather and schedule conflicts, Tillich attended the inauguration of President John F. Kennedy in January of 1961. He was greatly moved when he received one of 150 special invitations extended to a select group of American intellectuals. Tillich wrote John F. Kennedy that Kennedy's victory had rekindled his enthusiasm for politics. However, in October, 1961, Tillich became disillusioned after a discussion with Secretary of State Dean Rusk and James Reston of the *New York Times* on the use of atomic weapons in warfare. For Tillich, such a war could not be ethically justified because it would destroy what one wished to defend. Rusk, Reston and later the West German leadership saw Tillich's view as unrealistic and pacifist.[140]

In April of 1961, as the chief speaker at the Massachusetts Institute of Technology centennial celebration, Tillich stated that science was giving modern man means without ends. Technique had become an end in itself.[141]

It was also in 1961 that Tillich gave a series of significant lectures at Columbia University which were published in 1963 as "Christianity and the Encounter of the World Religions." [142] As early as 1958, Tillich had lectured on a similar subject at Wesleyan University and at the University of North Carolina. His trip to Japan, however, had caused the subject of world religions to have an even more important place in his thought. In these lectures Tillich dealt with quasi-religious (liberal humanism, fascism and communism) as well as the Christian-Buddhist dialogue. [143]

During the 1961–62 school year Tillich's health began to fail in a noticeable way. He had two serious illnesses which weakened him. In one case he was hospitalized. These illnesses and his forthcoming retirement from Harvard encouraged him to make arrangements to establish a Tillich archive at Harvard-Andover library. Upon his retirement, Tillich agreed to donate the great majority of his books and correspondence to the archive. Robert Kimball, one of Tillich's former assistants at Harvard, was appointed as his literary executor.

In terms of drama and high emotion few events in Tillich's career surpassed the farewell dinner in his honor on 24 May 1962. The setting, background and program made it what Tillich called "one of the great evenings of my life." The elegant dinner was served to 100 friends in the Busch-Reisinger Museum on the Harvard campus. All around the walls of the museum were old German wood sculptures. A string quartet played the music of Mozart and Hayden. Dean Samuel Miller of the Harvard Divinity School presided. Informal talks were given by Wilhelm Pauck, Rollo May, James Luther Adams, President Pusey and others. [144]

Tillich responded to the words of tribute by stating that Harvard had given him an opportunity as University Professor and professor in the Divinity School to carry through on what was the chief concern of his whole life, namely the reunion of what eternally belongs together but is separated—religion and the secular. In his concluding words Tillich urged Harvard to continue to be a *uni*versity which united the finite and the ultimate dimension in all of the realms of life. [145]

F. *Chicago* (*1962–1965*)

Since the days when Dean Jerald Brauer of the Divinity School of the University of Chicago had been Tillich's assistant at Union Seminary, he had high appreciation of Tillich's ability and significance as a theologian. He invited Tillich to become the first Nuveen Professor of Theology in the fall of 1962. According to Hannah, Dean Brauer and the Chicago friends did everything possible to make the Chicago experience a time of joy and fruitfulness. In turn, Tillich enjoyed the years in Chicago. (In introducing Tillich to a University of California at Los Angeles audience in 1963 the presider humorously observed that Tillich must be a saint because he actually liked Chicago.)

The Tillichs lived in an apartment in the Windermere Hotel on the lakefront near the University of Chicago. Dean Brauer provided Tillich with a suite of offices and a full-time secretary. He thoughtfully included in Tillich's contract an agreement that limited the number of Tillich's outside engagements. In turn, Brauer advised Tillich on which of his many invitations would be the most fruitful.[146] Tillich taught one course in the fall and spring quarters in the Divinity School in the school years of 1962–63, 1963–64 and 1964–65. The winter quarters in 1963 and 1964 were spent at the University of California at Santa Barbara.

In 1962, even before he began his lectures at the University of Chicago, Tillich was to receive an honor which for him crowned all others. On September 23 he was awarded the Peace Prize of the German Publishers Association. This coveted prize, first given to Albert Schweitzer in 1949, was a symbol of German freedom and democracy. The ceremony was held in St. Paul's church in Frankfurt. In the distinguished audience were the President of the West German Republic and the mayor of Frankfurt. A tribute was given to Tillich for opening the outside world to German scholarship after World War II. Otto Dibelius, Bishop of Berlin, gave an address of appreciation. He cited the fact that Tillich had forged a tie between Germany and the United States. Tillich responded with a speech on "Boundaries." He stated that the Germans must acknowledge the spiritual and intellectual boundaries which circumscribe them and then conquer these boundaries. He especially emphasized that the German people must remain open to the healing powers of eternity.[147] Tillich also stated that it was now time for the churches of Germany to return to the frontiers of culture and relate culture to the eternal.[148]

It has already been noted that Tillich was the subject of a *Time* magazine cover story in 1959. In 1963, Henry Luce, editor of *Time*, asked Tillich to be the principal speaker for the fortieth anniversary party for *Time* magazine in New York City. Luce, the son of missionaries to China, had known Tillich when Luce was a member of the Union Seminary Board of Directors. President Van Dusen had told Luce that Tillich was the most influential Protestant thinker in the United States.

Tillich delivered his speech on 6 May 1963, at the Waldorf Astoria Hotel before an audience composed of the subjects of 284 *Time* cover stories. These people represented all areas of American life. As each guest was introduced his or her cover picture was projected on a huge screen. Tillich spoke of the ambiguous character of all high achievement. According to Tillich, the United States had a free society, but it was one without depth. In the United States man is one-dimensional, expanding on a horizontal plane.[149] Tillich pleaded for the restoration of the vertical dimension in the United States and in Western culture. In referring to creative critics of society like himself as Socratic gadflies he suggested that the danger for such critics is that they will be "absorbed by the culture as another cultural good." [150]

On 2 June 1963, Tillich spoke at the Roofless Church in New Harmony, Indiana. This church was on the site of a German colony called Harmony. Harmony was founded in 1814 by a group of German Pietists led by George Rapp. In 1824, Harmony was taken over by Robert Owen, a Scottish industrialist. He called the village "New Harmony" and sought to build a socialistic, intellectual community and promote the arts and sciences. Because of human selfishness, New Harmony failed.

In 1950, Mrs. Kenneth Owen of Houston, Texas, the wife of Robert Owen's great-grandson, began a restoration of New Harmony. As a part of the restoration she commissioned the well-known American architect, Philip Johnson, to construct a "roofless church." As a part of the restoration, Mrs. Owen wanted to honor Paul Tillich. She did this by announcing plans to build a Paul Tillich park.

Tillich's visit to New Harmony was for the purpose of speaking at the dedication of the Paul Tillich park. He was given the privilege of suggesting the type of trees to be planted in the park. His choice was the German fir. In the completed park, on several large rocks in the grove of fir trees, the builders carved sentences from Tillich's sermons.[151] A bust of Tillich, sculptured and cast in bronze by Rosatti, stands on a pedestal among the trees.[152]

In 1963 the Tillichs fulfilled a long-anticipated desire to visit Egypt and Israel. Tillich's visit to Egypt was not successful. The tension between Jordan and Egypt meant that by going to Egypt Tillich had his Jordanian visa revoked. This kept the Tillichs from seeing the Old City of Jerusalem. The plans of the Islamic Foundation of New York to arrange lectures for Tillich in Cairo did not materialize. Despite the heat, the Tillichs did enjoy the pyramids and the mummies of the pharaohs. Tillich later stated that he preferred the more human Greek statues and temples to the quantitatively superhuman statues and temples of the Egyptians.

In contrast to Egypt, everything was well organized for the trip in Israel by the Israeli Foreign Office. Tillich was especially impressed with the Sea of Galilee. He also enjoyed the Jewish sector of Jerusalem. Tillich was saddened by the tragic, ever-repeated cycle of building, conquest and destruction in Israel. He came to the conclusion that the unifying power in Israel was the consciousness of a common tradition rooted in the Old Testament and preserved until today. In a perceptive analysis Tillich stated that the political developments in Israel may set Israel moving in a direction which will end by making it an unfit symbol of hope for the believing

Jews of the world. Tillich called for Israel to remain a symbol to Jews outside its boundaries. To do this it must maintain its ties to the prophetic spirit of Judaism.[153]

After leaving Israel Tillich went to the University of Zurich in Switzerland to conduct a seminar. Between seminar sessions, perhaps realizing it would be his last visit to Europe, Tillich traveled throughout Switzerland and Germany to see family and friends.

Karl Barth wrote Tillich a letter on 22 November 1963 welcoming him for a visit on December 1. In the letter Barth made humorous references to the Ground of Being and to Bishop John Robinson's *Honest to God* (which Barth said was horrible and Tillich praised).[154] Barth later reported that in this last meeting "I warned him that now might be the time to get himself straight. But he didn't seem to want to do that very much." Barth also remembered that they talked about Tillich's visit to Palestine. After Tillich's death Barth said that he thought that Tillich "now knows better about the inscription which he discovered in Nazareth and which he disapproved so much, saying 'Here the Word was made flesh.' " Barth went on to comment that one day we too will certainly know better.[155]

The year 1963 was another year of publication for Tillich when *Morality and Beyond* which deals with Tillich's view of the "transmoral conscience" and creative justice appeared. His third book of sermons, *The Eternal Now*, was also published in this year.

It was also in 1963 that Volume III of the *Systematic Theology* was completed, six years after Volume II. This volume constitutes parts IV and V of Tillich's system on "Life in the Spirit" and "History and the Kingdom of God." Parts of this volume contain the Gifford Lectures given at Aberdeen, Scotland, in 1954.

Part IV, "Life in the Spirit," is the longest part of the system and reveals the mystical roots of Tillich's thought. This section is Tillich's answer to the ambiguous nature of life where he affirms the reality of Spiritual Presence. This section also contains a lengthy discussion of the church.[156]

Part V discusses the ambiguity of history. History has structure, but human freedom and chance can upset the structure. The kingdom of God is the answer to this ambiguity. The kingdom of God as the Spiritual Presence of God is real in human history. It drives humanity to fulfill creativity, universality, and community. But the fulfillment is only fragmentary in history. The final answers are found in the kingdom as the end of history, or as eternal life.

Tillich rejoiced that he lived to see his system completed. In fact, some suggest that he felt that his vocation was fulfilled with the publication of his final volume of the *Systematic Theology*.[157]

One of Dean Brauer's purposes in inviting Tillich to Chicago was to afford Tillich a challenge to go on with his creative work after the completion of the *Systematic Theology*.[158] As we shall see, Tillich did continue to speak and publish and enter in a new way into the field of history of religions.

During the winter quarters of 1963 and 1964 Tillich conducted seminars at the University of California at Santa Barbara. The seminar of 1963 was published in 1965 as *Ultimate Concern: Tillich in Dialogue*. This book is one of the best primers available on Tillich's thought. The originally projected focus of inquiry for the seminar was on the problems raised by the contemporary encounter of major religious systems and the quasi-religious movements such as Communism, Fascism, Socialism and Nationalism. In actual fact, much of the seminar involved clarification of the meaning and nature of Tillich's terms and concepts.[159]

Tillich received a tremendous response from the students at Santa Barbara and at other California universities. In a lecture given at the University of California at Berkeley, 7,500 people attended.

Tillich remained active, vital and searching while in Chicago despite some health problems. One illness kept him from delivering a major address at the opening of the new galleries and sculpture garden of the Museum of Modern Art on 25 May 1964. In his prepared address, read by a friend at the opening, Tillich once again stressed that "the arts open up a dimension of reality which is otherwise hidden." Earlier in New York City, on 6 March 1964, Tillich attended a colloquium in his honor at the Cathedral of St. John the Divine. Some one hundred distinguished scholars from various fields attended.[160]

During the school year of 1964–65, his final fall school year at Chicago, Tillich cooperated in a two-semester, joint seminar with Mircea Eliade on the history of religions and systematic theology. Eliade states that despite his seventy-eight years, Tillich was more alert and resourceful than most members of the seminar. Tillich was primarily interested in the structures, historical concreteness and immediacy of archaic, traditional and oriental religions. He saw the significance of primitive and oriental religions for Christian theologians and for the world at large. Eliade states that in the seminar Tillich was renewing his own *Systematic Theology*.[161]

Some have commented that Tillich was at his dialectical best at the "Peace on Earth" conference in Chicago sponsored by the Organization for the Study of Democratic Institutions. The conference, convened by Robert M. Hutchins, on 18 February 1965, sought to explore ways to fulfill Pope John XXIII's peace encyclical of 1963. In his speech Tillich criticized the Papal Encyclical because it did not deal adequately with power and because it was too moralistic. In the light of man's ambiguity, Tillich states, genuine hope should be realistic and not utopian.[162]

As Tillich's fame increased, his writings were used widely as a source of authority. In 1965 the Supreme Court of the United States quoted from Tillich's *Systematic Theology* to defend a conscientious objector even though the objector was not a conventional theist. For Tillich, religion is a man's ultimate concern. This broader interpretation of religion accepted by the Supreme Court opened the way for many Americans to justify pacifism legally. This is ironic because Tillich himself was not a pacifist.[163]

On 2 March 1965, Tillich received an invitation to become the first person to hold the Alvin Johnson Chair of Philosophy at the New School of Social Research in New York City. It was an ideal arrangement calling for Tillich to teach one seminar and one public lecture course each year for an indefinite number of years.[164]

At almost the same time Tillich received an invitation to be a full professor at the University of California at Santa Barbara. Hannah was very much in favor of the Santa Barbara offer.

On 8 April 1965, Tillich accepted the New School offer to begin in March, 1966. In the words of Hannah, "the golden gates of Berlin, mirrored in New York, called again." [165] Later Hannah was to state that in a certain way, this new position would see his life in America return to its beginnings.[166] As we shall soon see, Tillich did not live to teach at the New School.

Tillich's last lecture (which was also his last public appearance) was given on 11 October 1965. He gave the concluding lecture for a History of Religions Conference at the Divinity School of the University of Chicago. His subject was "The Significance of the History of Religions for the Systematic Theologian." [167] After the lecture Tillich attended a social engagement at the home of Professor Joseph Kitagawa. Tillich reached home at midnight. In the early morning of October 12 he had a heart attack. He was to live for ten days.[168]

In her book, *From Time to Time,* Hannah describes in detail what Tillich called his "dying day." Tillich talked with Hannah about what happens to the centered self or human personality after death. The discussion also revolved around the Tibetan Book of the Dead and Buddhism. He reached out to touch a Greek New Testament. He asked forgiveness of Hannah for his wrongdoings. At about seven in the evening, on 22 October 1965, Tillich died.[169]

Because he had achieved widespread fame in the United States and Europe, his death resulted in extensive television, radio and newspaper coverage. A large article on his life appeared on the front page of the *New York Times* on 23 October 1965, accompanied by an editorial.

Memorial services for Tillich were held in Chicago, Cambridge, Massachusetts, New York City, Marburg, and Berlin. The author was on a sabbatical in New York City and attended a moving service at Union Seminary.

Tillich's body was cremated and the ashes interred in the East Hampton cemetery. Some seven months later, on 29 May 1966, Tillich's ashes were reinterred in the Paul Tillich Park in New Harmony, Indiana. A memorial service was held at the time of the reinterral in the Roofless Church adjacent to the Paul Tillich Park. In his address at the service, Rollo May stated that since Tillich's life began among German trees in a village in eastern Germany, it was fitting that his ashes should finally lie among the same kind of trees in a village in midwestern America.[170]

G. Significance of the American Period (1933–1965)

The significant external events in Tillich's life from 1933 to 1965 have been noted in some detail. These events represent Tillich's most fruitful period in terms of both literary production and theological influence. It has often been noted that these events are crucial if one is to understand Tillich's thought. His theology was influenced by his participation in the changing culture in which he lived. To some extent Tillich is led by these events, and he develops a theological interpretation of these events. To put it in another way, Tillich responds theologically to questions which are put to him or questions which he senses people are asking. On the other hand, Tillich had a particular theological and philosophical approach developed in his earlier years. Despite distinctive emphases in his American years, his American writings build on, update and continue his earlier work.

It will be helpful to note in a general way some of the distinctive developments of the American period as over against the 1919–33 period as well as Tillich's response to some of the new questions and insights which came out of the American period.

Tillich dealt more specifically with distinctively theological questions in the United States. It has been mentioned that Tillich lectured on artistic, social and political themes in relation to religion in Dresden and Frankfurt. In Europe his discussions tended to be with social and political scientists such as Horkheimer and Adorno in Frankfurt. In New York City, in a theological seminary, his concern necessarily was directed more to theological themes. The primary purpose of the seminary was to prepare ministers for parish work or for teaching religion.[171] Reinhold Niebuhr, for example, would direct conversations with Tillich in a more theological direction. By 1950, Tillich praised the more restrictive elements of his life at Union Seminary as a necessary discipline and corrective to the extreme individualism of his earlier academic career.[172]

In the United States Tillich found a different type of nonestablished church life. Although he had misgivings about the ability of the churches to provide a religious foundation for his hope for religious socialism, he did appreciate the fact that the churches were separated from the state.

This separation gave the churches a freedom to be more democratically open and socially concerned and interested in human rights than was the case with the established churches in Germany.

Closely related to the freedom in American church life was the freedom and nonhierarchical nature of life in general in the United States. The authoritarian nature of European life was not found in the family, schools and religion of the United States. Tillich, who had been known for experimentation in Germany, felt at home and prospered in this friendly and more open atmosphere in the United States.[173]

Tillich's message and personality were uniquely related to new developments in the United States in the late 1940s and early '50s. Before World War II, America was a rich land relatively untouched by the cataclysms of the world and was open to unlimited possibilities. World War II aroused many in the United States from naive optimism. The postwar period provided the "kairotic" moment for Tillich's approach. People became more concerned about the ultimate meaning of life and death. Life was no longer simple in an atomic age. America was powerful but insecure. In the midst of her wealth and riches she experienced a threat of meaninglessness. America was groping for answers.[174]

From his profound knowledge of biblical, Greek and European cultural history Tillich had the resources to speak to these questions. On university campuses and among disillusioned intellectuals, Tillich could fascinate an audience with his existential diagnosis and mystical answers. He was realistic without being cynical. In a different situation and in a different time Tillich had faced these questions, and he was now ready to adapt his answers to the American situation. Americans were ready to listen.[175]

John R. Stumme contends that Tillich's political period ended in 1945. From 1945–1965 social and political questions played a subordinate role in his life and thought. His emphasis on "kairos" and the opportunity for a new beginning and great change which he saw in Germany in the 1920s was modified. In the United States, in 1946, he spoke of a void developing. In this 1945–1965 period the ontological and priestly strain of his thinking overshadowed the eschatological, prophetic emphases of his earlier life. Existentialism and psychoanalysis largely took the place of Religious Socialism. He spoke more of the apolitical "courage to be" than of the concrete "socialist decision." The anxiety and meaninglessness of the upper and middle classes became the point of departure instead of the oppression of the under classes.[176]

Tillich was aware of this change and mentioned it in his discussion of the "void." This concept called attention to the relative social vacuum in his own work. It is a *relative* vacuum since the recital of the external events in his life has shown that he did continue considerable interest in social and political affairs.

Tillich identified his approach in America as a pragmatic, gradualist attitude to the political and social questions of his day. He contended that in spite of sharp differences there were continuities between this approach and his earlier one. Both his earlier and later approaches worked for the fragmentary actualization of the kingdom of God in history. But instead of an actual prophet he was more the guardian of the void who wants to keep the prophetic spirit alive in the church and in society.[177] This doctrine of the "sacred void" does imply, however, that there will eventually come a right moment in which to commence more positive, realistic and concrete programs of reconstruction.[178]

II. Tillich's Basic Purpose: Apologist to Intellectuals

Introduction

Tillich's basic purpose can be stated in a number of ways. According to Raymond Bulman, Tillich's chief purpose is to define the way in which Christianity is related to secular culture, from which the church had become isolated.[1]

Although there is some similarity to Bulman's statement of Tillich's basic purpose, Robert Schrader suggests a different formulation. According to Schrader, Tillich's basic purpose, especially as it is expressed in the *Systematic Theology*, is to be an apologist to intellectuals.[2] This basic purpose can be broken down into four separate aspects.

A. The first aspect is to *communicate* Christian faith to intellectuals. In fact, Tillich has been called an "apostle to the intellectuals speaking in their language." This description accurately conveys Tillich's conviction that his purpose is to be an interpreter of the Christian religion to intellectuals disaffected from the church and thrown into spiritual emptiness by secularization. The *Systematic Theology* may primarily be for the church, but it is for the church in conversation with humanistically educated skeptics.[3]

In a seminar at the University of California at Santa Barbara held in 1963 Tillich stated that he was concerned with those who are in doubt about, or in estrangement from, everything ecclesiastical. "My work is

with those who ask questions and for them I am here." [4] Tillich affirms
that he is attempting to lead "the cultured among the despisers" to rediscover
the lost dimension of cultural life which is the religious dimension.[5] Tillich
does not accept the criticism that he has surrendered the substance of
the Christian message because he has used terminology which deviates
from biblical or ecclesiastical language.

Tillich suggests that Karl Barth spoke to church people who were on
the boundary line of liberalism and who might have been led into a distorted
form of Germanic Christianity. Barth saved Christianity from this pitfall.
But, according to Tillich, Barth did not speak to the true intellectuals—
the people who think.[6] Tillich, however, sought to make faith possible
for these thinkers by removing unnecessary obstacles and searching into
the depths of the Christian tradition to find positive answers to their
questions.[7]

To accomplish his purpose Tillich sought to deliteralize, not demythologize, traditional symbols. Thus he spoke of faith as ultimate concern, of
God as Being-itself, of sin as estrangement, and of grace as acceptance.[8]
Tillich is not claiming that these words are necessarily better words than
traditional theological terms. Rather he is saying that an apologetic theology
directed to intellectuals will use the words they understand best.

B. The second aspect of Tillich's basic purpose is to develop a fresh
system of theology for apologetic purposes. In keeping with his desire to
communicate Christianity to educated people, Tillich advocated a systematic
approach because of its consistent nature.[9] Tillich is quick to deny that
he sought to write a complete *summa* such as that of Thomas Aquinas,
but he affirms that his system is more than an essay.[10]

For Tillich, *blatant* inconsistency turns away intellectuals. In fact, many
educated people have a particular need for and take a particular delight
in a system. Tillich himself states that it is impossible for him to think
theologically in any other than a systematic way. The smallest problem,
if taken seriously and radically, drove Tillich to other larger problems
and to the anticipation of an intelligible whole in which their solution
could be found.

Jerald Brauer of the University of Chicago suggests that Tillich's ability
to analyze and synthesize is a major reason for his impact on American
thought. Brauer describes Tillich's power of analysis and synthesis as an
artistic achievement. One evening Tillich outlined for Brauer an essay on
which he was working. As Tillich worked out the major concepts and relationship and their culmination, Brauer remembers that it was like listening
to a beautiful fugue unfold.

According to Brauer, Tillich saw as his primary task the construction
of his own theological system of meaning and coherence. This ability to
produce a system was one of the most compelling forces that attracted

and held the attention of his students. A synthetic mind which is truly constructive and creative is a rarity. Tillich's system may be criticized, but his systematic effort was greatly admired.[11]

C. The third aspect of Tillich's basic purpose is to *protect* the substance of the Christian faith from dangerous misinterpretations on the part of those within the church.

For Tillich, the misuse of reason must be fought with reason. A distorted doctrine leads to misunderstanding.[12] Tillich's book, *Dynamics of Faith*, was written in part to help overcome some dreadful distortions of the biblical idea of faith. For Tillich faith is distorted when it is conceived as either a knowing (intellectualism), a doing (moralism), or a feeling (emotionalism). In turn, he sought to define faith with an expression which suggests that faith is not merely a function of a particular faculty of the mind. Faith should be seen as involving both the depths and the totality of the self. Tillich defines faith as a state of being grasped by an ultimate concern.[13]

Another dangerous development in Christianity which Tillich seeks to uncover and correct is what is for him a wrong kind of literalism. For Tillich, a literalistic approach to Scripture is absurd and has less power than the existential-symbolic approach. Literalism leads intellectuals to reject the Christian message. Furthermore, the literalist himself has to stress the ultimate authority of his own reason. This leads to personal disintegration, fanaticism, and hostility toward others. Literalism often leads to dishonesty. Tillich seeks to "deliteralize" (not demythologize) biblical symbols for those who are able and willing to apply rational criteria to the meaning of religious symbols.

Tillich also seeks to point out and correct the danger of profanization. Profanization involves the process of transforming religion into a finite object among finite objects. The result is naturalism, humanism, and theological liberalism, which are powerless.

D. The fourth aspect of Tillich's basic purpose is to establish an *ontological* or *philosophical* base for the Christian faith. For Tillich, *some* kind of ontology is presupposed in almost *any* kind of discourse. Ontology is used by Tillich in its very broadest sense and is more or less equated with "presuppositions about reality." In *Biblical Religion and the Search for Ultimate Reality* Tillich affirms that ontology is implicit in biblical religion. In his other writings he seeks to establish his own understanding of ontology as an adequate orientation for the expression of the Christian faith. As will be noted in detail in the next section, Tillich's ontology is mystical, reflecting Plato, Plotinus, Augustine, the medieval mystics, and Schelling. Tillich admits that there is another type of ontology in the Bible which is more personalistic, nominalistic, moral, and prophetic. In the Christian faith both types of ontology are united—especially in the apostle Paul. The first or mystical type of ontology stresses participation. The second or moral type emphasizes judgment. According to Tillich, these two approaches differ not in principle but in emphasis.

In a 1958 letter to Tillich, Emil Brunner states that he believes Tillich is right in maintaining that ontology lies at the basis of biblical thinking. Brunner further states that what Tillich does with his mystical-ontological approach is noteworthy. But, according to Brunner, it is good that there are two ways, and there will continue to be two ontological approaches in the future.

Tillich emphasizes faith, experience, and inwardness because he thinks that these emphases are in danger of being overlooked. In other days perhaps he would have emphasized the more personal, moral, and prophetic approach. Tillich admits that he is perhaps overemphasizing the mystical side, which has been neglected, to achieve balance. He thus seeks to emphasize God as Being-itself in which we immediately participate. Tillich also emphasizes the "experience" of the New Being.

People who accept a Christianity devoid of mystical ontology will tend to become profanized (powerless) as in liberalism or hardened and demonized as in orthodoxy. The liberals, according to Tillich, without a mystical ontology will tend to identify religion with a set of ethical commands. On the other hand, without mystical ontology, the orthodox will become authoritarian and legalistic. Tillich admits that the neglect of the moral and prophetic ontology has its own dangers.

Tillich believes that the use of mystical ontology can help in the verification of the Christian faith for intellectuals. This verification is done on the basis of reason in the name of the universal *Logos*. Furthermore, Tillich affirms that mystical ontology helps all persons to penetrate beneath the surface of things and see their basic presuppositions. This uncovering helps us to see the common ground which is presupposed in our encounter with reality. We recognize that we have been given the need, the command, and the desire to find our common ground in Being, or God. This recognition opens the way for the presentation of the New Being as the power for reconciliation with God and with one another.[14]

III. Tillich's Basic Idea (Ontology): Essence, Existence, Essentialization

Introduction

Tillich's whole theological or onto-theological system derives its structure and form from his understanding that ultimate reality is involved in a movement of unactualized essence into existence and then in a return to fulfilled essentialization. This basic model incurs the risk of creating a stereotype, but the advantage of such a procedure is that it can serve to illumine Tillich's system of thought and more easily reveal the implications of his system. Wayne Proudfoot calls Tillich's system a monistic model, while Anders Nygren describes it as an onto-theology.[1] In any case, the essence-existence-essentialization categories which are sometimes only implied operate in each section of Tillich's system and seem to provide the key to the system itself. Consequently these three categories provide in large part (though not exclusively) the controlling structure and the dynamics of Tillich's system.[2]

By these emphases Tillich wants to show that the religious dimension of life precedes and informs in a potentially harmonious way every meaningful dimension of human life. According to Tillich, the loss of this participational view explains why the modern West has lost its sense of the presence of God as a source of life within life, and why, in most cases, the profession of the Christian faith leads to a break with humanity and culture.[3]

A. *Essence*

Essence is seen as both the principle of man's unity with God, and the basis of the intelligible and the good in man and creation. There is a twofold use of the term "essence" in Tillich's writing. First, essence is that which makes a thing *what* it is (logical character or ideal). Second, essence is that which appears in an imperfect and distorted way in a thing and which carries the stamp of value (valuation character). Essence, in this second sense, is what a thing should be but is not in its appearance in existence.[4]

The first or logical meaning of essence has many implications. Essence is the depth of things and gives them power of being. Essence is potentiality. The ontological priority of essence over against the universals makes the creation of universals possible. The realm of essence is a realm which our cognition can never entirely penetrate. This realm of essence is the source of existence. Essence is God or Ground of Being or the "really real" or the "depth of reality." [5]

Essence plays a structuring function. Essence and *Logos* are closely related. *Logos* is the principle of the intelligible manifested both within and without the divinity. *Logos* provides the principle of structure, both in the human mind and in reality. *Logos* correlates mind and reality. It is that which makes knowledge possible. It is in the essential structures of reality that God is present. However, these essential structures in existence are never more than partial reflections or expressions of the divine presence. Christ and God can manifest themselves in and through structures of reality without destroying these structures. Tillich sees the dialectical absence and presence of God in the essence-*logos* structure of creation. This view protects Tillich from pantheism.[6]

The second or valuational meaning of essence brings the note of good into the nature of essence. This good is the motivating power which drives existent man to seek to realize fully his essence. This essence stands over or within the existent man as his sustaining ideal. In virtue of the value of essence, existent or existing man strives onward toward greater good.[7]

B. *Existence*

In existence, man departed from this essential unity and so invited disruption. However, God and man are still related in the structures of essential man. Man retains essence in existence. The dynamic of man's own life (remnants of essential man) thrusts him toward essentialization.[8]

Existence is seen as the principle of distance between man and God and is thus closely related to alienation, guilt, and sin. In existence man is that finite being who is aware both of his belonging to and separation from the infinite. Tillich sees man's being religious and his being human as one and the same thing.

Tillich, however, disagrees with Hegel who sees man so attaining his essential nature in existence that there is an implied union with God whereby man sits in the center of the infinite. For Tillich, man never attains his essential humanity in this life even though the essential underlies his existential life.

There are only partial, distorted, and fragmentary appearances of essence in existence. The separation of power and form in existence accounts for the existential or disruptive side of actual creation. This separation also explains the dynamic in all of the created order, especially man. Man wants to preserve form and yet transcend form. Essence is always hidden yet shines through this existential distortion.[9]

Tillich's description of the transition to existence and the resultant existential state is given in a number of stages. 1. A transition is possible because of the structure of finite freedom. While finite freedom is unactualized, essential being is symbolized as dreaming innocence. Then dreaming innocence is exposed to temptation. Finite freedom thus becomes aroused freedom. Aroused freedom becomes actualized freedom. Actualized freedom is the loss of innocence and the loss of freedom. The actuality of existence has a moral element because man personally is responsible. On the other hand, the actuality of existence has a tragic element because it is unavoidable.

2. The transition to existence gradually becomes more extreme and desperate. It results in estrangement, guilt, and despair. Despair is the final abyss of man's predicament. The bondage of man's will means that man cannot break through his estrangement. This inability reveals to man his need to seek the New Being.

3. Finite freedom is that which makes man's transition to existence possible. Finitude in itself is limited, but this does not mean that it is estranged. Man, as finite freedom, is free within the contingencies of his finitude. He uses his finite freedom to contradict himself and his essential nature.

4. Under the conditions of existence Jesus is the only actual concrete manifestation of essential finitude without distortion.

5. The creation of finite freedom is the risk which the divine creativity accepts.

6. Man is caught between the desire to actualize his freedom and the demand to preserve dreaming innocence. In the power of his finite freedom he decides for actualization. Nature and universal existence, therefore, both share in man's guilt.

7. The state of existence is thus the state of estrangement. Man is estranged from the Ground of Being, other beings, and himself.

8. In Tillich's thought creation and the fall seem to coincide. The fall is both a fact and an act.

9. For Tillich, estrangement largely replaces what has been traditionally called sin. One of the most complex aspects of Tillich's system is his description of the ontological polarities which characterize man's state of estrangement.

10. Tillich indicates that man is given two choices: actualize his freedom or preserve his dreaming innocence. But as man who is essential goodness does actualize his freedom, he becomes a part of estranged existence.[10]

C. *Essentialization*

In essentialization through New Being there is a return to the integration of Trinitarian life and a unity from which man never fully departs in so much as he retains essence even in existence. In essentialized (reunited) man this participation becomes more intense as man's union with his essence becomes his union with God. Essentialization is thus a return to fulfilled essence. As we shall see, eschatology (last things) is correlated with essentialization.

As has been noted, Tillich describes essential creation as good in terms of man's unbroken and yet untried unity with God. He describes actual creation and the reality of fallenness in terms of a transition from this essential goodness to an ambiguous or mixed goodness in existence. Tillich's soteriology and eschatology endeavor to show how the dynamic of creation-fall can be reversed through participation in New Being. He describes this as the process of man's reunion with his essential unity with God. This is his concept of essentialization.

In Tillich's system this is expressed symbolically in the phrase "New Being" and translated philosophically into "essential being under the conditions of existence conquering the gap between essence and existence." In this saving transition from existence to essentialization the negativities of existence are negated. Hence, Tillich can describe the full sweep of his system in terms of a process moving "from essence to existence to essentialization." [11]

New Being is the restorative principle of the theological system of Tillich. New Being appears in the form of a personal life. Jesus as the Christ is the bearer of the New Being in whom man's existential estrangement is overcome. In Jesus the Christ essential finitude or New Being or "essential God-manhood" is actualized. The image of Christ shows what God wants man to be. Jesus the Christ shows what man essentially is and therefore ought to be. That which is potential in every man is actualized in Jesus as the Christ.[12]

The doctrine of salvation is described as "participation in the New Being" (regeneration), acceptance of the New Being (justification), and transformation by the New Being (sanctification). New Being is paradoxical in so much as it is contrary to man's self-understanding and expectation. Jesus is the medium of final revelation because as essential man he sacrifices himself completely to Jesus as the Christ.

Essentialization is more than a return to essence. Even conflicts and suffering serve the enrichment of essential being. In the transition to the eternal the negative is defeated in its claim to be positive. In total essentialization only the positive elements of existence and New Being are remembered. The negative elements are forgotten and discarded as nothingness which is the negative side of the symbol of ultimate judgment.

In the process from essence through existential estrangement to essentialization, the world-process gains something. The essences are enriched by a threefold process of actualization (existence), restoration (New Being), and finally the transition to the eternal (essentialization). The divine life is the eternal conquest of the negative. The negative pole in the dual aspect of life processes is still retained in eternity, but it remains as something which is eternally overcome. The essentialization of the individual person is a matter of degree, depending on how much positive there remains in a person after the negative in him is negated. This individual essentialization may result in a quality of life which can be characterized as extreme poverty or extreme enrichment.[13]

Anticipating the discussion of Tillich's Christology and the general evaluation of Tillich, it can be said at this point that the content of the meaning of Christ is in large measure determined by Tillich's philosophical usage of the essence-existence-essentialization concept.[14] Kenan Osborne, for example, contends that the axial concepts of essence-existence-essentialization are so all-dominating in Tillich's thought that they tend to predetermine how the God-man relationship may or may not be understood.[15] However this may be, it should be helpful to realize that the concept of essence-existence-essentialization, first articulated by Schelling and then developed by Tillich, dominates Tillich's entire theological work.

IV. Historical Influences on Tillich's Basic Idea and Basic Method

Introduction

Although Tillich did not call himself a technical historian, his mind was filled with a consciousness of history. His students were awed by his ability to trace from memory the history of an idea. The author participated in a number of Tillich's lecture courses and seminars in the history of thought and was greatly impressed by his grasp of philosophy and theological history. What some thought was Tillich's originality was seen at a deeper level as material borrowed and transformed by his erudite and synthetic mind.

Tillich held that the ideal of unbiased historical research which reports only the "naked facts" without any admixture of subjective interpretation was a questionable concept. The historian necessarily has a perspective and thus selects and organizes the facts from his interpretative viewpoint.[1]

Tillich openly states that he had an interpretative viewpoint. He was attracted to and thus influenced by thinkers who had an ontology grounded *on* the reality of divine immanence *in* creation and *in* human consciousness. If a thinker fails to ground the theological self-understanding of Christianity on the immanence of the infinite in the finite, Tillich sees the result as a dualistic theology. He frankly calls for a revival of the Augustinian sense of the divine immanence as the basis of a modern correlation between man (in both his personal and cultural life) and God. In fact, the history of theology is an ongoing drama of the efforts of philosophical theology to work out this correlation between faith and humanity in each age.[2]

To understand Tillich properly, some acquaintance with the theological and philosophical traditions on which he drew is necessary. In fact, it is difficult to understand Tillich's terms unless they are unraveled in the light of their history. A correlative benefit of this brief survey of representative historical influences on Tillich's thought will be to reveal that his thought is eclectic and formed from disparate historical elements.[3]

Tillich's uniqueness, creativity, and originality lay in the comprehensive scope of his vision and in the systematic consistency with which he developed the internal relations of the various elements of his philosophical theology. He was eclectic, but he was also creative and original.[4]

A. Ancient Period

1. *Parminedes (b. 510 B.C.) and the Pre-Socratics.* Tillich's love of the Greek language was a vehicle for his attraction to the Pre-Socratics and especially to Parminedes with his question of "Why is there not nothing?" [5] Tillich sees the principle of participation as originating with Parminedes.

He also appreciates the emphasis of Parminedes on the fact that being is older than becoming.[6] Some of Tillich's outstanding lectures were on the Pre-Socratics and the question of being.[7] In fact, Rollo May contends that Tillich was closer to the Pre-Socratics, such as Heraclitus, Empedocles and Parminedes, than he was to the Greek philosophers of the classical age.[8]

2. *Plato (427–347 B.C.).* Adrian Thatcher sees many of Tillich's concepts as having roots in or resembling the ideas of Plato. For example, Being itself in Tillich resembles Plato's Form of the Good. Likewise, Plato's forms resemble Tillich's essences. Tillich evidently drew from Plato's distinction of the Form "Good" from existence or becoming and Plato's idea that existence depends on the Good for its being and reality. Tillich's ideas of *eros* and participation also resemble those of Plato.[9] It is not surprising that Tillich defended Greek thought and its existential concern with the eternal against the criticism of Adolf von Harnack that Greek thought had distorted Christianity.[10]

3. *Plotinus and Neo-Platonism (A.D. 205–269).* Tillich was also influenced by the Plotinian vision of the ultimacy of the One. From Pseudo-Dionysius comes an emphasis on the God beyond God. The "God-above-God" of Tillich's *Courage to Be* is reminiscent of the Neo-Platonic search for the ultimate power of being in that which is beyond being—in the "good," the "pure actuality," or the "One." [11]

4. *Logos Theologians (ca. 2nd century A.D.).* With many of the early Christian theologians the *logos*, for Tillich, becomes the principle of God's self-manifestation to himself in the dynamics of his intra-Trinitarian life. The *logos* is also seen as the manifestation of God to creation as its structuring and thus its immanental and universal principle.

Tillich maintains that the theological use of the *logos* principle by Justin Martyr, Irenaeus, Clement of Alexandria, and Origen is the initial apologetic effort to relate the particularity of Christ to the universality of the human condition. For Tillich, a theology without *logos* is barbaric and fanatic. Such a theology would implicitly devaluate the created and the human, and imply that the divine comes wholly from without the created and the human.[12]

When Tillich called himself an apologetic theologian, he had in mind the example of the great second-century apologist Justin Martyr. For both Justin Martyr and Tillich, the *logos* doctrine provides common ground for the Christian and those outside organized Christianity. The *logos* doctrine makes it possible for men in all religions and cultures to have a partial grasp of the truth, a love of beauty, and a moral sensitivity.

Of the *logos* theologians, perhaps Origen had the greatest influence on Tillich's Systematic Theology. From Origen, Tillich adopted ideas relating to mysticism, the symbolic significance of religious language, and the doctrines of the *logos*, the Trinity, creation, the transcendental fall and universalism.[13]

5. *Augustine (354–430)*. It is especially in the writings of Augustine that Tillich finds his theological ancestry. In fact, he says, "If anyone wants to place a label on me, he can call me an Augustinian. . . . I am in basic agreement with Augustine with respect to the philosophy of religion." [14]

A number of concepts held by Augustine influenced Tillich. One is the concept of the goodness of creation founded in the structures of reality. It should also be noted that much of Tillich's understanding of essence and existence is related to Augustinian thought.

In his early years Augustine was a skeptic. He first turned to Neo-Platonism to escape the world and to unite with the One. Next he reversed the thrust of Neo-Platonism by placing the absolute for which he strove not beyond man and reality but *within* man and reality.

According to Tillich, with this concept of the location of God within man, Augustine created a new epistemology. Augustine used this epistemology of the "inner man" to refute skepticism by establishing an immediate mystical union with God in man's depth. This was also Augustine's answer to man's search for certitude.

It is obvious that Tillich appreciated and utilized much of Augustine's view on epistemology. According to Augustine, if the soul is the chief *locus* of God's presence to man, the cognitive union of man and God can best be described as the union of subject with subject and not as the relation of a human subject with God as object. Knowledge of God is man's union with God who is present to man in his human and rational structures. Thus, man's experience with God is man's most profound experience of himself. This further means that sensible knowledge of the exterior world is secondary in significance as a *locus* of worthwhile meaning.

A further implication of Augustine's epistemology which influenced Tillich is that man's search for truth is his search for the *logos* structure of reality and hence is a religious search. Consequently, philosophy and theology are involved in essentially the same endeavor. The Christian has much in common with the pre-Christian or non-Christian search for the *logos*. However, only the Christian can affirm that the *logos* has become incarnate.

Tillich uses some of Augustine's ideas to develop his Christology. The appearance of Christ as the *logos* is the unexpected appearance in existence of the human *logos* in its essential reality of unbroken unity with God. While the Christian may affirm and the philosopher may deny that the perfect *logos* of man has appeared, yet in their common quest for the *logos* they have a common ground which precedes the denial and affirmation of Christ as the *logos*.

Tillich is also appreciative of Augustine because Augustine was not an Aristotelian. In opposition to Aristotle's more rational, horizontal, and inductive approach, Augustine has an intuitive, voluntaristic, and more deductive approach. When Tillich speaks of these qualities in Augustine's thought, he is again speaking of qualities present in his own theology.[15]

B.   *Medieval Period*

Unlike many Protestants, Tillich had a muted appreciation for the Middle Ages. He was not a romanticist, but he did see in the Middle Ages a cultural organism in which the religious center had strong influence on all forms of cultic, legal, moral, and aesthetic activities. In fact, Tillich drew inspiration for his concept of theonomy from the romantic view of medieval society. Beginning with faith, especially in the thirteenth century, the mind was opened to see the reflections of the divine presence in all realms and facets of life.[16]

1. *Anselm of Canterbury (1033–1109).* It was Anselm who brought to a peak the ontological argument for God. For Anselm, man is immediately aware of the presence of God. From Tillich's perspective, this argument is superior to the arguments for the existence of God which reduce God to one object among many. For Tillich, these rational arguments for God's existence are blasphemous and often produce an atheistic response.[17]

2. *Francis of Assisi (ca. 1182–1226).* Tillich was impressed with the emphasis of Francis on a mystical religious fraternity with all of created reality both human and subhuman. Tillich saw this teaching of Francis as theologically founded on a perception of the divine presence as ground of all reality. He sees this insight of Francis as capable of bringing about a unified view of religion, culture, and nature itself.[18]

3. *Meister Eckhart (b. 1260).* According to Thatcher, Tillich was influ-

enced by several teachings of Meister Eckhart. These include the identification of God with Being-itself, the distinction between God and the Godhead, the concept of depth or *Urgrund*, and the idea of the *logos* in the soul of every man.[19]

C. Reformation Period

1. *Martin Luther (1483–1546)*. In the view of Carl Braaten, an important part of Paul Tillich's contribution to American Protestantism was his reinterpretation in contemporary terms of the message of the Reformation. There is no doubt that Tillich was greatly influenced by Martin Luther. Under his vital treatment the great doctrines of the Reformation became living symbols of the new relationship between God provided by Luther's reformatory work.

For Tillich, some of Luther's vital teachings have become distorted. For example, Tillich states that in the formula "justification by faith," faith has been transformed into a work which a man is exhorted to perform on his own conscious decision. This is contrary to Luther's view. To avoid this tendency, Tillich suggested that it might help to say justification *through* faith instead of *by* faith. This would mean that faith does not *cause* but *mediates* God's grace.[20]

From Tillich's perspective, the authoritarian, medieval church could not make the Christian faith religiously compelling. Christianity degenerated into legalism, quantification, and magic. At this point Luther entered. Tillich does not attribute to Luther a highly explicit and sophisticated participational ontology. He does state that much of Luther's power comes from his ability to reestablish the experiential basis of divine acceptance through his doctrine of justification by faith. This capacity is related to Luther's mystical appreciation of an immanent, divine presence in both its willful or dark side and its revelatory and reassuring side.[21]

Carl Braaten points out Luther's influence on Tillich's doctrine of correlation. Luther said that what makes a theologian is his ability to distinguish rightly between law and gospel. This means that law and gospel must be differentiated without being separated or being confused. This emphasis of Luther makes its appearance in Tillich's system as the methodological principle of correlation. Before Tillich would announce the Christian answer, the *kerygma,* he would carefully describe the human predicament as man's existence *under the law.* The presentation of the Christian answer offers the new possibility of life *under the gospel.* For Tillich, the proper theological method is always law (posing the question) before gospel (the attempt to answer). This is different from Karl Barth who placed the gospel (Christ) before the law (the analysis of man's actual situation). In Tillich's correlation approach, philosophy functions as law (raising the question) while theology functions as the gospel (the divine answer).[22]

Luther's "law of contrasts" in his doctrine of God (God's hiddenness and revealedness, wrath and love, left hand and right hand kingdoms) is reflected in Tillich's teaching that there are ontological polarities in the depth of the divine life. For example, Luther's idea of the devil as the agent of God's wrath is seen in Tillich as a negative principle, as the principle of nonbeing which is gnawing at the foundations of reality. This idea appears in Tillich's doctrine of the "demonic." [23]

Although Tillich had deep roots in the mystical-ontological-idealistic tradition, he placed this entire heritage under the criticism of the "Protestant principle." This principle came from the Pauline-Lutheran tradition. The estrangement between God and man is overcome and man is accepted even in his sin and doubt solely on the basis of God's grace without any merit or worthiness on man's part. Where this paradox of the divine-human relationship is understood and accepted, all ideologies are destroyed.[24]

2. *Jakob Böhme (1575–1624).* In a gathering of philosophers in the home of Nels Ferré, Tillich pronounced his famous dictum that his spiritual father was Schleiermacher, his intellectual father was Schelling, and his grandfather on both sides was Jakob Böhme.[25] Tillich was obviously influenced by Böhme in terms of his dialectical thinking in mystical-ontological categories.

According to James Luther Adams, Böhme's theosophy represents for Tillich the modern fountainhead of that dynamic, voluntaristic outlook which interprets the world as an emanation of tension between the ultimate ground and the abyss.[26]

Adrian Thatcher states that one must go to Böhme first to find the origin and significance of Tillich's concepts of ground of being and abyss. Böhme had coined his own word for abyss, *Ungrund,* literally "not-ground." Böhme, then, had considerable influence on Tillich's idea of a monistic God whose life consists of a violent interaction between two poles and a dualism internal to God himself. Nonbeing in this tradition is the originating principle in God himself, and the source of all change and potentiality in the created world. God is an eternal abyss, but within the abyss there is a "will" through which the abyss generates itself into a Ground. The eternal principle of becoming in God must be accorded equal status with the eternal principle of being. The principle of becoming is the good, creative element in the internal dualism within God.

In Tillich's thought, drawing on the Böhme tradition, the pair of concepts known as the ground of being and the abyss of being are almost synonymous with becoming and being. Ground and abyss are dialectically related to one another and in constant interplay between one another. The dialectical relation between ground and abyss mirrors the parallel dialectical relation in God between being and nonbeing. According to Tillich, this type of description of God provides a safeguard for the inscrutable mystery of God.[27]

D. Modern Period

According to Tillich, Protestant orthodoxy after the Reformation brought a needed conservative objectification to the Protestant reforms. This objectification, however, was gained at the expense of the diminishing of the power of the great inaugural experience of the Reformation.[28]

The reaction to the overemphasis on the objective contents of doctrine and ecclesiastical organization came largely from the Pietist tradition. Led by men such as Philip Jacob Spener, the Pietists put more emphasis on the "inner light," immediacy, and the subjective as well as the practical expression of Christianity.[29] It is in the doctrine of the inner light, which places ultimate truth and the reality of God within man, that Tillich locates the origins of the Enlightenment. When this inner light loses its religious aspect, it can be reduced to an identification with reason itself. It is in this sense that Tillich understands rationalism to be the daughter of mysticism, and the Enlightenment to be the child of the Reformation.[30]

1. *Immanuel Kant (1724–1804).* In a 1784 essay, Immanuel Kant stated that to be enlightened man must be free from the fetters of heteronomously imposed authority. True religion and true morality must find their basis within man himself and not be imposed from the outside in the form of external authority. Within limits, Tillich is to be classed among theologians who sought to work within the terms of the Enlightenment as defined by Kant.[31] He adopts and uses certain Kantian concepts such as the limitation of reason in existence, *a priori* concepts, and the *logos*-structure of the mind for responding to the *logos*-structure of reality. He finds in Kant's analysis of finitude, particularly of man's finitude, a clear expression of that quest or question which can only be answered by theonomy or by God's revelation. Tillich sees Kant seeking to overcome relativity through the discovery of something absolute in the moral imperative.[32]

From the beginning, however, Tillich rejected the view that theonomy or revelation is in some way antithetical to the hard-won autonomy of the Enlightenment period. In fact, he held that in a secular culture, made free from the domination of heteronomous religion, the divine *logos* may be more unambiguously seen in autonomous cultural spheres, such as art and philosophy, than in the more specifically religious sphere. For Tillich, there is a religious element in autonomy wherever the spirit of truth is present as unconditional demand or theonomy. Tillich calls theonomy a self-transcending autonomy.[33]

In Kant Tillich found much that was unacceptable. The native religiosity of the human spirit cannot rest within the limits of the finitude to which Kant's first critique had confined it. Furthermore, man cannot rest with the reduction of his religiosity to morality as described in Kant's second critique. Tillich wants to reaffirm the experience of the presence of God on a more holistic basis wherein man's experience of the religious cannot be reduced to any one of his capacities or experiences.[34]

Kant's "categorical imperative" is helpful for Tillich, but it is too abstract and limited. Tillich takes over the "categorical imperative" and connects it with the notion of "ultimate concern." For Tillich, it is in Christ, the Essential Man, that one discovers the material norm of the "what-should-be." Tillich also states that the doctrine of knowledge in Kant absorbed the question of being. Tillich emphasized the ontological over the epistemological and makes *logos*-ontology the center of his system.[35]

2. *Friedrich Schleiermacher (1768–1834)*. Early in his career Friedrich Schleiermacher spoke of the need to establish a perpetual alliance or pact in which the autonomy of neither the Christian faith nor modern knowledge would be threatened. His objective was to establish such an alliance on Protestant foundations. Yet, the two (the Christian faith and modern knowledge) were to remain distinct.[36]

Tillich appreciated Schleiermacher for many reasons. He appreciated, for example, the fact that Schleiermacher respected Kant but sought to surpass Kant by relocating the being of the infinite within the being of the finite. Schleiermacher did this in such a way as to preserve the demands of autonomous reason while pointing again to reason's theonomous depths. In other words, in his synthesis Schleiermacher kept the proper tension between God's transcendent discontinuity with man and the principle of the identity of God with man.[37] It must be remembered that Tillich kept alive the memory of Schleiermacher when it was generally popular in theology to debunk him. Emil Brunner had charged the ills of modern Protestantism to Schleiermacher.[38]

According to John Dourley, Tillich is indebted to Schleiermacher's analysis of man's religious experience of his creaturehood. Schleiermacher states that man's experience of a feeling of dependence is derived from that power on which he depends, which is at once both within and beyond him. Tillich chose to use "ultimate concern" instead of Schleiermacher's absolute dependence. In fact, Tillich criticizes Schleiermacher for using so vulnerable a word as "feeling" to describe this consciousness of dependence.[39]

John Clayton points out that Tillich's "ultimate concern" is active and Schleiermacher's "feeling of utter dependence" is passive. Furthermore, one can be utterly dependent in Schleiermacher's sense only upon God, but one can be ultimately concerned in Tillich's view about many kinds of things, only one of which is God.

In his concept of correlation Tillich sought to resolve what John Clayton calls the two conditions of Schleiermacher's dilemma concerning the relation of the Christian faith and modern culture. One is the autonomous condition and the other is the reciprocity condition. At least for Clayton, Tillich's concept of correlation does not finally resolve the dilemma set by Schleiermacher.[40]

3. *Georg W. F. Hegel (1770–1831)*. Hegel was even more radical in his synthesis. Going beyond Kant, he held that God comes to his own self-knowledge through man's finite consciousness. In so doing God completes himself and the enterprise of creation and history.

Tillich was greatly indebted to Hegel, but he also saw Hegel's weaknesses. Dourley has listed the following elements in Tillich's *Systematic Theology* which are influenced by Hegel's thought: the divine necessity to actualize its essential possibilities by creating beyond itself, essential or unactualized man as existing in a state of dreaming innocence, the close connection between creation and the fall, and an essentialism which lies deeper in Tillich's system than the existentialism which it grounds.[41] Tillich also saw Hegel's application of dialectic to the historical as a great accomplishment. He appreciated the fact that Hegel related politics and religion.

Like Hegel, Tillich viewed culture as belonging to man's "second nature" which he himself has created and in which he becomes conscious of himself as "spirit." He is similar to Hegel in holding that each particular time or group has its own character or spirit which can be directly grasped in its philosophy. Philosophy has a certain primacy over science and art. Tillich also follows Hegel in seeing the emergence of progressively suitable forms of expression until form and content are perfectly suited to one another. This perfection comes in the history of religion which leads to and finds fulfillment in the incarnation.

In the area of art, Tillich stresses that the expressionistic painters have distorted natural form in order to express more intensely the inner and largely hidden meaning of the object represented. This view is similar to Hegel's view of romantic art.[42]

As indicated above, Tillich noted weaknesses in Hegel's thought. Hegel ultimately removed ambiguity and contradiction from his entire process of ideas. In Hegel's thought history in its totality became a closed system and lost its openness and flexibility. Hegel's dialectic ceased when the final synthesis was reached in nineteenth-century Germany. According to Tillich, Hegel is wrong in making the dialectic (thesis-antithesis-synthesis) into a law of all-embracing necessity. Furthermore, for Hegel, there is no real fall. There is only a distance between the actual and the ideal.[43]

Tillich shows no patience with Hegel's view that faith in Christ is faith in a personified ideal. He states that the foundation of Christianity would be denied if the factual element in it were denied. Only if existence is conquered at *one* point—in a personal life, representing existence as a whole—is it conquered in principle. The "New Being" apart from Jesus of Nazareth is abstract and ahistorical and, therefore, not a sufficient statement of "the biblical picture of Jesus as the Christ." [44]

4. *Friedrich Schelling (1775–1854).* Tillich often tells of the time when he found a very rare first edition of the collected works of Schelling in a bookstore on his way to the University of Berlin. He states that "what I learned from Schelling became determinative of my own philosophical and theological development." [45] Tillich wrote two dissertations on Schelling. Wilhelm Pauck states that Tillich worked through Schelling's thought so deeply in his student days that its suggestiveness remained permanently embedded in his mind.[46] In fact, Tillich claims that Schelling was his intellectual father. John Clayton, however, maintains that the role of Schelling in Tillich's thought is frequently exaggerated both by Tillich and his commentators.[47]

Tillich was especially drawn to the later Schelling because it was later in his life that Schelling rejected Hegel's essentialism and its implied universal reconciliation. From Schelling's perspective, reality is not, in fact, transparently essential and so at one with and revelatory of its divine ground and matrix. In fact, according to Schelling, Hegel's essentialism is a negative philosophy. It needs to be complemented by a positive philosophy better able to reflect and address the nonessential, the irrational, and the unreconciled.[48]

Jerome Stone has carefully outlined the concepts from Schelling which Tillich transmutes and assimilates: (1) God is not *a* being but rather the *Urgrund* or Power of Being.[49] (2) The triadic structure of divine life [50] and, in a derivative sense, of human life. (3) The inbreaking of the potencies into the course of human life in the form of the demonic, the *Kairos* (especially in the entrance of the divine into the human in Christ), and in the coming Age of the Spirit. (4) The irrational event of the fall and the extrarational activity of the divine in myth and revelation. Existence has a quality of estrangement and resistance. Unlike Hegel, Schelling's concept of freedom opened the door to the irrational. The transition from essence to existence is an action based on free will. Essence remains before and after the leap from essence. So the transition or fall is not necessary, but is a free action.[51]

(5) The dynamics of culture and religion. a. Autonomy, heteronomy, and theonomy. Schelling describes escape from heteronomy as the necessity of turning autonomy from bondage to itself and rooting it in the unconditioned. b. Christianity as the fulfillment of paganism. For Schelling, the religious longings of mankind find fulfillment in the central revelation in Christ. c. The dynamics of Christianity. Schelling sees Catholicism as characterized by stability and Protestantism as characterized by development. Both of these emphases or polarities are necessary and a driving force in Christianity. d. The dynamic typology of religion. The movement in the history of religions occurs through inner principles of development which are both objective and subjective at the same time. These movements are in the development of human consciousness and in the real spiritual forces. Philosophical developments have a similar dynamic.

In adapting and utilizing Schelling's themes, Tillich purges the fantastic elements in Schelling's thought. As a theologian, Tillich also has a greater respect for the regulating influence of the Christian tradition. In Tillich's work there is a movement from the language of speculation to the language of symbol. Behind the symbols and metaphors, there is a divine mystery.[52]

5. *Sören Kierkegaard (1813–1855)*. Tillich clearly says both yes and no to Sören Kierkegaard and existentialism. Kierkegaard obviously helped Tillich break through the closed essentialist system of Hegel. He also considers Kierkegaard's view and later existentialism as a partial but important expression of the dynamics of twentieth-century man. Since existentialism expresses our age, our situation, and our questions, Tillich states that he must accept existentialism into his situational-answering theology, so that theological answers will have relevance.[53]

Tillich appears to have borrowed from Kierkegaard some of his dialectic which is related to the problem of human actualization. This dialectic sees man as torn between remaining in unactualized innocence and the inevitability of guilt through actualization.[54]

Existentialism for Tillich is not a philosophy. It has an underlying or implicit essential structure. If this essential structure is not admitted, Existentialism is destructive in the religious sphere when it is used to affirm the transcendence unrelated to immanence. It is not surprising that Tillich refuses to be called an existentialist. He is more fundamentally an essentialist. For Tillich, existence is negative and estranging while essence is positive and unifying. As far as the God-man relationship is concerned, Tillich's limited acceptance of Existentialism is seen in his definition of "essence" and "existence" and in his teaching on estrangement. Such Tillichian expressions as "ultimate concern" and "shock of nonbeing" are also related to Existentialism.[55]

6. *Karl Marx (1818–1883)*. In his autobiographical writing, Tillich states that his relation to Marx has always been dialectical, combining a yes and a no.[56] This approach could also be used to refer to the influence of some Marxists of the "Frankfurt School" with whom Tillich had contact both in Germany and in New York.[57]

The "yes" is based on the prophetic, humanistic, and realistic elements in Marx's passionate style and profound thought.[58] The reading of Marx after World War I inspired Tillich's involvement with the political movement of that period. Tillich states that he owes to Marx his insight into the ideological character not only of idealism but of all systems of thought, religious as well as secular. Often these systems of thought serve as power structures and prevent, even unconsciously, a more just organization of social reality.[59] According to Tillich, Marx helped awaken a definite self-consciousness in the industrial masses, and a social conscience in the Christian church.[60]

Tillich considered Marx as a kind of secular prophet whose atheism was a necessary protest against religious idolatry and heteronomy. For Tillich, however, this protest was transitional and dialectical, rather than a permanent account of reality.

Tillich also recognizes in Marx both a profound humanism and a strong historical realism. In his post-World War I period Tillich realized that his own previous idealism could stand as an obstacle to a full understanding of the historical and existential estrangement of man. For Tillich, the Marxist critique of a culture must be absorbed before any further advance can be made in a theory of culture. Marx gave Tillich's thought the necessary concrete grounding it needed in order to have political and social relevance.[61]

In contrast to Hegel and in apparent agreement with Marx, Tillich interpreted the period from the Enlightenment through the nineteenth century as having its real foundation in the economic conditions of existence. It is a period determined by the rise of capitalism. But, according to Tillich, the relative truth of Marx's economic view cannot become law for all of history or all societies. John Clayton contends that in certain respects Tillich remained more in the idealistic tradition and did not really assimilate the Marxist critique of the idealistic tradition.[62]

Increasingly, through the years, Tillich said no to Marx. Marx's atheism furthered human estrangement by broadening the gap between the sacred and the secular. According to Tillich, the utopianism of Marx had a strong residue of the Hegelian synthesis, reversed and brought down to earth, but moving on inevitably through historical conflict. Tillich affirmed that this utopianism lacked spiritual depth and would be ultimately self-destructive.[63]

7. *Friedrich Nietzsche* (*1844–1900*). As was noted in the biographical section, Tillich was greatly influenced by reading Nietzsche during World War I. Nietzsche, in turn, was influenced by Schopenhauer's voluntarism in his analysis of man as will-driven. Nietzsche refused, however, to accept Schopenhauer's negative conclusions about the death wish. Instead, Nietzsche affirmed life in his famous view of the will-to-power in the face of all that denied life. Included in the life-denying powers were Christianity and the limpid and pusillanimous spirituality which Nietzsche judged was endorsed by Christianity.[64]

Tillich confirms that the concept of power that qualifies his view of Being-itself relies specifically on Nietzsche's will-to-power. Tillich's admiration for, and dependence on this concept is expressed in considerable length in *The Courage to Be*, in which he states that courage which is related to will-to-power can show us what Being is, and Being can show us what courage is.[65]

It should be noted that Nietzsche's view of "will-to-power" was influenced by the Judaeo-Christian tradition. In fact, Guy Hammond thinks that Tillich's adaptation of this concept of God as Power of Being is a restatement of the biblical understanding of a dynamic God against the "Greek absolute." [66]

8. *Rudolf Otto (1869–1937)*. Tillich states that when he first read Rudolf Otto's *The Idea of the Holy* he understood it immediately and took it into his thinking as a constitutive element. According to Tillich, this book determined his method in philosophy of religion. Following Otto, Tillich started with the mystical, sacramental, and aesthetic experiences of the holy and advanced to the idea of God, not the reverse way. The ethical and logical elements of religion were derived from the experience of the presence of the divine, not conversely. Both Otto and Tillich were led by this existential interest to participate in movements for liturgical renewal and in a reevaluation of Christian and non-Christian mysticism.[67]

Tillich's notion of the divine mystery which is manifest both positively and negatively is derived in part from Otto's *The Idea of the Holy*. Tillich states that he interprets Otto's *mysterium tremendum et fascinosum* in this way. The *tremendum* is the abyss of being which is experienced as nonbeing. The *fascinosum* is the ground of man's being which is experienced as power of being, conquering nonbeing. Elsewhere, Tillich calls the *tremendum* the annihilating power of the Divine Presence and the *fascinosum* as the elevating power of the Divine Presence. In God, the abyss is what makes his being so mysterious that no revelation can exhaust it. The ground of being manifest as revelation is always qualified by the abyss which safeguards the mysterious character of the Divine.[68]

9. *Martin Heidegger (1889–1976)*. According to Adrian Thatcher, while earlier forms of ontology were important for Tillich, it is the Existentialism or "fundamental" ontology of the twentieth century, particularly that of Heidegger, which influenced Tillich most.[69] As was noted in the biographical section, Tillich joined the faculty at the University of Marburg in 1924 where Heidegger was teaching. At that time Heidegger was preparing to publish his *Sein und Zeit (Being and Time)*. Some years later Tillich would list that work as one of the books which most influenced his thought.[70] There is no consensus among Tillich scholars regarding the extent of Tillich's indebtedness to Heidegger. Both men had a similar philosophical heritage. But Tillich's explicit acknowledgment of his debt to Heidegger cannot be ignored.

Tillich's activity of "questioning" and "answering" gains a new and different significance in his work after the time at Marburg. Tillich admits that he came to a different understanding of the relationship between philosophy and theology as a result of his contact with Heidegger. The method of correlation was one of the eventual consequences of that new understanding.[71]

After leaving Marburg, Tillich went to the Technical Institute at Dresden. In his lectures there in 1927 entitled "The Structure of Religious Knowledge" Tillich states that man necessarily asks the question of the meaning of his existence. Implied in this question is the question of being as such. Up to this point Heidegger's influence is apparent. In fact, Heidegger states that the fundamental task of philosophy is the clarification of the question of the structure and meaning of being-itself. Tillich goes on to state that the question of the meaning of being also inevitably raises the question of that which lies beyond or transcends being. The philosopher can raise this question but it is not in his power as a philosopher to form an answer. The philosopher as philosopher cannot pass from the phenomenal to the noumenal. If the philosopher does not remain silent at this point he ceases to be a philosopher and becomes instead a theologian. The answer cannot be deduced from the analysis of human existence.[72]

According to Tillich, the question of being or the ontological question is produced by the shock of nonbeing. This shock confronts the layman in the form of his "having to die." Here the influence of Heidegger's thought on Tillich is apparent. Tillich has in mind Heidegger's description of man as a "being-toward death." The inevitability of death, and the possibility of death at any moment, provide man with a negative experience which shocks him into an appreciation and new assessment of the positive "givenness of his existence." For Heidegger, this question of death and "Why are there entities, why not nothing?" brings into relief both the awful reality of nothingness and the being which sustains entities from falling back into the nothingness from which they came. Tillich's conception of ontological shock and the ontological question is thus seen to be influenced greatly by Heidegger.[73]

In his biographical statement in the Kegley and Bretall volume, Tillich stated that it took years before he became fully aware of the impact of the encounter with Heidegger's philosophy on his own thinking. He affirms that he resisted but that he finally accepted this new way of thinking.[74]

Part Two

Tillich's Basic Method and Its Outworking in His System

Introduction

Tillich distinguished two emphases or approaches in presenting theological truth. One is called "kerygmatic theology" because it emphasizes the unchangeable truth of the message (*kerygma*) over against the changing demands of the human situation to which it is addressed. The other is called "answering" or apologetic theology. This approach starts with the human questions which are then answered by the Christian message. These questions and answers are those in which man is involved with his whole existence and which are therefore interrelated. This answering or apologetic theology utilizes the method of correlation, a term which Tillich used as early as 1924.[1]

The method of correlation is as old as apologetic theology. It seeks to satisfy two basic needs: the explication of the truth contained in the Christian message and the interpretation of this truth for every new generation. Tillich was convinced that theology should move back and forth between these two basic needs or poles. This made Tillich an apologetic rather than a "kerygmatic" theologian.[2] He was persuaded that the traditional symbols and forms used in theology, worship, and the Christian life generally were no longer understood properly and for many had become meaningless. He therefore attempted to reinterpret Christian symbols and forms of expression so that they would again be comprehended by contemporary man and thus become powerful.[3]

Because of the announced practical purpose of this particular study, more emphasis is given to the last three parts of Tillich's system. The first two sections of the system, "Reason and the Quest for Revelation" and "Being and the Question of God," are somewhat more speculative.

V. The Method of Correlation

In the biographical section it was pointed out that Tillich was a participating or existential theologian. John Dillenberger, Tillich's former student at Union Seminary and later his colleague at Harvard, indicates that Tillich's method of correlation is rooted in his own personal life. As we have noted, Tillich was a man of wide interests. He was interested in philosophy, the arts, and sciences, especially depth psychology. And, of course, he was a theologian. He was involved with each of these areas in his very being. No one of these areas had priority over the other.[1]

A. · Philosopher or Theologian or Both?

Rollo May, another of Tillich's former students and a prominent psychoanalyst, reports that Tillich is the only modern thinker he knows who lived on the boundary of philosophy and theology with an equal care for each discipline. Once an entire meeting of the American Philosophical Association was given over to a discussion of Tillich's philosophy. He has been criticized for riding two horses at the same time, but for Tillich these two disciplines of philosophy and theology, although distinguishable, are inseparable in his own person.[2]

It was not that Tillich was a philosopher who was interested in the arts and sciences and who approached theology through his philosophical interests. Neither was he a theologian who approached philosophy as a medium for his theological expressions, nor did he approach the arts and sciences for learned illustrations. Rather Tillich *was* a philosopher, a theologian, and a student of the arts and sciences. He was in fact a modern Renaissance man. His method of correlation is therefore not a contrived method, as a true method never is, but the very expression of everything for which he stood. He believed that all human disciplines must stand in their own integrity and never in isolation.[3]

Those who heard Tillich felt that he knew their basic questions and that he could speak to them helpfully. He was a daring theologian, unafraid of meeting the secular world on its own ground because he incorporated both the religious and the secular in his own person.[4] Moreover, he states that the most inspiring part of his work was the question and answer period, the "yes" and "no" in actual disputation. Tillich enjoyed dealing with questions which concerned people in their very existence. At the same time, however, he admitted that there is always a danger that the existential element might destroy the systematic consistency, or that the systematic consistency element might suffocate the existential dimension.[5]

For Tillich, Christianity and culture are not separate or identical nor can they be fused. Instead, the assumptions within any culture, which in their ultimacy have a religious character, are in a dialectical, or yes and no, relationship with the concrete assumptions of Christianity.

B.   *Questions, Quests, and Answers*

For Tillich, one *must* be a philosopher. But philosophy is not adherence to a particular philosophical position. Rather philosophy is seeing philosophical questions in their total range and asking questions noting that they quest answers. In the same way theological history with its answers implies questions. Philosophical questions and quests for answers are encountered by theological answers and quests. They have an inescapable interrelationship. Tillich was a philosopher and a theologian.

According to Tillich, the danger of the corruption of truth from one side or the other must be accepted as a hazard. We must recognize the danger. But we must not separate what in actuality cannot be separated at all.[6] By starting with the human situation as reflected in philosophy man is made more aware of his need. By seeing the Christian message in terms of that need, the message or answer is seen as not being arbitrarily imposed on a person.[7]

Tillich's correlation method is closely related to his basic idea which we have seen as essence-existence-essentialization. God's presence to man in the essential structure of man is dialectically both lost and retained after man's transition or "fall" from essence to existence. Man's separation from his essence in fallen existence is related to the disruption of man's vital processes. However, even in disrupted existence, man never totally divests himself of his essence and so of his relation to God and his quest for God. Even in existence, when man's essential relationship to God is diminished there is a recognizable quest or drive toward reintegration or reunion or essentialization.[8]

For Tillich, the being of man, even in fallen existence, is so grounded in the being of God that man asks existential questions and quests for theological answers. This gives Tillich a basis for his method of theology which we have noted is called "correlation" or "answering" or "apologetic" theology. Such a theology answers the questions implied in man's living situation in the power of the Christian message. Tillich draws on a type of ontological tradition which extends from the Pre-Socratics to the present. For Tillich the "philosophers of life" and existentialists are representatives of this tradition in the modern period. In his last years, Tillich was seeking to broaden his base to include questions raised by the Far Eastern religions and culture as well.

But in the main, for Tillich, Existentialism best expresses our age or our situation. It expresses our questions. According to Tillich, the theologian must study the existential expression of the contemporary mind if his theological answers are to have any relevance at all.[9]

Tillich clarifies his method of correlation by insisting that theology is related only to that which concerns us ultimately. Theology should never leave the area of ultimate concern and try to play a role in matters of preliminary concern such as matters of technical history and science.

In his autobiographical section in *My Search for Absolutes,* Tillich points out that he has tried to show that within the different realms of man's encounter with reality (cognitive, ethical, aesthetic, and social-political) there are structural absolutes. In each of these structural absolutes there is a point of self-transcendence toward the absolute itself. For example, in the cognitive realm the point of self-transcendence is Being-itself. In the ethical realm, the point of self-transcendence is love which contains justice. Something is holy to everyone, contends Tillich, even to those who deny that they have experienced the holy. Religion in the larger concept, beyond organized religion and nonreligion, appears as that depth dimension of ultimate reality which grasps one with an ultimate concern. This dimension of depth is also found in secular structures, although it is often hidden in these structures. This conception of religion gives positive religious meaning to secularism.[10]

Furthermore, Tillich affirms that that which concerns us ultimately is that which determines our being or our nonbeing. At the border of our finite being there are only two ontological alternatives: nonbeing or the Ground of all Being. At this boundary line man confronts the shock or threat of nonbeing or the estrangement of his finitude. Man in his disruptive existence has a yes and no, or dialectical relationship with God, or the Ground of Being. This dialectical relationship involves man in a continual quest for help and answers. Tillich's entire systematic theology gravitates around the polar relationship between man's disruptive existence and his quest for a solution to his existential dilemma.

C. Five Crucial Areas of Man's Concern

From the standpoint of method, Tillich describes five crucial areas of philosophical or existential concern, noting that in each area there is a quest for fulfillment. He then shows how each quest is answered. For example, reason quests for revelation. Being quests for God. Existence quests for the Christ. Life in its ambiguity quests for an unambiguous life or spiritual presence. History quests for the kingdom of God.[11]

Robert Scharlemann points out that Tillich really has three main forms of questions or quests (being, existence, and life). Reason is an aspect of being, and the quest of history is an aspect of life. There are also three main forms of the answer (God, Christ, and the Spirit).[12]

It should be noted, however, that the question of existence answered by the New Being in Jesus the Christ is central for Tillich. He believed that Christology should be the heart of every Christian theology. Moreover, the confession that Jesus is the Christ contains, in principle, Tillich's whole theological method and system.[13] Tillich's theology is consequently both thoroughly correlational and Christological.

D. Philosophy and Theology: Contrast, Similarity, and Relationship

In summary, Tillich's method of correlation requires that every part of the system should include one section in which the question is developed by an analysis of human existence and existence generally, and one section in which the theological answer is given based on a systematic theology which is rooted in the Christian tradition. Philosophy deals with the structure of being in itself. It is more detached and ideally looks more objectively at the whole of being and the whole of reality. Theology deals with the meaning of being for us. It is involved and participates with passion, love, and commitment in relationship to the logos manifesting itself in a particular historical event.

Tillich admits that only a philosopher influenced by the Christian tradition thinks as he does. However, Tillich states that he ceases to be a philosopher if he tries to be intentionally Christian in his philosophical thinking. On the other hand, no philosophy which is obedient to the universal logos can contradict the specific or concrete logos which is revealed in Jesus the Christ.

Tillich acknowledges that there is a convergence between the philosopher and the theologian. The creative philosopher also has an ultimate concern whether or not he is fully conscious of it or admits it. The philosopher is thus a theologian to the degree in which his existential situation and his ultimate concern shape his philosophical vision. But the divergence remains because the philosopher does not intend to be a theologian. He tries to turn away from his existential situation, including his ultimate concern, toward pure reality. In conclusion, Tillich states that the divergence between philosophy and theology is such that there can be neither conflict nor synthesis between them. When a theologian enters the philosophical arena he must enter it as a philosopher. Only as a philosopher can the theologian be in conflict with another philosopher. That is, he must make his appeal to reason alone.

The apologetic power of the system is impressive, especially to those inclined toward the mystical side of Protestant theology and yet desirous of a realistic ontology and Christology. As will be seen, many criticize Tillich because he does not have a higher Christology or does not rely more on biblical terminology.

It may be, therefore, that Tillich's greatest contribution is in his methodology rather than in his theology as a whole. Tillich emphasizes, however, that his method and his system belong together. His method determines the shape of his system, and the method itself is shaped in the construction of his system.[14]

The *Systematic Theology* was written in its final form as Tillich was having conversation with American students of theology in the 1950s and '60s. These were students who lived during the Eisenhower era but were primarily political followers of Adlai Stevenson, Hubert Humphrey, and John F. Kennedy. The students were neither revolutionaries nor socialists.

At the particular time Tillich was creating his theology, the seminaries did not have a large number of third-world students who were conscious revolutionaries. Unlike today, there were not many blacks or radical feminists in the schools. Tillich thus wrote his *Systematic Theology* at a time when he did not have the proletariat in his theological view. His emphasis, therefore, was to fight dehumanizing forces in the society rather than try to restructure society. Utilizing his method of correlation, if he were writing today, Tillich would no doubt adjust his theology to deal with some of the questions which have arisen in a more dramatic way since 1965.[15]

VI. Reason and the Quest for Revelation

It would appear that Being and the Question of God should be considered before Reason and the Quest for Revelation. Logically, the question of being is prior to the question of knowledge since the science of knowing is part of the science of being. Tillich has chosen for reasons outlined in the introduction to the *Systematic Theology* to begin with an analysis of man's rationality and its quest for revelation.[1]

In the section on Tillich's basic idea or ontology, it was shown how Tillich's idea of essence-existence-essentialization provides the key to the understanding of his theological system. This key applies to reason just as to every other aspect of life. The motif of his basic idea will help us to understand Tillich's idea of reason and man's quest for revelation.

A. *Definitions*

1. *Essential Reason.* For Tillich, there is no break between reason and revelation as if revelation were superadded to reason. For theologians trained in a two-storied, natural-supernatural framework there is a profane world, a profane ego, and a profane history in contrast to the supernatural world. For philosophers trained in a scientific, empirical framework there is *only* a profane world, profane ego, and a profane history. For Tillich there is a continuity without identity between man and God, between the natural and the supernatural and thus between reason and revelation.[2] Tillich affirms this continuity when he develops his idea of essential reason. Essential

reason in its perfection is reason "in unity with being itself." Essential reason is at one with God. Even in fallen human existence there are remnants of essential reason which prompt fallen reason to seek a reunion with essential reason. Tillich calls this essentialization. When reason is essentialized and at one with God, it then knows that essential reason is coextensive with "the content of revelation."

2. *Ontological reason and technical reason.* Tillich considers his view of reason as consistent with what he calls the "classical philosophical tradition." Reason in the broadest sense is for Tillich the *logos* structure of both mind and extramental reality which enables the mind to grasp and shape reality. All of reality is intelligible because of this structure. He calls this view of reason "ontological reason." Ontological reason is present in all of the operations of human reasoning including the cognitive, aesthetic, practical, and technical.[3]

According to Tillich, the victory of technical reason over ontological reason in the twentieth century results in humanity's being subjected to technical manipulation. Human beings are treated as means rather than as ends. He thus has a negative attitude toward technical reason separated from its ontological base. Reason used in this technical sense stands in danger of becoming a mere ploy of logical forms or a means to control knowledge. Applied to man this view of reason denies man's subjectivity. Applied to God, it serves to reduce God to a calculable object.[4]

Technical reason is valid if it is guided by the tradition of ontological reason for the fulfillment of worthwhile human purposes. Ontological reason is reason in the service of God for explicating the *logos*. The attainment of truth through ontological reason takes on the aura of a mystical experience between man and ultimate reality. Verification for the attainment of essential truth is experiential, participational, and based on its validity for the life-processes of the individual and mankind. In contrast, technical reason does not involve the whole man and does not participate in the depth dimension of essential structures as does ontological reason. Thus technical reason does not deal with the ultimately meaningful.[5]

3. *Subjective and objective reason.* Tillich's view of ontological reason holds that there is a *logos* structure in both mind and in reality. This means that there is a distinction between subjective (the structure of mind) and objective (the structure of reality) reason. In the interaction between subjective and objective reason, subjective reason grasps or receives the objective *logos* and also shapes it to some degree. In the receiving or grasping, subjective reason captures essential truth. In fact, Tillich describes revelation as "receiving knowledge in its fulfillment." This implies that revelation introduces man into the essential dimension of reality in a certain fullness.[6]

4. *Theory and practice.* Another important facet of Tillich's view of

ontological reason is that theory and practice are interdependent and inseparable. This is true because man transforms reality according to the way he
sees it, and he sees reality according to the way he is capable of transforming
it. Thus for Tillich there is a close relationship between the knowing subject
and the known object. There is a necessary separation of the knower from
the known, but a unitive experience results in a healing because it unites
the knower with the known through their mutual relation to the *logos*
structure of reality. This unitive experience involves an emotive or affective
dimension. This means that knowing the truth at the essential level is
not only a cognitive recognition of reality but a participation in transforming
reality.[7]

5. *Depth of reason.* Another term used by Tillich is "depth of reason."
Depth refers to the presence of the absolute or God in the essential structures
of mind and reality, but in such a way that the mind is never fully at
one with the absolute and yet never fully separated from it. In theological
terms, Tillich is affirming the presence of God to the mind. God remains
the creative source of all creativity. It is from the presence of God to the
mind in the depth of reason that the mind in each of its functions derives
its awareness of the absolute. Cognitive reason points to the truth itself;
the aesthetic sense points to beauty itself; legal reason points to justice
itself; and communal reason points to love itself.[8]

6. *Myth, cult, and the symbolic.* It is also in the depth of reason that
Tillich locates the source of myth and cult. We remember that for Tillich
essential reason is reason at one with God and so essential reason is closely
related, if not identified, with the depth of reason. In existence, however,
essential reason is both at one with, yet separated from, union with God.
Because in existence man's reason is no longer identical with the *logos*
structure expressed in God, man must express his relation to, or experience
of God in myths. Despite man's fall into existence, his reason retains essence
and reflects the structural presence of God to man himself. Man must
express this essential but ambiguous relation to God. In his fallen state,
this cannot be done with clarity and preciseness, but can only be expressed
in mythological language and cultic reenactment.[9]

Tillich contends that myth and symbol are inevitable for man in his
fallen existence. This means that the symbolical and mythical dimensions
of religious experience can never be rationalized away or dismissed. There
is a mutual inherence between God and the structure of the mind. This
implies for Tillich that symbols, unlike signs, may participate structurally
in the reality toward which they point. Thus conceived, religious symbols
may be said to have the power to unite the knower with a deeper dimension
of his own psyche and with the deeper dimension of reality or God. Symbols
die only when the religious experience out of which they have grown is
no longer the experience of the group which holds the symbols.[10]

Thus it can be seen that Tillich's view of symbols presupposes his basic idea of essence-existence-essentialization and a doctrine of knowledge based on the immediate presence of God within the structures of the finite mind and reality. All reality, especially the personal, participates in God and points to God symbolically when the ultimate manifests itself through its structures. All reality is thus potentially the material for religious experience and so potentially sacramental. On the other hand, no manifestation of God through created structures can be identified with God, for Tillich's system contains an inherent safeguard against idolatry.[11]

Like everyone else, the theologian participates in ultimate reality by means of religious symbols according to his faith. However, he also has the task of conceptualizing, explaining, and criticizing these symbols. He should never allow his rationalizing to divest these symbols of their participational import and creative potential.

B. *The Conflicts and Contradictions of Ontological Reason in Its Existential State*

As will be remembered, Tillich's basic ontology is that man has fallen from the essential into existence, and the process of salvation or reunion with God is seen as the process of the essentialization of fallen existence. In the area of reason, revelation would be the essentialization of fallen reason. Christ as the final revelation would be the one in whom reason is fully at one with its essence. What happens, therefore, to man's reason in the transition from essence to existence? According to Tillich, there is a disruption of the vital balance of the polarities whose proper interaction characterizes essential reason. This disruption occurs as human reason experiences a transition or fall from its essential to its existential state.

Tillich presents these conflicts first, in accordance with his method of correlating philosophical questions with theological answers. Later he will seek to show in a theological discussion how these conflicts are overcome and reason is reintegrated in the Christian revelation.

In the area of reason, Tillich identifies three sets of structural polarities, which, in existence, are in conflict.

1. *The conflict between structure and depth as the conflict between autonomy and heteronomy.* In existence there is a tension between structure and depth and this leads to a conflict between autonomous reason (structure) and heteronomous reason (depth). Autonomous reason is rooted in the *logos* structure of the mind, and this structure is rooted in divine and natural law. But in existence, autonomous reason is not aware of the depth dimension of its structure. Heteronomous reason is reason which speaks to man from outside yet in the name of the depth of reason. In existence, heteronomous reason is seen as an authority coming from without, minus depth. And

so, in existence, these two forms of reason are in conflict. Some elements of essential reason remain in existence, and so reason quests for revelation as the reconciliation of structure and depth.[12]

2. *The conflict between the static and dynamic as the conflict between absolutism and relativism.* In existence, the pole of dynamics or growth denies the absolute pole and tends toward a dynamism and emphasis on change which fails to find any stable form of expression. This results in positivistic relativism or cynicism. The pole of form or self-preservation denies growth in the name of fixed absolutes such as a revolutionary absolute or conservatism. The essential element in existential reason, however, causes one to look for resolution even in the midst of conflict. This resolution would have to be in the concrete absolute which will satisfy both the demand for the absolute or static element in reason, and yet do so in terms of a dynamic individual who embodies the absolute.[13]

3. *The conflict between the formal and emotional poles of reason.* In existence, the pole of formalism at the intellectual level appears in the controlling, logical, legal, and objectively cognitive functions of reason. The pole of emotionalism reacts by asserting the need for the unifying or loving dimension of reason. The essential element in existential reason causes one immersed in the conflict to look for a resolution in revelation. Revelation will satisfy the formal structures of reason but at that level where it provokes and evokes in one a commitment which is at once both rational and emotional.

Thus for Tillich each of these poles of reason is valid, if it is in balanced tension with its corollary. This balanced tension or integration can only be found in revelation.[14]

C. *The Meaning of Revelation*

1. *Introduction.* Revelation and faith for Tillich must not be seen as alien antitheses but rather as expressions of man's truest self which proceed from those depths in man where his presence to God is immediate. In speaking to man God is really speaking from a presence that was immanent and real from the outset. Revelation is really a revelation to man of his truest self which emerges from his ontological union with God. Faith becomes an expression of this union. A heteronomous God and an autonomous man are united in theonomy which means man's reunion with a God who is immediately present to him and closer to man than he is to himself. Religious knowledge proceeds from that experience wherein man becomes conscious of his union with God's presence. Tillich maintained that when this principle of identity or immediacy was denied, as in the thirteenth century by the adoption of Aristotle's philosophy, then the process of the secularization of the Western world began.[15]

For Tillich, reason, even in its fallen or existential state, contains something of essence, and this essence includes something of revelation. Even in its fallen state, existential reason is not profane. It is so structured essentially that the transcendent continues to break through it immanently. Through the sheer goodness and graciousness of the Creator, reason has a *telos* or meaningful directedness toward revelation. Reason is thus made for revelation. It is made for Christ. In its fragmentary state there are essential elements left in existential reason. This means that reason in its fallen state has enough of its essence left that it quests after revelation, New Being and total essentialization.

Tillich is opposed to any kind of natural theology. Natural theology implies a dualistic view of the universe. For Tillich, there can be no natural or profane or nonreligious revelation. Existential or fallen reason retains essence and so is God-related, even in its fallen state. Of course, in its fallen or existential state reason quests for a *fuller* essentialization or God-unitedness. To avoid the overtones of a dualistic view which simply divides the natural and the supernatural Tillich chooses to call for a new relationship called "theonomy." This term describes the new situation after the experience of revelation.

2. *Revelation as a revelatory constellation.* Revelation, for Tillich, can be seen as a revelatory constellation involving four dimensions. The first aspect, from God's perspective, is God's self-revelation. The second, from man's perspective, is his reason grasped by the unconditioned, or as Tillich calls it, ecstasy. The third, from the view of the knowledge imparted, is the experience of mystery. For Tillich, mystery, even in the revelatory constellation, remains profoundly mysterious. Only the experience of mystery is grasped. The fourth aspect is constituted by the media of revelation, namely the word and the sacrament. It is word when the revelation occurs through the medium of a *logos*-being. It is sacrament when revelation occurs through a non-*logos*-being or a nonpersonal object.

These four components have no independent meaning outside the constellation. They are all dialectically interdependent, continuous but not identical.[16]

3. *Three concepts of revelation: mystery, ecstasy, and miracle.* Another way of perceiving Tillich's understanding of revelation is to see it as founded on three interconnected concepts which he designates as mystery, ecstasy, and miracle.

(1) *Mystery.* Mystery refers to the appearance of the ultimate in the structures of reason in a certain revelatory correlation of reality and mind. For Tillich, the mystery appears when human reason is driven beyond itself to its ground and abyss or to that which precedes reason, to the realization of the fact that being is and nonbeing is not, to the original fact that there is something and not nothing.

Tillich further describes the revelatory experience of mystery in terms of its negative and positive polarities. The negative aspect, which is virtually a precondition of the positive dimension of revelation, consists in the shock of man's experience of his finitude and the threat of nonbeing, with which the experience is accompanied. This shock of possible nonbeing is the beginning of all genuine philosophy while also being a specifically religious experience of the abysmal element in the ground of being. This negative side of the appearance of mystery in revelation which causes man to be aware of his finitude and possible nonbeing is possible only because of his awareness of his potential infinity or the fact that he belongs to Being-itself. Thus the negativity implies an awareness of God.

The positive aspect of the mystery which Tillich calls "actual revelation" arises not only from one's perception of the abyss dimension of God but from one's awareness of God as "ground" or "the power of being conquering nonbeing." Mystery always remains mysterious, but it is now experienced as that power of being within which the negativities of existence are over-come. In this actual or positive side of revelation as mystery God is seen as ground, as supportive, and as the basis for human courage in the face of man's finitude.[17]

(2) *Ecstasy.* The appearance of mystery in the revelatory union of the mind with its depth always occurs in the interrelationship between the subjective and objective *logos.* Subjectively this union is experienced as "ecstasy," whereas the objective counterpart of this ecstasy is called "mira-cle" or sign event.

Ecstasy is the state of mind in which reason rises beyond its subject-object structure. In ecstasy reason is at one with God, who is the source of both the subjective and objective *logos.* Thus reason in ecstasy participates in God as source of the subject-object structure of reality and in so doing transcends both by experiencing God where being and truth are one. It should be noted that ecstatic reason encounters God as both abyss and ground. This God who is revealed in ecstatic reason has always a living and so a Trinitarian character.

It should also be noted that ecstatic reason does not destroy the structures of the subjective *logos* through which it appears. Rather, ecstatic reason or revelation fulfills reason by uniting its rational structure with its basis in God. Revelation is the manifestation of both the depth of reason *and* the Ground of Being. Thus for Tillich revelation can never be merely a matter of the conveyance by God of knowledge relating to the subject-object structures of reality. This would mean that God as revealer and savior would violate his created structures and so establish a dualism between himself as creator and revealer. This would dehumanize man and demonize God.[18]

(3) *Miracle.* Just as ecstasy unites subjective reason with its depth so does *miracle* unite objective reason with its depth. Thus in every revelatory

experience the depth of the subjective and the depth of the objective *logos* exist in correlation. A "miracle" or "sign event" is an occasion which astounds us and which conveys to us a consciousness of the mystery of being. A genuine miracle is primarily an unusual, shaking, astonishing event which does not destroy or contradict the rational structure of reality. A genuine miracle is an event which points to the mystery of being at that juncture where it expresses its relation to us in a specific way. It must be received as a sign-event in an ecstatic experience. In every revelatory event there is a concurrence of an objective happening received by ecstatic reason or faith. The relations of the mind in faith to the object of its faith are so intimately connected that ecstasy can be attributed to reality and miracle to the mind.[19]

What is given to us, therefore, in revelation is no new body of information. There is no increase in our knowledge of nature, history, and man. The insight which comes to us through a miracle and is acquired through ecstasy is perhaps best described as a new awareness of, or a new perspective on, that which is already known. We get knowledge about the revelation of the mystery of being, not just additional information. What we already know is clarified and its experiential value heightened by our discovery of its union with the ultimate.[20]

For Tillich, the prime example of the revelatory correlation between subjective reason in ecstasy and objective reason in miracle is found in the revelatory event of Christ. Jesus was the Christ because he was received as Christ by the community of faith. This reception accounts for the ecstatic dimension of the revelatory event of Christ. Yet Christ was the Christ because he stood in perfect union or full participation with the Ground of Being and as such attained that perfect self-sacrifice. Here Christ stands the double test of finality: uninterrupted unity with the Ground of his being and the continuous sacrifice of himself as Jesus to himself as Christ. Thus Christ in unbroken unity with God in the conditions of existence constitutes the miracle of the Christ-event. Peter's profession of faith, "Thou art the Christ," constitutes the ecstatic side of the Christ event. Christ could be the Christ because he fully participates in the being of God and because this participation was recognized by those who received him out of their participation in the same ground.[21]

D. *The History of the Preparation and Reception of Final Revelation*

1. *The period of preparation.*

(1) Universal revelatory experiences are transformed into sacramental objects by religious leaders. This is called *conservation*. Unfortunately, this sacramental-priestly approach tends to transform the medium of revelation into the content.

(2) If this idolatrous situation is to be avoided, the interpreters must

take a *critical* approach. This approach may appear in three forms: a. *Mysticism* rejects the demonic identification of anything finite with the Ground of Being; b. *Rational* persons such as Spinoza can also help avoid a false identification of medium and content; and c. *Prophetic* groups such as monastic communities and Reformers may also attack distorted sacramentalism. The revelation through the prophets of Israel is the direct, concrete preparation for the final revelation. In the process of the prophetic struggle with distorted sacramentalism, the Old Testament revelation moved progressively toward the universal revelation. According to Tillich, the eventual breakthrough to final revelation must happen in a personal life. Christianity claims that it has happened with the arrival of Christ.[22]

2. *The period of reception.*

(1) The bearer of the receiving revelation is the Christian church. All religions and cultures outside the church are from the Christian perspective still in the period of preparation. And there are many groups and individuals in the Christian nations and churches which have never received the message of the final revelation in its meaning and power. There are also nominal Christian groups which on occasion relapse into the preparatory stage.

(2) This means that the Christian church, based on the final revelation, must be involved in a continuous process of reception, interpretation, and actualization. This revelation occurs through the Spirit of Jesus as the Christ. The Christian church affirms that, at least for this space-time continuum, no new revelation can surpass this event of final revelation. Although this final revelation has been accomplished in history, the invitation to accept this revelation must continue to be extended in all times and places where the final revelation has not yet been acknowledged.[23]

E. *Final Revelation Overcoming the Conflicts in Reason*

Already we have noted the conflict in the three sets of structural polarities in fallen or existential reason. Tillich declares that Jesus as the Christ is the decisive, fulfilling, unsurpassable revelation, the criterion of all other revelations. Christ as the final revelation is the perfectly theonomous man and so resolves the conflicts between these polarities in reason in himself and for those who participate in his theonomous humanity in the Spirit.

1. *Jesus, autonomy, and heteronomy.* Christ can resolve the conflict between autonomous and heteronomous reason. Jesus' unbroken unity with the Father through the Spirit unites autonomous reason with its depth. Because Jesus sacrifices himself to his being as the Christ, he cannot become a heteronomous law and thus falsely replace one heteronomy with another.[24]

2. *Jesus, the dynamic, and the absolute.* Jesus reintegrates the dynamic and absolute poles of reason. In Jesus, man's essential relation to God was fully realized in existence, and so the absolute appeared in the concreteness of a human life. This reconciliation of the absolute and the concrete

in the biblical portrait of Christ makes it possible for one to understand clearly the nature of Christian love. The law of love portrayed in Christ is absolute but it must be experienced and applied in a dynamic way in terms of the particular and concrete.[25]

3. *Jesus, formalism, and emotion.* Jesus overcomes the conflict between the formal and emotional poles of reason. Man's reason grasps, or is grasped by, Christ in his totality. This includes reason in both its formal, and in its emotive and unifying capacity. The *logos* which detached philosophy or scientific reason grasps, and the *logos* which reason grasps through love in its depth dimension, is the same *logos* which appeared without distortion in Jesus as the Christ. This unification in Christ can lead to the reconciliation of science and theology.[26]

F. The Ground of Revelation

1. *Reason, revelation, and the Trinitarian interpretation of the divine life.* In the crucial introductory section of the *Systematic Theology* on "Reason and the Quest for Revelation" Tillich sees the integration of man's reason through reason's participation in the integration of intra-Trinitarian life. For Tillich, the doctrine of revelation is based on a Trinitarian interpretation of the divine life and its self-manifestation. It is the abyss-character of the divine life (Father) which accounts for the mysterious dimension of all revelation. It is the *logos*-character of the divine life (Son) which makes revelation possible by giving concrete and particular definition to divine life. It is the dynamic-character of the divine life (Spirit) which unites depth and form within the Trinity. The Spirit, therefore, brings about the correlation of ecstatic reason in the mind, and miracle in objective *logos* through which revelation occurs. Thus any perception of God, or experience with him, is of the living and Trinitarian God.[27]

2. *Final revelation and the Word of God.* The five different meanings of the term "Word of God" are all united in one meaning which is "God manifest."

(1) First, God as the Ground of Being has the *logos*-character of self-manifestation.

(2) In contrast to a Neo-Platonic process of emanations, the Word or *Logos* creates by mediating between the silent mystery of the abyss of being and the fullness of concrete, individualized beings.

(3) The Word manifests the divine life in the final revelation which is Jesus as the Christ. The *Logos* becomes a being in history under the conditions of existence revealing to us "the heart of the divine life." The Word is the being of Christ, of which his words *and* deeds are an expression. Thus the Word cannot be identified with Christ's words separated from his deeds. Tillich views any identification of the Word with language, and particularly with written words, as the Protestant pitfall.

(4) The Bible is seen as the Word of God in two senses. First, it is

the written, literary document of the final revelation. Second, the Bible as a whole participates vitally in the church's ongoing experiences with the final revelation.

(5) The Word is the message of the church as proclaimed in her preaching and teaching. The human words proclaimed become the divine self-manifestation when they are spoken in power and received by the listener in correlation.[28]

G. Reason, Revelation, and Essentialization

In Tillich's system the essentialization or reintegration of the polarities of reason in existence is but one significant instance of the essentialization and reintegration of life itself. As we will note in the following sections, Tillich acknowledges other polarities or ontological elements besides those operating in the area of reason which are in need of reconciliation for the essentialization and reintegration of life.[29]

VII. Being and the Question of God

Just as reason quests revelation, so finite being (man) when he analyzes himself, necessarily asks the question about Being-itself (God). Between finite being (man) and Being-itself (God) there is correlation.[1]

A. The Nature of Being

As has been indicated, Tillich's philosophical categories and structures are rooted in German classical Idealism. To understand Tillich's discussion of Being and God, one must therefore be familiar with the language and assumptions of this Idealism. Finite being, for example, means primarily man, *logos*-being. Man alone has realization of being and is a potential participant in all being. He is a microcosmos because he can think in universals. For this reason, finite being (man) when he analyzes himself, necessarily asks the question of the foundation of his finite being. As we shall see, this analysis results in anxiety.[2]

The analysis of finite being (man) in this section primarily analyzes the formal structure of being prior to its actualization in existence. The next section on "Existence and the Quest for the New Being" will begin a more detailed exposition of actualized existence as fallen or estranged.[3]

B. *The Structure of Being*

Following his method of correlation, Tillich first presents an analysis of the structure of being which helps one understand how the question of God arises in human experience.

1. *The ontological principles.* The character of everything that is, insofar as it is, raises the basic ontological question or the question of being as being. The ontological question arises in the shock of nonbeing as expressed in the question: "Why is there something; why not nothing?" Man knows the power of being in himself, but he is also separate from it in his finitude. He must therefore search for an understanding of the ground and power of being in everything that exists.

The doctrine of being, "ontology," consists of principles, categories, and concepts which are *a priori* in the sense that they are presupposed in every actual experience. Tillich describes various levels of these ontological principles and concepts.

(1) *Self and the world.* The *first* level of the basic ontological structure is *self* and *world*. Since man is a microcosmos in whom all levels of the world are incipiently present, he experiences directly in himself the structure of being as a whole. Man experiences an unconditional element. This involves his need to express himself as a "self," and the need to acknowledge a "world" to which he "belongs." Man, however, is not completely bound to his environment but transcends it by knowing and willing according to universal ideas and norms. The self-world structure underlies the subject-object structure of reason. This basic ontological structure of reality must simply be accepted.[4]

(2) *Elements of being.* The *second* level of the ontological structure is that of the *ontological elements.* This level consists of three pairs of elements in polarity with each other. These three pairs of elements are individualization and participation, dynamics and form, and freedom and destiny. The first element in each pair corresponds to "self" and the second to "world" in the basic ontological structure.

a. The first polarity is *individualization* and *participation.* Individualization is characteristic of every self. But the individual self as a rational being participates in the universe with its structures, forms, and laws. This participation makes all kinds of knowledge possible, and what is even more important is the fact that the participation which the finite has in the infinite is the source of man's awareness of God.

b. The second polarity is *dynamics* and *form.* In human experience, dynamics and form appear as vitality and intentionality. Man's vital power is conditioned by his intentional relation to objective and meaningful structures. This polarity does justice both to creativity and permanence.

c. The third polarity is *freedom* and *destiny.* Freedom is the capacity of man to determine his acts by the self-conscious center of his total being. Destiny is formed by nature, history, and the structural limits of finite being. This polarity does justice both to the existentialist emphasis upon freedom and responsibility *and* the determinist emphasis upon the limitations imposed by nature and history.[5]

(3) *Being and finitude.* The *third* level of the ontological structure is *being* and *finitude.* Finitude, according to Tillich, is being, limited by nonbeing. Everything which is finite is mixed with nonbeing. Nonbeing appears as the "not yet" and the "no more" of being. This nonbeing is dialectical nonbeing which has the potentiality of being. In fact, God's own being must include dialectical nonbeing or potentiality in itself if God is to be regarded as "living" and as concerned with the processes of life and history. Life and history necessarily involve the actualization of potential being. This dialectical nonbeing in its resistance of being also accounts for the presence of structural evil in the universe and for the potential of existential evil in man. In summary, dialectical nonbeing is that which can become being if it is united with essence but, in the case of finite being, can resist or threaten being.[6]

2. *The categories and the question of finitude.* When man becomes aware of his finitude he becomes anxious. This anxiety resulting from the general threat of nonbeing is always present. This omnipresence of anxiety is revealed in an analysis of the four major categories or forms of finitude: time, space, causality, and substance. Each of these forms is capable of expressing being (courage) but also the nonbeing which threatens it (anxiety).

(1) When man has the courage to accept his transitoriness and inevitable death *time* may be creative. However, time may be experienced negatively when one's refusal to accept his transitoriness gives rise to anxiety. This raises the question of the ultimate foundation for this ontological courage. On what grounds does one affirm courage?

(2) Man needs physical and social *space.* But the threat of the loss of space causes insecurity and anxiety. Man, however, may have the courage to affirm the limited space he has and to face the threat of losing it. What is the source of this courage? How can a being who cannot be without space accept both preliminary and final spacelessness?

(3) *Causality* is that form which necessitates that every finite being depend upon something else. When this contingency is recognized in human experience it causes anxiety. What is the source of man's courage to accept his contingency?

(4) *Substance* is the basis of that which is relatively unchanging. Anxiety arises on the human level because change reveals a lack of substantiality, and the final loss of substance in human experience is death. What is

the source of the courage to face and accept such a loss? It may be concluded therefore that anxiety is caused by the potential loss of *being* in all of these categories.[7]

3. *The elements and the question of finitude.* Anxiety is also aroused because of the tendency of the polar elements in finite beings to draw away from each other and destroy the unity of the whole. The tension between individualization and participation can give rise to self-centeredness and loneliness or to a loss of individuality in collectivization. The tension between dynamics and form can lead to rigid form and loss of creativity or to chaotic formlessness. Finitude can thus lead to the loss of *essential being* and meaning through the disruption of the polar elements in the self and the consequent disintegration of the self.[8]

4. *Essence and existence.* The tension between the polar elements does not necessarily lead to destruction. However, existence *universally* involves a distortion of essential being. This is in keeping with the Christian affirmation of the essential goodness of creation and the split between the created goodness of things and their distorted existence. This distinction and contrast between *essence* and *existence*, the created and the actual world, as we have seen, is at the heart of Tillich's theological thought. This threat of nonbeing as loss of being and loss of meaning gives rise to anxiety and drives man to the question of an ultimate source for the courage to accept and overcome his anxiety.[9]

C. *The Logical Arguments for God*

Before coming to Tillich's theological statement of God as Being-itself, which is the answer to the question of God implicit in human finitude, it is important to note the way in which a philosophical analysis of existence gives rise to the question of God.

1. Tillich rejects the traditional arguments of natural theology for the existence of God. It is important at this point to remember Tillich's concept of existence as defined in the chapter on his basic idea or basic ontology. For Tillich, the concept of existence is not applicable to God. God is beyond essence and existence because he is the creative ground of both. Furthermore, as the creative ground, he cannot participate in the tensions and disruptions of existence.[10] According to Tillich, the contemporary idea of existence is drawn from modern Existentialism and cannot be applied to God because it signifies estrangement and nonbeing and implies that being has fallen away from essence. God cannot exist since existence is synonymous with estrangement. It should be observed that for most theists the term "exists" is not meant in an existential sense parallel with the term estrangement.[11]

2. Tillich further maintains that the traditional cosmological and teleolog-

ical arguments for God are failures as arguments. In these arguments God is derived from the world and therefore he cannot be that which infinitely transcends the world. The traditional arguments are of value only as expressions of the question of God which are implied in human finitude. They cannot answer the question of God.

3. Tillich's view of the traditional arguments reminds us that he is in the Augustinian or ontological rather than the Thomistic tradition in his approach to the knowledge of God. The Augustinian tradition affirms that man may be estranged from God in his existence, but he is not separated from him (as in Aquinas). Man has the possibility of overcoming his estrangement because he and God essentially belong to each other. Man is immediately aware of God with certainty, so that he does not need to infer God's reality. Eternal and unchangeable truth is present in the quest for knowledge and even doubt presupposes the existence of this truth. According to Tillich, the ontological argument does not prove the existence of God as *a* being, but it points to the awareness of an unconditional or ultimate element which is present in man's encounter with reality.[12]

4. A subordinate use of the cosmological argument can be made, according to Tillich, to show how the unconditional element of which we are immediately aware can be recognized in nature and culture. The cosmological argument from contingent being to a necessary being raises the question of God as Being-itself who is able to conquer nonbeing and give one courage in the face of anxiety. The teleological argument is another means by which man expresses his question regarding God as the ground of meaning who is capable of overcoming the threat of meaninglessness. These arguments serve primarily to help make clear man's need for God.

However, George Thomas maintains Tillich should have shown that the philosophical arguments for God could show belief in the God of theism is *reasonable* even if it is not *demonstrable*. According to Thomas, Tillich's failure here makes the distance between philosophical "quest" and the theological "answer" wider than it needs to be.[13]

D.   General Definition of God

Following his correlation method, Tillich next proceeds to present the theological answer to the question raised by his philosophical analysis of being. The answer is described as God as *Being-itself*.

First, Tillich describes the *meaning* of God as that which concerns men ultimately. To be really ultimate, God must transcend everything concrete and finite. And yet the transcendent must be mediated through concrete objects—or beings of various kinds which point to the divine beyond themselves but avoid becoming idolatrous or demonic by being seen as holy in themselves.

Tillich's typology of religion is based largely upon the tension between the requirements of concreteness and ultimacy in the divine or holy. *Polytheism* is an expression of the religious demand for concreteness in the divine. *Monotheism* emphasizes ultimacy as a reaction against this concreteness. *Mysticism* transcends all concrete expressions of the divine and tends to become idealistic monism. This leads to *pantheism* in which the many finite things disappear in the unity of being. Pantheism and mystical religion are dangerous unless they are combined with an emphasis on monotheism and the absolute transcendence of God. Christianity provides the answer to these dilemmas with its *Trinitarian monotheism* which can balance the legitimate but dialectical demands of ultimacy and concreteness.[14]

E.   *The Doctrine of God and the Answer to the Universal Question of Being*

1. *God as being.* Tillich's typology of religion prepares the way for his attempt to synthesize the mystical and the pantheistic conception of God as Being-itself with the theistic conception of God as transcendent. God is not *a* being alongside others or above others but God is Being-itself or the Ground of Being. To call God *a* being is to subject him to space and substance categories. As Being-itself, God is the power inherent in everything and the power resisting nonbeing. But he is transcendent in that he transcends every being and the totality of beings. God is both creative as the power of being and depth or abysmal in so much as he infinitely transcends all beings.

2. *God as knowable.* The only nonsymbolic statement we can make about God is that he is *Being-itself*, for that statement does not point beyond itself. Everything else which is said about God is symbolic because it is drawn from some finite experience which points beyond itself to him. Finite reality can become the basis for symbolic assertions about God because every finite thing participates in Being-itself. This conception of religious symbolism implies that the meaning of all religious symbols is characterized by some ambiguity. However, this very ambiguity is invaluable in that it helps one avoid absolutizing things which are only relative.

The assertion that God is Being-itself rather than *a* being expresses the pantheistic and mystical elements in God. This form of expression is balanced by Tillich's recognition that the primary symbols for God are derived from the self or subject-side of the structure of being such as individualization, dynamic process, and freedom. This emphasis on personal quality, actions, and relations in speaking about God expresses the theistic or personalistic element in God. By thus describing God in a series of symbolic assertions, Tillich combines the pantheistic and mystical elements with the theistic element.

3. *God as living and personal.* Tillich seeks to move beyond both the

Thomistic, static substance view of God and the modern process model. While granting that both a static element of rest and a dynamic element of becoming reside compatibly in the being of God, Tillich believes that there is no potentiality in God which is not actualized—for the "not yet" is always balanced by an "already" in God. God is therefore living in the sense that he is the stable and dynamic ground of all life.[15]

Tillich regards the symbol "personal God" as absolutely necessary for an existential person-to-person relationship with God. On the other hand, in a manner that is quite controversial, Tillich rejects the traditional theistic view that God is *a* personal Being who resides above the world and mankind distinct from the world. God as personal means that as Being-itself he is in some way the ground of everything personal and surely not less than personal himself.[16]

4. *God as Spirit and as Trinity.* Both the apostle Paul and modern Idealism influenced Tillich in his strong emphasis upon the Spirit as the fulfillment of life. The urge of life is for one to become spirit and to fulfill oneself as spirit. The Spirit unites power and meaning and includes all of the ontological elements in union with one another. The symbol of the Spirit provides the philosophical presupposition for the Christian doctrine of the Trinity. Through the Spirit the divine fullness is posited in the divine life as something definite (e.g., the *logos*), and at the same time this spirit of definiteness is reunited in the divine Ground.

The doctrine of the Trinity stands for the outgoing of God from himself and the reunion of God with himself. God is infinite because he has the finite (with its nonbeing) within himself united with his infinity. Tillich appears to interpret the Trinity through the Hegelian dialectic in order to safeguard the doctrine of God as living, or God as being in tension and movement with himself.[17]

F. *The Doctrine of God as the Answer to the Question of Finite Being*

1. *God as Creator and as immanent and transcendent.* For Tillich, God is immanent in the world as its permanent creative Ground, and he is transcendent to the world through freedom. Man is created good in his essential being, but he universally actualizes himself at the cost of becoming estranged from God. Tillich insists that this does not imply the *necessity* of the fall because the Fall is the product of individual freedom as well as universal destiny.[18]

In the introduction to Volume II of the *Systematic Theology* Tillich points out that his view differs from both supranaturalism and naturalism, or naturalistic pantheism. For Tillich, supranaturalism makes God an individual substance and a cause alongside other causes. Naturalism denies the infinite distance between finite things and their infinite ground. Tillich's view is that God is the creative Ground. Tillich's view seems to synthesize the pantheistic element of immanence with the theistic element of transcendence in a way that leans toward panentheism.[19]

For Tillich God is Being-itself, and finite beings are contained within him although they are also transcended by him. According to George Thomas, this view raises the philosophical question of how a finite being can be both *within* God and assert his freedom *against* him. The fundamental religious question concerns the distance or gulf between God and creatures which is disclosed in the experience of God as the "holy." Tillich appears to be influenced to a large extent by an idealistic ontology which minimizes the distinction between God and the world because of the fear that traditional supernaturalism will lead to dualism. Tillich affirms the mutual interpenetration of the finite and the infinite and yet at the same time asserts the reality of an absolute distinction, or infinite chasm between the finite and the infinite.[20]

2. *God as directing creativity or providence.* According to Tillich, faith in providence gives meaning to historical existence in spite of experiential meaninglessness. This view is different from the view that all things are so ordered as to serve human happiness. For Tillich, God directs everything toward its fulfillment. Providence works through the freedom of man and the structure of creatures in general. Tillich's view sees providence as a general divine condition or quality of inner directedness present in every situation. There is a continuity of the structure of reality as the basis for being and acting. But there is no special divine activity in particular historical conditions. God will not alter the conditions of finitude and estrangement. But the doctrine of providence affirms that no situation can frustrate the fulfillment of man's eternal meaning. Since this view of providence is not connected with special events and expectations, it does not lead to disappointment and cynicism.[21]

3. *God as eternal and temporal.* For Tillich, the divine eternity includes time and transcends it. God is essentially and actively related to time. In God's life, however, the moments of time are not separated from one another. Eternity is an eternal present which moves from past to future without ceasing to be present. This means that the future is open and that which is new can happen in history.

Faith in God as eternal in this sense can thus give man the courage to face his anxiety concerning the past time and the future time, since the separated moments of time are united through God in eternity. Thus faith in God as eternal is the basis for man's confidence that he may participate in eternal life. Man's hope, according to Tillich, is therefore not based on the belief that the substance of his soul is innately or naturally immortal but on his participation in the eternity of the divine life.[22]

4. *God as knowledge and will.* Since God cannot be brought under the

subject-object structure involved in human knowledge, the doctrine of the *omniscience* of God does not mean that God possesses the faculty of a highest being who is supposed to know all objects. Rather, the concept of omniscience is a symbolic way of saying that nothing is strange, dark, hidden, or outside of the centered unity of God's life and the *logos* structure of being. The abysmal quality of life cannot swallow the rational quality of the divine life. Since Tillich has denied that God is *a* being, the concept of divine knowledge seems, in a rather vague sense, to involve the inclusion of everything within the rational structure of the divine life.[23]

5. *God as divine love and justice.* Love involves the reunion of essence and existence. Since reunion presupposes separation, love cannot be realized where there is no individualization. Thus love is fully realized in man. The New Testament *agape* love is the affirmation of the other person unconditionally, apart from any desirable qualities. It also involves the acceptance of the other in spite of his resistance, and moreover implies the willingness of one to suffer for and forgive another. This kind of love can be asserted of God in a symbolic way because he works for the fulfillment of every creature and seeks to bring into unity with him all who are separated or estranged.

Justice is an expression of love. Justice acknowledges and preserves the freedom of the beloved and does not force obedience or forsake him in his disobedience. The resistance and condemnation of those who are unjust is the reaction of love which is violated or rejected. The divine love as shown in grace and reconciliation is the just and ultimate answer to the questions implied in the finitude, disruption, and estrangement of human existence.

The symbols for God's holy love, power, and justice are Father and Lord. "Father" expresses the originating, sustaining, and directing creativity of God, as well as his activity in justifying man by his grace. The symbol "Lord" expresses the power, majesty, rule, and justice of God. God remains Lord and Judge in the midst of the reconciling power of his love. This discussion prepares the way for the next section where we will find the manifestation of the Lord and Father as Son and Brother under the conditions of existence.[24]

VIII. Existence and the Quest for the New Being

Introduction

Just as the question of being, "Why is there something and not nothing?" drives man to the question of God, so the question of existence drives man to the question of New Being or Christ.[1] Since Tillich claims to be a Christian theologian, this part of his system is crucial for an evaluation of his entire theology.[2] This section of his *Systematic Theology* has occasioned some of the deepest and most widespread discussion.[3]

Tillich divides this area of his *Systematic Theology* into four sections. *First*, he gives his analysis of man's existential situation or predicament. In a departure from his usual procedure, Tillich opens this section with reference to his doctrine of the fall, rather than a philosophical analysis. The fall, for Tillich, is an expression of man's existential predicament.

Second, Tillich presents the question which arises out of the fall, which is man's quest for New Being. The fact that man *must* ask about what he has "lost" means that he has lost something of his essential being. The fact that man *can* ask about his essential being indicates that he has not lost it altogether. Man quests for a power that can undo or counteract the destructive structure of his existence.[4]

Third, Tillich gives the revelatory answer which is the New Being in Jesus as the Christ. In this connection, he presents his dogmatic assertions concerning the being of Christ who in his life, death, and resurrection makes possible the fulfillment of man's quest for New Being.[5]

112

A. The Human Predicament

1. *Essence and existence.* According to Tillich, an ontological understanding of the relationship between essence and existence is the foundation of theological thought. The term "essence" is akin to Plato's "idea" or "form." Essences transcend the empirical world. They form a higher level of being which is realized only imperfectly in the realm of existence. The essences are the causes of things. Essence stands behind existence and everything within existence.

Since essence is the true and undistorted nature of things, it is the basis of value judgments.[6] In contrast to the emphasis of the Enlightenment, for Tillich, existence entails defect of essence, or the falling away from what man is essentially. This philosophical idea of the estrangement of man in existence from essence is theologically related to the Christian interpretation of the fall.[7] As we shall see, essences actualize themselves in existence and in so doing become distorted.

2. *The transition from essence to existence and the story of the fall.*

(1) *The fall and finite freedom.* Tillich sees the Genesis story of the fall as a religious expression which rises out of man's existential awareness of the universal human predicament. Tillich translates the story of the fall into abstract philosophical and psychological terms. For him, man's fall or transition from essence to existence is not an event that happened once upon a time. The state of essential being which the fall presupposes is not an actual stage of human development.

Ontologically, the fall precedes everything that happens in time and space. This fall is the original fact, for everything that exists in time and space is affected in some way by it. But the fall is not a determined necessity since every person affirms with finite freedom, and therefore with responsibility, his state of estrangement. Man's predicament is therefore neither a matter of destiny alone nor freedom alone.[8]

If Tillich is asked to give a rationale of man's fall, he seeks to explain the need for man to exercise his finite freedom which is always in polar unity with destiny. This exercise of power through freedom makes man his own center rather than centering his life in God of whom he is an image. Why does man do this? This is the insoluble mystery, an irrational evil, and absurd. Only man made in the image of God has this power to separate himself from God.[9]

According to Bulman, Tillich's theological perspective on the fall is related to Schelling's philosophical doctrine of a Transcendent Fall. This Transcendent Fall is rooted in the Godhead, yet it is so free from dialectical necessity that Schelling calls it a leap or a tearing loose from the Absolute and true reality.[10]

(2) *Dreaming innocence, temptation, moral responsibility, and tragedy.*

a. *The stage of the transition from essence to existence.* This is portrayed by Tillich as taking place in a number of stages.

First, essential being, which is good, is symbolized as dreaming innocence. This stage precedes actual existence and has potentiality only in the divine mind and not in actuality. However, dreaming innocence does contain the real and the actual in terms of anticipation. It is akin to the child's original innocence in regard to his sexual potentialities.[11]

Second, dreaming innocence is in turn exposed to temptation. This natural or creaturely temptation is portrayed biblically and symbolically in God's prohibition not to eat of the fruit in the story of the fall. Such a prohibition presupposes on man's part the desire to sin. This Tillich calls "aroused freedom." Thus temptation occurs when finite freedom becomes conscious of itself. There is then a transition from the nonaroused to the aroused consciousness.

Third, aroused freedom or consciousness next becomes actualized freedom. Man wishes to use his freedom to actualize his independent self, but at the same time he is commanded to maintain his dreaming innocence. Actualized freedom therefore involves both loss of innocence and the loss of freedom itself. With this loss of dreaming innocence the transition to existence becomes actual. The actuality of existence has both a moral element (man is personally responsible) and a tragic element (it is unavoidable). This transition is both a cosmic event and the universal personal transition from essential goodness to existential estrangement.[12]

b. *The Garden of Eden and "dreaming innocence," and the fall.* Tillich attaches importance to the "nonactual" state of "dreaming innocence." However, difficulties arise because Tillich's terms give the impression that he believes in some kind of actual "before" and "after" in a spatio-temporal sense. The word "transition" also implies the crossing from one realm to another. It appears to refer to a happening or a process.

But for Tillich, dreaming innocence refers to dream states that are both actual and nonactual at the same time. It is a "motif," an "image," or a "psychological symbol" used in an analogical sense.[13] According to Thatcher, there is a basic weakness in Tillich's allowing the symbol "dreaming" to refer to the realm of essence or potentiality. If existence is that which has fallen from essence, then the realm of essence should have a fullness of being and an ontological priority which is incompatible with the symbol "dreaming innocence." Dream-contents may but do not necessarily become actual.

Another problem in Tillich's thought, according to Thatcher, is Tillich's weak representation of what is involved in moral choice. It appears that Adam could preserve his essential nature only at the cost of never making decisions at all. This would raise a problem of how freedom can be a part of man's essential nature.[14]

In Tillich's discussions with students at Santa Barbara he praised the biblical story of the snake and the "tree of the knowledge of good and evil," insisting that without this experience in the Garden of Eden man would always have remained in "dreaming innocence." The state of innocence in the Garden implies a relationship to God where full humanity and man's intended freedom for love never have developed. For Tillich to "exist" means to "stand out" of that kind of nonbeing which is mere potentiality. Consequently, the fall brings a guilt that is necessary in order to prepare man to actualize his potentialities. Only if we are able to say No to God can we really love him.[15] But man's self-actualization is a matter of freedom, and thus man is guilty.[16]

For Tillich, the Genesis story comes from man's retention of his essential nature in existence which enables him to "remember" his original unity with God and project this backward to account for his origin. The Genesis story is thus a religious expression of both man's dialectical unity with God and his sinful estrangement from God in time.[17] Man's actual situation provides the material for a story to be told. Tillich grants, however, that in spite of its inevitability and universality, this transition from essence to existence is irrational.[18]

(3) *Creation and the fall.* An important point in Tillich's doctrine of the fall is that man and nature are equally involved, partake mutually in the transition from essence to existence, and are both subsequently involved in estrangement. Tillich denies, however, that this is a tragic view because despite destiny there is freedom. Sin is not a structured or determined necessity. He further states that creation is good in its *essential* (merely potential) nature or character. Man's distortion in existence cannot be blamed upon his essential goodness. However, actualized creation and estranged existence are evil, so *actual* creation is not good. Thus the fall is not a logical necessity but simply a fact. While man must choose to actualize himself in order to *be* (which choice involves nature), he nonetheless is personally responsible and guilty for the estrangement which follows.[19]

Tillich thus sees the world of nature as fallen in so far as it participates in man's estrangement. And it does participate because *man* is never without his natural environment. The world is so dependent on man, that, in the traditional meaning of the words, it has no independent ontological status.[20]

3. *The marks of estrangement and sin.* Tillich prefers the term "estrangement" to "sin" because estrangement expresses the truth that one belongs essentially to that from which one is estranged. "Sin," however, must be used because it expresses that man is responsible. Osborne is quite right when he contends that sin is more ontological in Tillich than moral or theological. Salvation is thus more of an overcoming of a distortion than a re-establishment of the God-man relationship.

The marks of estrangement are unbelief, *hubris* or pride, and concupiscence. Unbelief is turning away from God. This leads to *hubris* or the self-deification of finite man. This in turn leads to concupiscence, which is unlimited desire for control and possession in all of man's relations.

For Tillich, it is impossible to separate original sin (as fact) and actual sin (as act). The fact is original and precedes the act, but the act is a matter of freedom and responsibility.[21]

4. *Existential self-destruction and evil.* Estrangement means that man contradicts his essential being and destroys its structure. The ontological elements are destroyed and disrupted. Freedom separate from destiny becomes arbitrariness. Destiny becomes mechanical necessity. The dynamic quality of life loses form and becomes oppressive. Form loses dynamism and becomes oppressive and formal law. Individualization without participation becomes loneliness, and participation without individualization falls under the power of the object in which one participates.

In the section on God we noted that man in his *essential* finiteness before the fall overcomes the threat of nonbeing by the ontological courage to be. The situation of existential, or estranged, finite being is different. While death is a natural ontological necessity, sin gives it a sting. Man is guilty because he uses his freedom. Therefore, existential man needs more than courage to be what he is. He must ask for New Being.

In the state of estrangement the categories of time and space are likewise involved. Having rejected God's eternity, man tries to prolong and continue time and cannot—and so is in despair. Having lost God's omnipresence, man does not belong anywhere and is therefore homeless.[22]

B.   *The Quest for the New Being and the Meaning of the Christ*

Although existence would reject Christ, the essence in estranged man quests New Being and Christ.[23]

1. *The failure of attempts at self-salvation.* In spite of man's estrangement he continues on his own to seek salvation and his lost unity with God and his essential manhood. But every attempt in a free act is bound to the tragic destiny of the fall.

Religious law shows that man's essential nature is used by man to seek salvation by actually trying to keep the law in the state of estrangement. Asceticism, self-negation, and mystical practices are used as attempts to force the reunion with God. Ritual is used to seek to induce the divine presence, and intellectual belief is used in an attempt to reunite the *logos* quality of man with the intelligibility of God.

These quests for self-salvation indicate that man is questing New Being and that New Being is already present in a limited fashion. In actuality, man is questing the Christ for he is the One who brings the New Being and restoration to essential unity with God.[24]

2. *Expectations of the New Being.* The quest for the New Being is universal. For Brahmanism and Buddhism the New Being is predominantly non-

historical in perspective and therefore is sought *above* history. Jews, Christians, and Muslims with their linear, historical perspective seek the New Being *in* and *through* history.[25]

3. *The symbol of Christ and paradox.* Tillich saw in the Christ an appropriate symbol for the universal quest of mankind for the New Being. Christianity claims that in Jesus as the Christ the different forms of the universal quest are fulfilled. Jesus as the Christ unites the horizontal or historical dimension of the quest with the vertical or transhistorical counterpart.[26]

In Jesus as the Christ, and in him alone, the absolutely universal and the absolutely concrete coincide. This assertion that New Being has appeared in Jesus as the Christ is neither irrational nor nonsensical but the claim is paradoxical. A paradox is that which contradicts the common opinion based on ordinary human rational experience. According to Tillich, Christianity cannot reduce this paradox without denying its own originality and its very reason for being. This is the fundamental paradox of Christianity and the basis for all other paradoxical elements within it.[27]

For Tillich, paradox is the impossible possibility. From man's side it is impossible for human essence to be actualized without the estrangement of existence. From God's side, however, it is possible for Essential Manhood to appear under the conditions of existence without being overcome by them. Although this appearance of Essential Manhood in existence is beyond man's capacity for understanding, he can seek it. The fulfillment of this quest can come only from God and is solely a matter of God's grace.[28]

C. *The Being of the Christ*

1. *The historical and biblical witness to Jesus as the Christ.*

(1) *Jesus as the Christ: fact and reception.* Tillich preferred to speak of "Jesus as the Christ" instead of Jesus Christ because he wanted to emphasize equally two elements of the Christ-event. One is the *fact* of Jesus of Nazareth and the other is the *reception* of this fact by those who received him as the Christ. Jesus is the "anointed one" in that he *received* the office of the Christ or *became* the Christ. For Tillich, the reception of the Christian event is as important as its ontological givenness. Christianity was born in the moment in which a follower said, "Thou art the Christ." Undoubtedly Peter and others made this statement as an ecstatic confession and existential commitment. Christianity will live as long as there are followers who experience this commitment and repeat this confession.[29]

In a dialogue with scholars contained in the book *Philosophical Interrogations* Tillich stated that he tried to emphasize in Volume II of his *Systematic Theology* the historicity of the event upon which Christianity is based. A. T. Mollegen believes that for Tillich the incarnation happened once in time and space. The incarnational events were photographable and the physical actions and words of the human individual who is the Christ could have been heard and recorded. The New Testament portrait of the historical and biblical Christ is all we have, and this is normative for Tillich. But, of course, for Tillich this picture is an expressionistic portrait. The total factual elements cannot be recovered through scholarly research in the sources. Therefore, for Tillich, Christology is not totally dependent upon proven facts about Jesus of Nazareth. Tillich maintained that neither the conservatives nor the liberals can reconstruct or destroy the New Testament portrayal of Christ. The best that scholars can do is to establish reasonable historical probability.[30]

The church lived for seventeen hundred years without scientific verification of Christ's life and when this method of verification was finally tried it proved to be useless, for the biblical sources did not intend to present a scientifically verifiable biography. Thus Tillich states that historical research can neither give nor take away the foundations of the Christian faith. The basis of the Christian faith, therefore, according to Tillich, rests on the unity of the historically probable accounts of Jesus and the reception of him as the Christ.[31]

(2) *The question of the factuality of Jesus and the experience of personal transformation.* The basis of faith for Tillich is a confluence of fact, appreciation, and interpretation of fact. This is similar to and compatible with the correlation of "sign-event" and "ecstasy" in his view of revelation. The problem of the knowledge of Jesus as the Christ is solved existentially— not theoretically—in the moment of appropriating faith. That which faith alone can guarantee is New Being. No historical criticism can question the immediate awareness of those who are transformed into the state of faith. Object (fact) and subject (reception) have become a unity in a mode of transformed existence possessed by those in the church.[32]

In Tillich's dialogue at Santa Barbara, published as *Ultimate Concern,* he emphasized that the biblical records of Jesus do reveal the power in him as it impressed itself on his disciples—this cannot be denied. We can say that the impression which Jesus made on the disciples caused this image to appear. Reality and image are not contradictory terms. Image is the way in which reality expresses itself and is handed down from one generation to another. The personal reality behind the gospel story is convincing. It shines through. Without this personal reality and event, Tillich states that Christianity would never have come into existence. The final proof occurs when individuals are transformed by the reality of Jesus as the Christ. Thus Christianity is not a faith based on insoluble historical problems.[33]

According to Tillich, this experience always was, and remains, the basis for the certainty that "eternal God-manhood" has appeared in a personal life under the conditions of estrangement without being conquered by them. This assertion is a matter of immediate awareness. There is no possible doubt regarding this awareness. The immediate awareness guarantees the past event. On the other hand, the immediate awareness does not guarantee one's interpretation of the cause and the various components of the elements *in* the present or *in* the past event. The *present* elements of awareness are objects which are subject to psychological analysis. The elements in the *past* event are objects of historical construction. The only unfalsifiable truth is that the early disciples encountered somebody who showed qualities that grasped and transformed them. They called it saving power, new creation, or the presence of the kingdom. Beyond this statement no historical research can go.[34]

(3) *The uniqueness of the constellation of events related to Jesus of Nazareth.* In Tillich's Santa Barbara dialogue he stated that the events related to Jesus and his reception could not happen again. It happened *then* and *there* and has become the symbol of Christianity. The question of whether someone else could be "Jesuslike" in that situation could hardly be answered. Christianity separated from Jesus as the Christ is an impossibility. There cannot be a repetition of the whole constellation of events involved. So the whole situation is a "providential event" which, as such, is unique. The conditions were fulfilled at that moment of time. We should not deviate from the biblical tradition which never isolates Jesus of Nazareth from the context of history. Such isolation is the worst sort of liberal theology.[35]

2. *The New Being in Jesus as the Christ.* For Tillich, the New Being is essential being acting under the conditions of existence, overcoming the discrepancies between essence and existence. Since in Jesus as the Christ existence and essential being are united, the law as judgment of existence by essential being is not applicable to him. Jesus as the Christ overcomes existence as it is expressed in estrangement, conflict, and self-destruction.

Jesus as the Christ bears the New Being in the totality of his being which transcends the conflict between essential and existential being. Particular aspects of Jesus' life, therefore, must always be subordinated to and interpreted by his being. His words and his deeds are important as they express his peculiar being in which we may participate, but which we cannot imitate. The suffering of Jesus is also to be seen as an integral expression of his being but not as something extraneous to be abstracted from his being as Eternal God-manhood.

The life of Jesus at every point contradicts the life of existential estrangement and bears witness to and confirms him as the New Being. In the life of Jesus there are no traces of unbelief or self-evaluation. In the temptations he rejects the unlimited desire for food, knowledge, and power. When one speaks of Jesus' sinlessness and goodness these are but ways of describing the New Being as it overcomes the estrangement of existence.

If Christ's temptations were real, could he have succumbed? If he could not have succumbed, how can it be said that his temptations were real?

To answer these questions Tillich utilizes his concepts of the polarity of freedom and destiny. The resistance of Jesus to temptation is his decision and yet it is a result of divine destiny. Beyond acknowledging this unity we cannot go.

Tillich points out that the marks of Jesus' finitude are many. He participated in the tragic element of existence and was subject to the conditions of existential estrangement. But he was not defeated by them. He conquered them by bringing them into his unbroken unity with God. Jesus is the Christ by virtue of his being and because of the continuous self-surrender of the Jesus who is Jesus and the Jesus who is the Christ.[36] Jesus as the Christ is totally transparent to God and under all conditions his unity with God is maintained. However, Jesus as Jesus does not cease to be a personal or a complete individual. Nor does Jesus as the Christ, the New Being, cease to be such a complete individual in virtue of his complete transparency. This means that we may *participate* in New Being because he *is* New Being.[37] The estrangement of our existential being from our essential being can be conquered both in principle and progressively in power through Jesus as the Christ.[38]

3. *Evaluation of Christological dogma.*

(1) *The value of the creeds and councils.* In his dialogue at Santa Barbara, Tillich states that the protective conceptualization in the Nicene Creed was a legitimate protection against the very dangerous theology which made Jesus a half-god. The creed states that Christ was fully God and fully man. For Tillich, this means that God's image was not distorted in Jesus. He was not merely half-true, as in all the pagan half-gods that represent only one side of God.

On the other hand, the idea of a metaphysical son is simply a pagan incarnation motif. Most pagan religions, including Indian religion, claim that their deities have incarnations. The special concept in Christianity is that the essence or heart of the divine appeared in Jesus. From *both* sides— from God's essence, his heart, namely his *agape*, and from man's essence, his full humanity—the divine appeared in Christ. We are therefore, according to Tillich, not obliged to take the conceptual ideas of a Hellenistic Christology as solutions for the twentieth century and its pluralistic cultures.[39]

Tillich did believe, however, that Nicaea threatened a true understanding of the humanity of Jesus and failed to account for his full participation in man's existential predicament. Fortunately, Chalcedon emphasized the historical-dynamic character of the New Being in Christ. Thus in the two great councils of the early church both the Christ-character and the Jesus-character of the event of Jesus were preserved.[40]

(2) *The constructive Christology of Tillich.* In the Santa Barbara dialogue Tillich further seeks to simplify his evaluation of Christological dogma and set forth his own view. A student asked why it was necessary for

Jesus to be tempted in the wilderness by God if Jesus was the Son of God. If God sent him to earth as his Son, Jesus would have known the answer immediately without any testing. Tillich states that the student's view represents monophysitism. The early church rejected this view which states that Christ had only one nature, the divine nature, without a full human nature. The church rather maintained with Paul that Jesus was also human and therefore stood under the law because human existence is existence under the law.

For Tillich, the true interpretation comes from the baptismal scene: "Thou art My beloved Son. Today I have chosen Thee." The gospels see a man who is driven by the Divine Spirit to his work as Messiah and as one who proclaims the coming of the kingdom of God as his message. Jesus was a full man. This means that he was full of weakness, full of *eros.* He was involved in all human tragedies, but he maintained his relationship to God.

For Tillich, in Jesus as the Christ, at one decisive point, the relationship between God and finite man was not interrupted and thus existential estrangement is overcome. This relationship might have been approached elsewhere, but the relationship of Jesus to God always remains the ultimate criterion. In Jesus this relationship has appeared for the first time in its full measure. For this reason, Tillich calls Jesus as the Christ the center of history.[41]

Furthermore, Tillich attempts to give a constructive correction of the Christological dogma. The early church wanted to emphasize the saving power of Christ. They thought that this could be done by a high Christology which emphasized his divinity. However, for Tillich, only a "low" Christology which emphasized Christ's humanity is adequate for the salvation which he brings. Tillich therefore suggests dropping the creedal statements "human nature" and "divine nature" when speaking of Christ. Jesus as the Christ had only man's essential nature and did not succumb to man's existential or estranged nature. God has no "nature" since he is beyond essence and existence. He is who he is. So the term "divine nature" cannot be applied to Christ. Jesus the Christ, unlike God, is not beyond essence and the temptations of existence. Christ was a person, born into and subject to the trials of existence.

Tillich's solution is to speak about the dynamic, eternal God-man-unity rather than to utilize the static concepts of Christ's human and divine nature. Instead of "human nature" it is better to speak of Christ as "essential man" for essential man represents the original image of God embodied in man.

Tillich explains that the New Testament gives two analogies which help to express this eternal God-man-unity. The term "adoption" is necessary because if the eternal unity of God and man is actualized in existence, it can happen only through an act of finite freedom. God chose to "adopt" the man Jesus as the Christ. Jesus in turn chose to accept his adoption through obedience. However, Christ's free choice is not contingent—it is destined. Furthermore, this unity actualized in Jesus as the Christ is not finite but eternal. Therefore, the term "incarnation" is necessary to show the eternal character of the relationship between Jesus and the Being of God. The incarnation seeks to express the paradox that Jesus who transcends the universe appears in it and under its conditions.

Tillich's use of "incarnation" is not the traditional metaphysical concept that "God has become man." The danger of this traditional theme is that it is usually or often interpreted in terms of an impersonal mythological metamorphosis whereby God assumes human substance. For Tillich, the incarnation of the *Logos* is not a metamorphosis but the dynamic manifestation of God in a personal life-process as a saving participant in the human predicament. Thus Tillich believes that the analogy of "adoption" provides the best theological basis for a positive reconstruction of Christological dogma.

Tillich's Christology should be seen in correlation with his doctrines of man and revelation. For Tillich, no revelation takes place that is not received by man through his own categories of understanding. This means that in the revelation of God in the event of Jesus as the Christ the activity of man must be relatively independent and free. On the other hand, God must not cease to be absolute and transcendent. For Tillich, God's "otherness" can be better protected if his relation to Christ is seen as a "choosing of" or a "manifestation through," rather than a metaphysical "unity with." [42]

(2) *Evaluations of Tillich's Christology.* According to Alexander McKelway, Tillich will not say with the incarnational Christologies of Nicaea and Chalcedon, that Jesus Christ was "truly God and truly man." Tillich's emphasis is rather on an adoptionist position that God chose Jesus and Jesus obeyed God and became the Christ. [43]

Thatcher points out that critics not only call Tillich's Christology adoptionistic but Nestorian, Sabellian, Docetic, Dionysiac, and Gnostic. This demonstrates, for Thatcher, how difficult it is to judge a largely philosophical vocabulary (essence-existence-essentialization) according to traditional theological norms. [44]

D. *The Universal Significance of the Work of Jesus as the Christ*

1. *The uniqueness and universality of Jesus as the Christ.* Although Jesus was a concrete reality, the New Testament pictures him as of universal significance. He answers man's questions and fulfills man's quest. The universal meaning of the event of Jesus of Nazareth was expressed in dramatic symbols. These symbols must be deliteralized but not removed as the vehicle of religious expression.

2. *The cross and the resurrection.* The two central symbols of the total

participation of Jesus in man's existential estrangement and his victory over estrangement are the cross and the resurrection. Christ's subjection to existence is expressed in the symbol of the "Cross of Christ." The conquest of existence is expressed in the symbol of the "Resurrection of Christ." These two symbols are interdependent.

The cross is both an *event* and a symbol. The resurrection is both a *symbol* and an event. The character of the event of the resurrection is not clear, but the certainty of it was grasped by the despairing group of followers and the church was born. The disciples called this experienced event the "Resurrection of Christ." Faith in the resurrection of Christ can be neither positively nor negatively determined by historical research. Rather faith is based on the experience of being grasped by the power of the New Being. Faith is its own guarantor.

Tillich calls his view of the resurrection the "restitution" theory. This restitution is rooted in the personal unity between Jesus and God and in the impact of this unity on the apostles. In an ecstatic experience, the concrete picture of Jesus of Nazareth becomes indissolubly united with the reality of the New Being. Tillich tends to blend the resurrection, Pentecost, and the ascension into one event, although the ascension has a finality to it which is lacking in the other events associated with the Resurrected One. Tillich thus holds an immanent view of the resurrection which is confirmed by one's faith in Jesus as the Christ by the presence of the Holy Spirit.[45]

In the Santa Barbara dialogue, Tillich makes much of the various New Testament images of the resurrection. For Tillich, Christ's spiritual presence, as it appears in resurrection vision, is something that transcends the historical image. These resurrection stories are unique. They gave the disciples victory and hope instead of their distress and despair.[46]

McKelway notes the lack of biblical references and exegesis in Tillich's approach to the resurrection. There is only a brief allusion to the crucial passage about the resurrection in 1 Corinthians 15.[47]

3. *The New Testament symbols which undergird the cross and resurrection.* For Tillich, the New Testament has many symbols and stories which undergird and describe the cross. The accounts of Jesus' birth, poverty, flight into Egypt, and the descriptions of low estate, loneliness, and suffering are all part of the same story. They show that the divine self-manifestation subjected himself to the conditions of existential estrangement and could therefore conquer these conditions in the power of the New Being.

The story of the resurrection of Christ, according to Tillich, is also anticipated in a large number of events and symbols such as pre-existence, post-existence, virgin birth, transfiguration, and certain miracle stories. Other symbols which are related to the resurrection are the ascension, Christ at the right hand of God, Pentecost, millennium, the second coming, and the last judgment.

(1) *Pre-existence and the virgin birth.* The New Testament language of pre-existence points to the presence of the eternal principle in the divine self-manifestation in Jesus of Nazareth. Virgin birth expresses the conviction that the divine spirit and historical destiny determine the nature of the bearer of the New Being even before his birth. For Tillich, the literalistic character of the New Testament accounts of the virgin birth is fraught with many problems because this deprives Jesus of full participation in the human predicament.

(2) *Miracle stories.* In the miracle stories, Jesus appears as the victor over the demonic or the suprapersonal structures of destruction. The saving power of New Being has power over these enslaving structures of evil. For Tillich, the miracles are not supranatural interference in ordinary events but rather witnesses to the power of the New Being to overcome the self-destructive consequences of existential estrangement in the created structures of reality.

(3) *Ascension and millennium.* The New Testament portrayal of Christ sitting at the right hand of God shows that God's creativity is working with the New Being in Christ. The millennium concept conveys the prophetic theme that there is an inner-historical fulfillment of history before its final consummation. However, even in this period of millennium the demonic power while subjugated to New Being is not totally eradicated.

(4) *The second coming of Christ.* The second coming of Christ expresses that Jesus, at least in the present space-time framework, cannot be transcended by anyone else who may appear in history. The symbol of the second coming also shows that we are in a period of waiting. Although the demonic is broken in principle, there is a sense in which the full power and victory of the New Being have "not yet" been realized.

(5) *The last judgment.* For Tillich the last judgment is an immanent judgment which is always going on in history. It points, however, toward an ultimate separation of the ambiguous elements of reality. It also includes the purification and elevation of the essentialized aspects of man into the transcendent unity of the kingdom of God.

All of the symbols listed above undergird the central symbol of the resurrection of Christ. According to Tillich, these symbols must be deliteralized and reinterpreted in order to unite their cosmic and existential qualities. These symbols may die, but the New Being is not dependent on the symbolical form in which its ontological reality is expressed.[48]

4. *Jesus the Christ as the power of salvation.*

(1) *The meaning of salvation.* Tillich interprets "salvation" in correlation with the idea of negativity. One is saved from ultimate negativity. Salvation is essentialization, which means reaching that state in which the negative is exposed as negative and the positive is exposed as positive. This means that salvation saves us from the negativity of existence and gives us essential being in contrast to existential estrangement.[49]

Salvation can also be experienced in terms of healing. Healing reunites that which was estranged and overcomes the alienation between man and God. Salvation reclaims one from the old order and transfers him into the new realms and relationships of New Being.

Tillich affirms that there have been prior historical manifestations and processes of healing (a line of revelatory and saving events) which proceed from and lead toward the center of revelation, salvation, and healing found in Jesus Christ. He goes further to state that in some degree all men participate in the healing power of the New Being. Otherwise, they would have no being. The self-destructive consequences of estrangement would destroy them. But no man in this life of existence is ever totally healed existentially, not even those who have encountered the healing power as it appears in Jesus as the Christ. Jesus Christ, however, remains the ultimate criterion of every healing and saving process. In him the healing potential is complete and unlimited.[50]

(2) *The atonement.* For Tillich, the traditional distinction between the person and work of Christ must be abandoned. The being of Christ *is* his work and his work *is* his being which is the New Being.

For Tillich, therefore, the doctrine of the atonement is the description of the effect of the New Being in Jesus as the Christ on those who are grasped by it in their state of estrangement. Atonement is always both a divine act (removing human guilt) and a human response (man's acceptance of reconciliation in spite of guilt). Tillich sees value in both the objective (Origen, Anselm) and subjective (Abelard) approaches to atonement. Tillich prefers to transcend Anselm's substitutionary view by his concept of participation which balances the objective and subjective approaches.

Tillich's central thesis is that God's atoning activity must be understood as his participation in existential estrangement or unconquered negativity and its self-destructive consequences. God's participation can lead man from existence to essentialization. When unconquered negativity becomes conquered negativity we have salvation. Thus we see that Tillich's interpretation of the atonement is correlative to his basic ontology of essence (the positive factor), existence (the negative factor), and above all essentialization (the ultimate exposure of the negative as negative and the positive as positive without the threat of negativity).

For Tillich, man's essence retains an irremovable dialectical relationship to God, even under the distortions of human existence. Salvation, in Tillich's terms, is, therefore, basically not a reestablishment of the God-man relationship, but rather the overcoming of this existential distortion.

As we have seen, the overcoming of the distortion of existence cannot be obtained by one's own efforts (Judaism, asceticism, mysticism, sacramentalism). Salvation can only come as God's gift through Christ for Christ is the final, complete, unsurpassable revelation of God. In Christ one finds total transparency to the revealing God which means that all the potential existential distortion which might be involved in Christ's existence as man is removed. Christ's Essential Manhood allows the fullness of the infinite to shine through. In this one point, Jesus as the Christ, existence has been conquered. Atonement is thus the conquering of negativity so that man's essence can be essentialized. This is due to God alone. Christ on the cross merely "manifests" this process by his total transparency to the divine and his total surrender to the *Logos*. [51]

Osborne suggests that Tillich's view of atonement is dominated by his basic ontology of essence-existence-essentialization. Thus Tillich removes redemption from the crucial theological area of the God-man relationship to the more philosophical concerns regarding essence-existence. Consequently, Christ has a restricted role in this salvation as a mere "manifestation." [52]

(3) *The threefold character of salvation.* Tillich's basic idea or ontology (essence-existence-essentialization) is reflected in his doctrine of salvation as regeneration, justification, and sanctification. Regeneration or new birth is a *reunion* of the self as estranged existence with its originally intended essence. The individual enters this new relationship with the essence of his personal being by participation in the New Being manifest in Jesus as the Christ. The subjective consequences are fragmentary and ambiguous, but faith in Jesus as the bearer of New Being gives a real though yet incomplete self-realization.

Justification is the *acceptance* of man by God. This comes *after* regeneration because justification presupposes faith and this means that one is already in the state of having been grasped by the Divine Presence. Faith must be seen as the work of the Divine Spirit and not as an intellectual or moral work of man. Man is justified or accepted *after* being grasped by the New Being. The wording of the phrase "justification by grace through faith" must be clearly understood. The cause of justification is God alone (by grace), but the faith that is willing to believe that one is accepted is the experiential channel through which grace is mediated to man.

In fact, for Tillich, regeneration and justification are one. Both describe the reunion of that which was previously estranged. Regeneration depicts the actual reunion. Justification portrays the paradoxical character of this reunion by declaring that God makes those just who are not just, and accepts those who are not acceptable.

Finally, sanctification is the *process* in which the power of the New Being transforms personality and community both inside and outside the church. This process is the work of the Spirit in history. It will be treated more fully and appropriately in our exposition of the fourth and fifth divisions of Tillich's system, "Life and the Spirit," and "History and the Kingdom of God." [53]

IX. Ambiguous Life and the Quest for Unambiguous Life

Part four, "Life and the Spirit," is the most complex and intricate part of Tillich's entire system. In this rather lengthy section Tillich not only analyzes "life," its ambiguities and dialectical tensions, but also deals with the doctrines of the Spirit, the church, ethics, and culture. Enough detail will be given to illustrate how Tillich continues to develop his basic ontology (essence, existence, essentialization) and apply his method of correlation.

A. Question: Life and Its Ambiguities

1. Life as a multidimensional unity.

(1) Life as essence and existence. For Tillich, life is a form of being which involves the two fundamental aspects of reality, essence and existence. Since life is and contains essence, it is positive and good. But life as man experiences it in himself and in others is existential, which means that it has negativity, estrangement, conflict, distortion, and death.[1]

Life is thus a mixture of essence (man's essential nature in its unity with God) and existence (man's fallen state in estrangement from God). This juxtaposition makes life "ambiguous."[2] If there is any quest in life, it comes from the essential possibilities of life longing for unambiguous fulfillment.

(2) Life as multidimensional. Since life is a unity, it should not be thought of in terms of levels or degrees of hierarchies beginning with the inorganic and ascending to God. The concept of levels divides life into

watertight compartments or separateness into the two-level world of supra-naturalist dualism.

Tillich prefers the term "dimension" to express the distinctions between the inorganic and the organic, the spiritual and the historical, because it also includes and expresses the idea of unity. This expression permits man to be seen as a multidimensional unity in whom all the dimensions of life are actual. Man is the most evolved grade of being and contains many dimensions: inorganic, organic, psychological, and spiritual. The dimension of spirit, which is also called "the dimension of depth, the ultimate, or the eternal," is peculiarly dominant in man.[3]

For Tillich, the dimension of spirit in man supplements and transcends but does not remove the inorganic or psychological dimensions. J. H. Randall, Jr., sees Tillich as being in the lineage of the philosophers of "emergent evolution" such as Lloyd-Morgan, Samuel Alexander, A. N. Whitehead, and Nicolai Hartmann.[4] Tillich notes the influence of organic and even inorganic processes on man's intellectual, creative, and spiritual activities. He speaks of "spirit" as a dimension of material organic life, which is present potentially even in the inorganic life. The spiritual dimension of man becomes actualized and distinct only when constellations occur in the lower dimensions which support it.[5]

The dimension of spirit in man includes those cognitive and moral functions of life in which the personal center sees itself in relation to the world and acts upon its world. Human "spirit" is thus the unity of "power and meaning" in man which is grounded in material organic life.[6] This view is diametrically opposed to Descartes' idea of the soul as a "ghost in a machine."[7] Rather Tillich combines on the one hand the Hebrew and Indo-Germanic view of spirit as the breath or power of life and on the other hand the Western philosophical conception of spirit as mind or intellect.[8]

Tillich, with his doctrine of the multidimensional unity of life, rejects the teaching that at a certain moment God added an "immortal soul" to an otherwise complete human body, with this soul bearing the life of the spirit. This "addendum" view, for Tillich, threatens one's understanding of the unity of the psychological and spiritual dimensions. As we will see, in part five of his system, Tillich also rejects the idea of a "natural" immortality of the soul. According to Bulman, Tillich's doctrine of the multidimensional unity of reality and his preference for the term "centered self" or "personal center" rather than "mind" or "soul" are reflective of the views of a number of New Testament scholars.[9]

2. *The functions and ambiguities of life.* Tillich next describes the three functions of life as they are actualized in the spirit of man and notes their ambiguities. The ambiguities in turn lead man to a quest for the Divine Spirit.

For Tillich, life is a process. It moves out and away from a personal ontological center and then back toward it. The three functions of life can be seen within this recurring process.[10]

(1) The function of *self-integration* (individualization, centeredness, participation, and the moral acts). The first function is the self-integration of life. This is a circular movement within the polarities of individualization and participation which establishes the center of self-identity.

Tillich thus sees man as constituting his personal self in the moral act. Man realizes that he is a personal center over against another personal center. Real participation requires that one person must acknowledge the other as a person. This existing and acknowledged relationship with the other person is the basis for morality and ethics. The "ego-thou" relationship thus developed is the ground for the "oughtness" of the moral imperative. The very character of the ego-thou relationship is constituted to demand and expect *agape* love. The recognition of the oughtness of *agape* love gives concreteness to the categorical imperative and also gives centeredness to a person.

In actual life, the very "law of love" which is the basis of the moral imperative is subject to ambiguities. *Essentially*, man's spirit is questing for the fulfillment of individualization and participation. Existentially, man's spirit expresses resistance to such fulfillment. If a person becomes too individualistic, he becomes separated. On the other hand, participation holds the danger of the loss of individuality. There are likewise ambiguities when the categorical imperative (the law of love) is applied to concrete circumstances. In some cases the moral law produces hostility against God and other men. Thus man is driven to quest for a morality which fulfills the law by transcending it. This is given in *agape* love which can reunite and integrate man with God. Man's moral ambiguity, therefore, drives him to quest for and ask for *the Spirit* of love.[11]

(2) The function of *self-creativity* (dynamics, form, growth, and culture). In the context of the polarities of dynamics and form, the spirit of man is seen as self-creative, which means dynamics as growth within form. This self-creativity finds expression in culture. For Tillich, culture can be summarized under the headings of language, the cognitive realm, and the aesthetic realm. The language functions of communication and denotation reflect the basic self-world structure of man's life. The cognitive act grasps the ontological structure of reality and seeks to bridge the gap between subject and object in terms of truth. The individual strives for personal growth or the attainment of his essential humanity. The social group strives for justice.[12]

Essentially, there should be no cleavage but only correlation between the dynamic in man's intelligence (the *logos*-structure of the centered-self) and the form (the *logos*-structure of the objective world). In man's *existential* situation, however, cleavage is present. In fact, both man's mind (dynamics) and the object (form) are involved in existential distortion. As a result, the linguistic, cognitive, and aesthetic realms of the spirit, as expressed in culture are, while potentially valuable and real, nevertheless ultimately inauthentic.

In praxis, the spirit of man is striving for essential manhood and for universal justice. Man in existence resists this striving. However, spirit-as-essence quests the Divine Spirit in which it will find essential manhood, universal justice, and unambiguous eschatological fulfillment.[13]

(3) The function of *self-transcendence* (freedom, destiny, and religion). The self-transcendent function of man is a vertical movement within the polarities of freedom and destiny in which life drives itself toward the sublime or toward ultimate and infinite being. The life that can transcend itself under the dimension of spirit is free, even if it is never separated from its destiny, for in transcendence is found the unity of freedom and destiny.[14]

Existentially, however, man offers resistance to such self-transcendence. This is done, first by his profanization or secularization, which does not see the "religious" or "holy" quality in things. Existence distorts and negates man's essential drive toward self-transcendence and toward his experiencing the holy.

Another possible ambiguity related to the function of self-transcendence appears when something finite is elevated to infinite value. *Essentially*, man's spirit should be self-transcendent only toward the authentically divine or unconditioned.

The Greek hero who approaches the sphere of the divine does not usually aspire to divine equality. He touches the divine sphere, is rejected by it, and embarks upon a path of self-destruction, but he does not usually claim divinity for himself. If he should claim divinity for himself, the demonic appears. The demonic occurs in religion when it seeks to claim ultimate significance for certain moral and cultural forms which are really only media of revelation.[15]

3. *The quest for the unambiguous life*. Tillich thus portrays all of the dimensions of life as being involved in the paradoxical union of the essential and the existential and consequently subject to ambiguity. But only in man, who is the bearer of the spirit, do the ambiguities of life and the quest for the unambiguous life become conscious. Man makes this quest primarily in the realm of religion. He attempts to transcend his estrangement and reunite with his own essential being and with God. This is impossible through his own resources and so man quests for an answer to his condition. In keeping with Tillich's basic method of correlation, his description of the spirit as man's unique dimension establishes the form in which the answer to man's dilemma needs to come—namely redemption through the Divine Spirit.[16]

The Divine Spirit is "God present." For Tillich, the Spirit of God is not a being separated from man and reality, so he prefers to use the symbol "Spiritual Presence." The symbol "Spiritual Presence" is directly correlated to the human spirit. However, in order to be present in the human, the Divine Spirit must be present in all of the dimensions which are actual in man. This means, as indicated above, that the Divine Spirit is present in all the dimensions in the universe.

In Part Five of Tillich's system, he will present the other two main symbols for unambiguous life—the Kingdom of God, and Eternal Life. The three symbols, Spiritual Presence, Kingdom of God, and Eternal Life, are mutually inclusive but they are applied in Tillich's system to represent different dimensions of the same reality. As noted above, Spiritual Presence indicates the conquest of the ambiguities of life in the dimension of the human spirit. The Kingdom of God shows the conquest of the ambiguities of life in the dimension of history. Eternal Life, in turn, shows the conquest of ambiguities in the dimension beyond history. The emphasis in each symbol is different but the language refers to the same substance, the same unambiguous life.[17]

B. *Answer: Spiritual Presence*

As Tillich explained in Part Three of the System, the concept of New Being in Jesus as the Christ is normative and central for his theology. New Being, however, is created in man by the Spiritual Presence. The theology of the Divine Spirit, therefore, is crucial for Tillich. In fact, he is called a "theologian of the spirit" and sees himself as a theologian of experience and inwardness in the tradition of the apostle Paul.[18]

It has already been noted that Tillich's analysis of ambiguous life is related to human spirit, which is his name for that psychic function of life which characterizes man as man. This analysis shows the problem which causes the human spirit to quest for a theological answer in terms of the Divine Spirit.

1. *The Spiritual Presence in the spirit of man.* The Divine Spirit dwells and works *in* the human spirit. However, while breaking into the human spirit, the Divine Spirit does not remain at rest. It drives the human spirit out of itself and into meaningful self-transcendence. The human spirit is grasped by something ultimate and unconditional. The classical term for this state of being grasped by the Spiritual Presence is "ecstasy."

In the driving of the human spirit beyond itself toward ecstasy, the Spiritual Presence does not destroy man's rational structure or the personal center of the individual. But the gift of God in Spiritual Presence creates unambiguous life—at least in a fragmentary way appropriate for man, who remains a creature. The Divine Spirit and the human spirit are relationally but realistically united. A good example is prayer, in which God is not merely an object but is also a subject at the same time, so that God as Spiritual Presence prays to himself through us.

Spiritual Presence is often confused with chaotic behavior and irrationalism. This confusion causes psychologists to attempt to "explain away" Spiritual Presence. For Tillich, however, it is primarily through the dynamics of the ecstatic, self-transcendent consciousness that the Divine Spirit brings meaning-bearing power to human experience. Spirit-given ecstasy is creative while more self-destructive excitement is not.

The Spiritual Presence is mediated to men through the Word and the sacraments. Reality comes to us by the silent presence of an object or by the vocal self-expression of a subject.[19]

(1) The importance of the sacraments. For Tillich, an object or event becomes "sacrament" in the broad sense when the transcendent is seen to be present. Tillich thus saw nature as the finite expression of the ground of all things.[20] If this larger sacramental sense is disregarded, then sacraments in the narrower sense lose their significance.

In the narrower sense, "sacrament" refers to some particular object or event in which the Spiritual Presence has become embodied in such a way as to allow the Spiritual Community to actualize itself. As symbols and media of the Spirit, the sacraments unite two essential factors: a relationship to nature and a participation in salvation history. The sacrament "uses" the power of being in nature to "enter" man's spirit. In principle, anything may convey the Spiritual Presence. Certain elements, however, such as water, bread, wine, fire, and oil have inherent qualities which make them adequate and even irreplaceable for their symbolic function. The twentieth-century rediscovery of the unconscious concern with such basic elements causes us to realize anew the necessity of using the powers of nature to mediate the Spirit to the total man.[21]

Words may appeal to our intellects and move our wills, but the sacramental reaches the unconscious as well as our conscious beings. In neglecting the sacraments, Protestantism has been led to either an intellectualization or a moralization of the Spiritual Presence. Communication to and from the Spiritual Presence can, however, occur through actions, gestures, and forms as well as through sounds and syllables. On the other hand, the Roman Catholic stress on sacramental efficacy has, according to Tillich, distorted the sacraments into nonpersonal acts of quasimagical technique. This view tends to separate the sacramental object from an active faith on the part of the participant.[22]

A balance may be found in what Tillich calls "Protestant principle and Catholic substance." Catholic substance sees the holy as primarily incarnate. It is a present reality, represented by holy persons, objects, and functions.[23] This view sees the sacraments as ontologically related to their sacramental function. As such, they (water, fire, oil, bread, wine) have "inherent" qualities which make them adequate and irreplaceable for their sacramental function.

The sacraments, however, are in the ever-present danger that ritual actions, which represent the holy, will claim holiness for themselves. They tend to become identified with grace itself. To counteract this tendency toward the distortion of the sacramental principle, Catholic substance needs to be maintained in polar tension with the Protestant principle.[24]

The prophetic churches look upon the holy as dependent upon a decision by the participants and related to one's personal moral and spiritual condition and development. For the Protestant, a sacramental symbol is neither a thing nor a sign. It participates in the power of what it symbolizes, and therefore, it can be a medium of the Spirit. Tillich calls his alternative view of the sacraments "realistic" as opposed to a merely metaphoric *or* ritualistic interpretation.[25]

Tillich believes that all sacramental acts must be subject to the criterion of the New Being in Jesus as the Christ. They must somehow refer to the historical and doctrinal symbols which have emerged within Christianity such as the crucifixion or eternal life. The number of sacraments depends on tradition, evaluation of importance, theological issues (marriage and divorce, priesthood and laity), and criticism of abuses. Another decisive question is whether the sacraments possess, and are able to preserve, the power of mediating the Spiritual Presence.[26]

(2) The importance of the "Word." The *Word* is crucial, even to the sacraments, because language is the basic expression of man's spirit. According to Tillich, the Bible does not contain the words of God, but it can, and has become the "Word of God." Its uniqueness rests in the fact that it is the document of the central revelation. Every day, by its impact on people both inside and outside the churches, the Bible shows that it is the Spirit's most important medium in the Western tradition.

Other religions and cultural documents and even human conversations can become the Word of God if they work on the human mind in such a way that an ultimate concern is created. The biblical words, however, constitute an ultimate touchstone for what can and cannot become the Word of God for someone. They point out that nothing is the Word of God if it contradicts the faith and love which are the works of the Spirit and which constitute the New Being as it is manifest in Jesus as the Christ.

Tillich expresses gratitude for the "inner word" or so-called Spirit movements of history. However, in their emphasis on the Spirit's freedom from ambiguous form, their term "inner word" is misleading if it implies that God speaks to man without a medium. "Inner word" actually means refocusing into contemporary relevance the words from the Bible and traditions and former experiences under the impact of the Spiritual Presence. The reformers opposed the "inner word" or Spirit movements of their time because they were afraid that the ultimate criterion—the New Being in Jesus as the Christ—would be lost in the name of the immediacy of the Spirit. The reformers thus interpreted the Spirit as being inseparably bound to the biblical message of the Christ.[27]

In an anticipatory way the Spiritual Presence overcomes man's ambiguities by creating the transcending union between man and God in the unambiguous life. Faith and love form the "content" of this union. Faith is the state of being *grasped* by the transcendent unity and love is the state of being *taken into* that unity. In faith, one is grasped by God, and in love one adheres to him. In this sense "love" means reunion between God and man. It is *agape* and is characterized by God's unambiguous love for his creatures. Thus love is only possible for man within the union with God given by Spiritual Presence.[28] The Spiritual Presence through faith and love creates the New Being beyond the conflict between essence and existence and thus, in a fragmentary way, above the ambiguities of life.[29]

2. *The Spiritual Presence in historical mankind.* The invasion of the human spirit by the Divine Spirit does not just occur in isolated individuals. Social context is important, so the Spirit invades the human spirit in and through social groups and communities. Mankind is never left alone. This participation by man in unambiguous life as an individual and in social groups is always fragmentary in its manifestation in time and space. The complete transcendent union or unambiguous actualization awaits the future beyond history.[30] This fragmentary unambiguous life in mankind as a whole is an anticipation and preparation for the central manifestation of the Divine Spirit in Jesus as the Christ.[31]

(1) Jesus as the Christ as the criterion of all spiritual experiences. Since mankind is never left alone, there is a common experience of the Spiritual Presence in all religions. When religions are compared in a phenomenological way, there are differences. For Tillich, however, there is an identity of the dimension of the Spirit or Spiritual Presence in the various religions. But it is only in Jesus as the Christ that the Divine Spirit was present without distortion. In Jesus, the New Being appeared as the criterion of all spiritual experiences in the past and future. In Jesus as the Christ, we find the keystone in the arch of spiritual manifestations in history. It is true that Jesus was subject to individual and social conditions, but his human spirit was entirely grasped by the Spiritual Presence.[32]

Tillich's adoptionism is once again apparent. Jesus was grasped by the Spirit at the moment of his baptism. This event confirmed him as the elected "Son of God." The Divine Spirit found a vessel in which to pour itself. Tillich is here drastically altering the classical declaration that the Spirit proceeded from the Father and the Son as expressed in the Western version of the Nicaean Creed.

(2) The Spiritual Presence in the Spiritual Community. The Spiritual Presence is not only manifested in the Old Testament and in all religions but in the Spiritual Community or the church. In fact, Christ is not the Christ unless he is *received* as the Christ. The place where he is received is the Spiritual Community. This Community is existential New Being as created by the Spiritual Presence, but it is fragmentary as it appears under the conditions of finitude.

The unambiguous life present within the Spiritual Community has certain distinguishing marks. These marks are seen in the Spiritual Community created at Pentecost (Acts 2). This Community overcame the disruption of mankind symbolized by the Tower of Babel. The Spiritual Community is a community of *ecstasy*, *faith* (reestablished by the Spiritual Presence after Jesus' crucifixion), *love* (expressing itself in mutual service), and of *unity* (seen in the uniting of nationalities and traditions). The Spiritual Community is also characterized by *universality* (expressed in missionary outreach), *holiness*, and a *unity of morality, culture*, and *religion*.

The Spiritual Community has a dialectical relation to the historic Christian church—it is a relation both of identity and nonidentity. This means that the historical, institutional churches which are marked by ambiguity are actualizations as well as distortions of the Spiritual Community.[33]

(3) The latent and manifest Spiritual Community. Tillich also speaks of the Spiritual Community as both latent and manifest. This is not to be identified with the interpretation of the invisible and visible church by Calvin. Rather it refers to the general and universal manifestations of the Spiritual Presence as opposed to its specific and Christian manifestations. It emphasizes the existential difference between a "before" and "after" relation to the event of Jesus as the Christ. The *latent* church reveals the impact of the Spiritual Presence, but without its ultimate criterion in Jesus as the Christ. Tillich gives a number of examples of the latent church in various religions and philosophies such as Christian humanism, Islamic devotional communities, mythological groups, and the mystical religions of Asia and Europe.[34] He appears to have been influenced by Clement of Alexandria, Augustine, and Luther in their teaching regarding an invisible church when developing his concept of the latent church.[35]

Although the "latent" church manifests in some ways the impact of the Spiritual Presence, it does not have the ultimate criterion of Jesus as the Christ. This means that the latent Spiritual Community is open to profanation and demonization without the ultimate principle of self-negation, reformation, and transformation which is potentially present through the cross. The latent Spiritual Community also lacks an organization which can withstand paganism. The various expressions of latent Spiritual Community are unconsciously driving toward the Christ (even though they reject him).[36]

The church is the Spiritual Community in its *manifest* stage. Individual churches are judged against the marks of the Spiritual Community at Pentecost which we have already identified as ecstasy, faith, love, unity, and universality.

3. *The divine Spirit, the churches, and the individuals in the churches.* We have noted Tillich's description of the ambiguities of life. He has also stated that the Divine Spirit solves these ambiguities. Tillich endeavors now to describe the way in which the Divine Spirit raises life to a transcendent unity above its ambiguities in religion, culture, and morality.

(1) The Spiritual Community and the churches. Spiritual Community is not a religious group but is a power and structure inherent in all religious communities which are determined by an ultimate concern. A religious group can be called a church, in the strict sense of the word, only if it is consciously based on the appearance of Jesus as the Christ.

The Spiritual Community constitutes the spiritual essence or essentiality of the churches, but the churches inwardly distort the Spiritual Community. So one must make the distinction between the sociological and the theological aspects of the churches. Both these dimensions must be emphasized equally. This will help avoid devaluating the empirical churches (as Spirit groups do) and it also helps prevent the indifference to the Spiritual Community as an ideal (as liberal Protestants do). In summary, the Spiritual Community is the inner *telos* of the churches and is the dynamic source of everything that makes them churches.

It is obviously wrong to ignore the churches because they do not completely embody Spiritual Community in their concrete reality. Within the ambiguities of their social existence, the churches embody unambiguous Spiritual Community. In terms of both the members and the institution, the churches are "holy" because of the holiness of their foundation, but they are not holy in themselves.[37]

(2) The life, struggles, and functions of the churches. Initially it was a risk to belong to a church, but now church membership is often simply a cultural shelter. This lack of existential commitment in the churches has produced many ambiguities in religious life. But faith remains in the churches because the Spiritual Presence remains in them, grasping the members. *Agape* love in the churches and their members also continues to fight against disunity and division among individuals, races, and cultures through the power of the Spirit.

Creeds are unavoidable attempts to formulate conceptually the implications of the basic assertion that Jesus is the Christ. But the creeds are ambiguous. Likewise, the expression of *agape* love in the church is real yet ambiguous. Even though a Christian is cognizant of the churches' ambiguities, he is grasped and held by the power of the Spiritual Presence in his own life and in the life of the churches.[38]

To better describe the churches, Tillich sets forth their seven functions.[39] All of these functions are performed in the name of the Spiritual Community, but they are also performed by ambiguous sociological groups called churches. The aim of the functions, however, is to conquer the ambiguities of life in the power of the Spiritual Presence.

a. The *first* function of the church is the *constitutive* function. This means that a church receives the New Being, responds to it, and mediates it to others. The response involves both a confession of faith and worship. This response requires respect for tradition and a constant reformation. Faith is confessed in creeds but also in prose, poetry, symbols, and hymns. Worship is expressed personally and communally and should both acknowledge and transcend the subject-object polarity. There is an identity and nonidentity of him who prays and him who is prayed to.

b. The *second* or *expanding* function of the church includes missionary, educational, and apologetic activity. This involves both adaptation to culture and a maintenance of verity and integrity against the prevailing culture.

Missions is the first function of expansion. For Tillich, missions is a transformation of the church's latency into manifestation all over the world. People are not outside of God. Rather, they are grasped by God on the level in which they *can* be grasped. It is a distorted level, but it is not nonreligion. It is the reality of the Divine preparing in paganism for the coming of the manifest church.[40] The proof that Christianity is universal is its assertion that Jesus is the Christ.

Education involves both understanding and participation. Evangelism calls for both evangelistic preaching and practical apologetics. Apologetics involves both a silent witness of faith and love and an attempt to break through the intellectual walls of skepticism and dogmatism which are not only erected by the churches' critics but exist within the lives of church members. Evangelistic preaching gives witness to the possibility of a transforming experience of Spiritual Presence which conquers estrangement and creates New Being.

c. The *constructing* function of the church attempts to correlate all of the cultural dimensions of life with the experience of New Being. All of these constructing functions operate within the polarity of form-affirmation and form-transcendence. The church takes styles, methods, norms, and relations and then transcends them. The Spirit breaks into the finite forms and drives them beyond themselves. There is a danger here. In spite of the form-transcending character of religious art, for example, aesthetic rules must be obeyed.

The aesthetic function expresses in ever-renewing styles the meaning of the church's life through poetic, musical, and visual symbols. Honesty does not allow an artist to repeat styles which have lost their expressiveness. Expressionism, for Tillich, lends itself more readily to expressing ecstatic transcendence. But no style should be forced upon the artist. It is regrettable that the Protestant fear of idolatry has led to its neglect of the visual arts.

d. The *cognitive* function of the church is operative in the formulation of its theology. The meditative element of cognition is necessarily directed toward the symbols of the original revelation. The discursive element of cognition analyzes and describes the substance of the original revelation in a form in which it can be grasped. For Tillich, the philosophical model, or style, of existentialism best lends itself to form-transcendence because it asks the experiential questions of human existence and of man's predicament. But this philosophy must not be forced upon theologians.

e. The *communal* function works to actualize and manifest Spiritual Community within a historical group. The church struggles to overcome the limitations of exclusiveness by enabling persons to participate in a spiritual community which transcends social, racial, or national boundaries. Inequality among persons is overcome by the realization that all are sinners and all may experience forgiveness from God. The inherent danger of hierarchical leadership and power groups is overcome by the constant challenge of prophets. The threat to the vitality of the spiritual life which is posed continually by legal and structural forms is difficult to overcome this side of the *eschaton*. But structures and forms are needed.

f. The *personal* functions in the church develop methods to make the individual transparent to the Spiritual Presence while preserving his humanity. An asceticism which negates the material world and pleasure is to be avoided. However, an ascetic discipline which helps a person fulfill his human potentialities is desirable.

g. The *relating* function of the churches is unavoidable since as sociological groups they cannot avoid acting upon and receiving from other sociological groups. There are three ways in which relation happens: silent interpenetrations (priestly function), critical judgment (prophetic function), and political establishment (kingly function).

Through silent interpenetration the church radiates the Spiritual Presence into society. The church draws its forms from society which in turn allows the church to preserve its substance and convey its message to society. By critical judgment the church exposes and protests the negative qualities of the society in which it lives. Since the church proclaims high standards, society is justified in criticizing the churches which contradict justice and individual saintliness.

By being involved politically the church attempts to influence social groups (both local and international) so that the church can exercise its priestly and prophetic functions. In political action, however, churches cannot use means which contradict the character of Spiritual Community such as military force, a mind-control type of propaganda, or the arousal of groups through religious fanaticism. Churches should further avoid both a totalitarian control of all realms of life and the mere subjection of the church to the role of servant to the state. This function would probably involve some form of political compromise.

According to Tillich, the church must maintain a polarity between social mutuality and opposition. The church must relate to the world and yet be against the world. Catholics and Protestants have tended to extremes in this area and both could learn from one another.

(3) The life of the individual in the churches. For Tillich, the consideration of churches as institutions is not complete without consideration of the individual members. As the Spiritual Community is the community of spiritual personalities so the Spiritual Presence is the dynamic essence of every active church member.

a. Objective approach and infant baptism. This raises the question as to which is ontologically prior, the church or the individual member. The practice of infant baptism is commensurate with the *objective* approach which emphasizes the church over the individual. This approach points to the fact that the Spiritual Community is a reality which precedes the changing, disappearing, and reappearing acts of personal faith.

b. Subjective approach and believer's baptism. The *subjective* interpretation of the church emphasizes the need of individual conversion, for there must be a conscious turning away from estrangement and an affirmation of the New Being. In other words, the latent Spiritual Community must become manifest. The church as a manifest Spiritual Community builds upon latent Spiritual Community. In fact, Tillich believes that his concept of Spiritual Community can largely overcome the duality between the objective and subjective approaches to the church.

c. Regeneration before justification. Foremost, for Tillich, is the importance of the participation of the individual church member in the New Being. He therefore reverses the order of the Reformers and places regeneration before justification. This order makes more clear the fact that salvation begins as man is accepted by God and given New Being. Grace is primary. Justification comes after regeneration. God alone can reunite us to himself. No human claim or work is valid. Luther's formula must be replaced with "Justification or acceptance by grace through faith."

d. Sanctification. Tillich believes that Calvin's idea of the law as a positive guide for the Christian life is in danger of leading toward a legalistic perfectionism and moralism. Tillich likewise sees weaknesses in Luther's idea of freedom because this can so easily engender uncertainty of faith and lack of moral discipline. Tillich's solution is to interpret sanctification as a process of increasing consciousness of the work of the Divine Spirit. The Christian becomes progressively more aware of the ambiguities of life and of the demonic. But in the sanctification process one experiences also an increasing freedom from the law, a fuller realization of one's *essential* nature, a more loving relationship to others, greater self-fulfillment, and a more complete participation in the holy.[41]

(4) Religion, the Spiritual Presence and the Protestant principle. Tillich claims to be in the line of New Testament thought when he states that the effectiveness of the Spiritual Presence in the churches and in the lives of Christians is measured by its ability to do away with religion as a specific function of the human spirit. Christ came to transform the old state of affairs and not begin a new religion. Both the traditional and legalistic forms of religion along with the secular order are transcended through the Spiritual Presence.[42]

This idea of the conquest of religion by the Spiritual Presence is, according to Tillich, yet another dimension of his Protestant principle. This principle does not allow any absolute claim to be made by a relative entity, not even the church.[43] No person can grasp that by which he is grasped—the Spiritual Presence. For Tillich, the relevance of the Protestant principle, which arose in the Reformation era as a protest against the tragic and demonic self-elevation of religion, is not restricted to the Reformation churches. It is, moreover, a legitimate declaration of the victory of the Spirit over religion.

4. *The Spiritual Presence and culture.* (1) The union of religion and culture in Spiritual Presence. As we have seen, in existence culture and religion are separated. Under the impact of Spiritual Presence they are united. In fact, the Spirit can speak prophetically through men and women who are outside the manifest church. This creates the "latent" church. For Tillich, the holy and the secular belong to and need each other. Religion (as ultimate concern) is the substance of culture, and culture (as the combined structure of society) is the form of religion.[44]

(2) Theonomy. The presence of the Spirit in culture creates what Tillich calls "theonomy." This term is used in contrast to autonomy and heteronomy. An autonomous culture such as the Enlightenment lives primarily out of meanings which are self-created. A heteronomous culture imposes meanings which are felt to be strange or arbitrary as exemplified by the era of Protestant scholasticism. A theonomous culture is one in which the self lives under God without arbitrariness or imposed authority. The self lives out of a transcendent source of meaning. The clearest example of this type of culture in the past is, according to Tillich, the classical period of the Middle Ages.[45] In more formal terms, Tillich defines theonomy as the directedness of the self-creation of life under the Spirit toward the ultimate in being and meaning.

Theonomy implies that there is a split between subject and object in culture which should be overcome. The approach of mysticism swallows subject and object into an ecstatic unity. Some forms of love submerge the lover into the personal center of the loved.

Theonomy seeks to overcome these splits by directing life toward the transcendent unity of all being. In relation to language, it elevates language to symbols and thus witnesses to the sublimity of life beyond subject and object. In relation to cognition, it gives knowledge a direction and Spirit-determined wisdom. In the realm of communal relations, the Spiritual Presence presses toward the universal. In reference to inequality, the Spiritual Presence provides an ultimate equality which places existential inequality under judgment.[46]

These examples reveal how theonomous culture under the Spiritual Presence seeks to overcome the ambiguities of culture even if the result is fragmentary.[47]

5. *The Spiritual Presence, morality, and healing.*

(1) Spiritual presence and morality. The concepts of autonomy, heteronomy, and theonomy are important in Tillich's discussion of morality. If the moral commandments are seen as expressions of a divine will, a will which is sovereign and without criteria, they can become heteronomous and destructive.[48] Specific ethical duties are constantly changing because of the changes in context and situation. A theonomous ethic should be created by Spiritual Presence. In this case the religious substance (ultimate concern) is discovered and expressed through the process of free argument and discussion.[49] Ethics, therefore, comes within the province of philosophy and not of theology. This is because theology is always in danger of placing heteronomous authority over ethical analysis. When philosophy is free and objective in its analysis, it may, if grasped by the Spiritual Presence, provide the basis for theonomous ethics. According to Tillich, autonomous, philosophical ethics alone is free to interpret in an unprejudiced manner the changing forms and bases of the moral imperative. It alone is used by the Spirit for the creation of theonomous morality in a given society.[50]

By living under and within the Spiritual Presence a person can know how much or how little of life should be sacrificed for the sake of others. Furthermore, Spiritual Presence reveals that law is not an external ought to be obeyed but rather grace working in us to give us realistic motivation for our ethical attitudes and actions.[51]

Thus it can be seen that Tillich has more in common with contemporary situation ethicists than with divine command ethicists. John J. Carey suggests that Tillich's approach to ethics should perhaps best be classified as an ontological, self-realization ethic.[52] Justice (treating others as a "thou") and *agape* love must be yoked as a means of enabling selves to come together. Love is thus the ultimate norm because it is both unconditional and flexible.[53] It alone can liberate us from bondage. Tillich also emphasizes cumulative moral wisdom as constituting a helpful guide. All of these emphases point toward a self-realization ethic which actualizes our potentiality as persons.[54]

McKelway contends that Tillich would improve his position if he emphasized that the Spirit which is the basis of morality and ethics is the Spirit of Jesus the Christ in whom the command of God takes a gracious and saving form. If he did this, there could be no thought of oppressiveness or heteronomy in theological ethics. Rather, ethics would find in Jesus Christ the loving claim of God.[55]

(2) Man's essence and Spiritual Presence. Dourley explains that Tillich seeks to use his essence-existence-essentialization thesis to build an ethic which is at once philosophical and Christian. Tillich sees man's *essential* nature retained in existence as standing over against the existential distortion of this nature as both its judge and potential fulfillment. Law and conscience are expressions of man's essence which derive from his partial unity with his essence in existence.

Fulfillment of the law and conscience become man's progressive assimilation of his essential humanity. It is in this need for progressive assimilation that Christianity becomes operative in Tillich's system. Man senses his inability to recover his essential humanity and thus must accept it from the Spirit. It is thus the Spirit, in the salvation-grace reality, which heals the breach between man's existence and his essence.[56]

(3) Spiritual Presence and healing. Tillich affirms that wherever life comes under the impact of Spiritual Presence, it is healed, even if in a fragmentary way. This correlationally leads us to anticipate the final fulfillment of Eternal Life and the Kingdom of God where there is total healing and salvation.[57]

6. *The Trinitarian symbols, dogma, and reinterpretation.* Dourley is no doubt right when he suggests that the Trinity is much more extensive in Tillich's theology than his explicit treatment would indicate since, for Tillich, there is even a latent awareness of Trinitarian reality in man's natural apprehension of God.[58] One is therefore not surprised to learn that Tillich ascribes the foundation of the doctrine of the Trinity to three closely related processes. The *first* process is based on the conflict within man's ultimacy and concreteness in that toward which his concern is directed. The drive toward ultimacy results in assertions of monotheism. This drive is, however, based on an ultimate contradiction within the polytheistic teaching which maintains that there are many contending gods. Yet the drive to concreteness produces the need for mediators between an absolute transcendent God and finite, particular man. One needs for God to be experienced concretely and for him to be personally related to man. The Trinity, therefore, provides the only adequate correlation of these needs in that it points to a God who is absolute and transcendent and yet is capable of manifestation through concrete mediators.

The *second* process which gives evidence for the Trinity is the inevitability of a triadic understanding of God if God is to be understood as *living*. A living God must himself exemplify the dynamics of life. God does this through the interaction of self-relatedness, self-alternation, and reunification. Thus the Divine Life is an ontological reunion of otherness with identity in an eternal process. All of life is thus Trinitarian insofar as it successfully unites depth and form in the Spirit. The Spirit is the principle of integration.

These two natural theological considerations precede and yet give meaning to the Christian affirmation of the Trinity which arose to deal with the nature of the reality of Christ's saving power. This is the *third* process. The existential reality of man's salvation through Jesus the Christ eventually led to the affirmation of Nicea that Christ was divine. Soon the theologians were led to a declaration regarding the deity of the Spirit. This came when they realized that the Spirit of Christ was not Christ's human spirit but the divine reality which accounts for the New Being in Christ, and in those who in history participate in the New Being through him.[59]

Although Tillich begins the exposition of his system with anthropology or an analysis of man's existential questions, he correlates his doctrine of the Trinity with man's questions in such a way as to show how the Trinity has been operative throughout the system. For Tillich, the Trinity is therefore a symbol for both the reality of the divine life and the ultimate answer to the predicament of human life.

The ontological conflicts between essence and existence are posited by Tillich as being in God where their tension is overcome in a balanced and harmonious life. The Father as a symbol of creative power expresses himself and his otherness in the *Logos* as the principle of his self-manifestation or objectification through the union of the Spirit. The Spirit unites man with God and thus unites man with himself and others. The Spirit does this by effecting in man a realization of the intra-Trinitarian integration. So man's essentialization in a reestablished union with God is harmonized with the healing integration of the polar dynamics of human life. In the essentialization process, man's union with his essence becomes his union with God and brings about the integration of his humanity through its participation in the divine integration.[60]

X. History and the Quest for the Kingdom of God

Introduction

The topics of history and the kingdom of God constitute the conclusion of Tillich's *Systematic Theology*. This section on "History and the Quest for the Kingdom of God" is actually an extension of the section on "Ambiguous Life and the Quest for Unambiguous Life." History is a dimension of life and is actualized only in the realm of the spirit. But it is given a separate treatment in the *Systematic Theology* because "history" is the most embracing of all the life-dimensions and the "kingdom of God" embraces and expresses the fulfillment of salvation. This historical dimension adds a new note of finality to the other dimensions. It looks to the fulfillment of power and meaning and describes the direction of the process of actualization.[1]

History and the kingdom of God were the central concerns for Tillich in his early theological career in the midst of the chaos in Germany just after World War I in the 1920s.[2] In the biographical section we noted that Tillich acknowledged that many of his most important concepts, such as the Protestant Principle, *kairos*, the demonic, the *Gestalt* of grace, and the ideas of theonomy, heteronomy, and autonomy, were worked out for the sake of a new interpretation of history. History thus became a major theme in his theology and philosophy because of the historical reality which he found when he returned from the first World War.[3] As was also noted

144

in the biographical section, Tillich later shifted from an almost exclusive concern with the corporate-historical aspects of human existence to a point of view more inclusive of individualistic dimensions; however, he never gave up corporate history as an important concern.[4]

For Tillich, there can be no solution *in* history for the meaning *of* history. But this does not mean that history is ever without the presence of meaning and purpose. This section provides another example of Tillich's basic affirmation that finite reality is estranged, but never completely separated, from the ground of being. As we have seen, Tillich believes that this *essential* connection between man and God can be recognized in the relationships between the universal *logos* and revelation, the unity of being and the being of God, and the New Being and Christ. In history this essential connection between God and man is interpreted by Tillich with the concept of *kairos* or "the right time," which refers to the presence of the kingdom of God in history. For Tillich, Jesus as the Christ is the center of history, and thus Jesus is the basic or normative *kairos* in which the aim of history becomes real for man. But the eternal also breaks into human history to judge and to reform it in other moments of history or *"kairoi."* [5]

Tillich's correlation method in this section is similar to the approach used in the other four sections of his *Systematic Theology*. First, man's situation in history is described. Second, the problem or question of the meaning of history is presented in terms of the ambiguities of man's historical existence. Third, the answer to this question is found for both historical existence and life beyond history in the kingdom of God.

It should also be noted that Tillich's basic ontological thesis, "from essence, through existence, to essentialization," which describes the whole process of his thought, is operative and normative for his interpretation of history.[6] The drama of history is therefore composed of the movements from man's essential union with God to the existential conditions of history that are the consequences of the fall, and back to the essential union of salvation. This drama is enacted both in the life of each individual and in history as a whole.[7]

A. The Question of History and the Quest Which History Creates

1. The nature and structure of history.

(1) *Man and history.*

a. *Definition of history.* Following the implication of the Greek word *historia*, Tillich states that history is both subjective and objective. The interpreting subject singles out certain facts and imparts significance to them. The ideal of unbiased historical research which reports only the naked facts without a subjective interpretation is a questionable concept. A subjective mentality or view precedes events, not temporally, but in the sense that this subjective view determines which facts shall be remembered and the meaning which they shall bear.

Furthermore, this subjectively oriented interpretation of history takes place in the context of a "historical consciousness" or "tradition." A tradition is related to the needs, desires, and recollections of a particular social group. In epics, sagas, and legends, such recollections are remembered and reformulated in a highly symbolical way. But even the more objective methods of a modern historian are related to his own participation in a group with its special tradition and memories. This recognition of an historian's own historical consciousness does not deny the importance of strictness, accuracy, and honesty in his historical research. But the historian must admit his *a priori* understanding of the meaning of life. In this connection, Tillich admits that his own concept of history is unavoidably influenced by Christian symbolism.

b. *The historical dimension.* Actually, for Tillich, historical events with their interplay of the subjective and objective are peculiar to humans. In the first place, historical events move in a horizontal direction since they are motivated by human purpose. Second, man exercises freedom in the selection and execution of his purposes. Freedom stands in polarity with destiny, but destiny and the historical situation never totally destroy a person's freedom. Third, because historical events are the products of freedom, they produce human relationships and contexts that are new. And fourth, historical events produce events of unique significance since the events are new in meaning and value.

All of these ideas relate to Tillich's basic idea of essence, existence, and essentialization. Historical events are the actualization of essential human potentialities which thus represent moments in the development toward the fulfillment of history. Such developments related to freedom and purpose do not occur in the realm of higher animals or in the astronomical universe. Outside of the human realm, history may be anticipated, but not actualized.

c. *Prehistory and posthistory.* Tillich states that we do not know when the first spark of historical consciousness dawned in the human race, but we can recognize expressions of this consciousness. We do not know the moment of transition because of the mixture of slow transformation and sudden leaps in all evolutionary processes. According to Tillich, historical man is new, but he was prepared for and anticipated by prehistorical man.

Tillich notes that Jesus and the New Testament refuse to put the statements regarding the end of history and eschatological symbols into a chronological sequence or frame. Jesus said that he did not even know when the end would come. This leaves the future of historical mankind open for possibilities derived from present experience. The self-destructive power of man could bring historical mankind to an end. It is also possible that man could lose his motivation toward the future. According to Tillich,

this type of mankind that "knows everything and is not interested in anything" is described in Huxley's *Brave New World.* A third possibility is
for mankind to drive on toward the new until the gradual or sudden disap-
pearance of the biological and physical conditions for the continuation of
historical mankind. According to Tillich, these possibilities for historical
mankind must be recognized and projected metaphysically, while at the
same time they are liberated from a literalistic interpretation of the biblical
symbols of the "end of history."

d. *The bearers of history.* For Tillich, the direct bearers of history are
groups rather than individuals. Individuals are only the indirect bearers
of history. This is true because man actualizes himself only in a community
according to the polarity of individualization and participation. Thus human
history is the history of a group.

If a group is history-bearing, it must have a certain quality. It must
be able to act in a centered way which means that it possesses the power
to maintain itself from within and protect itself from without. In times
past, this group role has been fulfilled by families, clans, tribes, and cities.
In present times, it is fulfilled by the modern state. This history-bearing
group is not based primarily on force (although it sometimes uses force),
but on a feeling of communal identity or affinity expressed in blood relations,
language, and traditions.

Since history flows in a linear or horizontal direction, a history-bearing
group must have an aim, purpose, or destiny which Tillich calls "vocational
consciousness." Such a vocational consciousness may be different for each
group in each era. Examples are Rome (the ideal of law), Italy (rebirth
of civilization), Spain (Catholic unity), France (leadership of intellectual
culture), England (worldwide Christian humanism), Soviet Union (Greek
Church or Marxist prophecy), and the United States (concept of new beginning and missionary zeal for democracy). These aims show that any area
of life may constitute a center, but since the political realm insures the
basic cohesion and centeredness of the group, Tillich sees the political as
predominant. The biblical symbol for the fulfillment of history is the kingdom of God. According to Tillich, this is a political symbol and is thus
an appropriate symbol for correlating communal and individual human
needs and divine resources and fulfillment.[8]

Since human freedom is so dynamic and thus disruptive, in past eras
the drive toward unity and centeredness has not, generally speaking, made
mankind as a whole the bearer of history. In light of new historical developments, Tillich does speak of the possibility of a supranational center of
power.[9] He also states that the technical conquest of space is producing a
unity which makes possible an inclusive or holistic interpretation of the
history of mankind. The general tenor of his thought indicates, however,
that Tillich sees only the beginnings of a stirring toward a united mankind.

This means that for a long time to come, particular groups will be the bearers of history. Even in the future a united mankind would act according to the pressure and leadership of particular groups.[10]

Tillich refrains from either personifying groups apart from individuals or elevating individuals to history-bearing roles. The individual is important, but the individual is the bearer of history only in relation to acting in and through a group. Biography is not history. It is true that certain individuals such as Caesar or Napoleon have special historical significance. But they are significant only because they symbolically represent their community.[11]

(2) *The categorical structure of history* (*time, space, causality, and substance*). In his discussion of "Being and the Question of God" Tillich presents the ontological categories of time, space, causality, and substance in their relation to finitude generally. In the topic before us he applies these categories to the dimensions of life under the inclusive dimension of history.[12]

a. *Time and space.* Time and space belong together. We can measure time only by space and space only in time. Time and space, however, are independent in a proportionate way. For example, in the inorganic realm space is predominant, and this means that the category of time is not as crucial for the understanding of that realm. Although the inorganic realm exists in time, the various spaces and different moments in it are not necessarily united in one's interpretation. But in the organic realm where, for example, a tree exists, the spaces (roots, leaves, and so on) and the times of these various elements are united in the process of growth. In the animal realm, through memory and self-directed movement, the animal can enlarge its empirical encounter with time and his space. But in the realm of human life (the dimension of the spirit), both time and space are unlimited except by the limitations of a concrete situation. The spirit may transcend a given temporal and spatial environment, but a person is always forced to return to the concreteness of some space (a house, a city, or country) at some time.[13]

One of the tensions in Judaism today is over the Zionist argument that in order to be, a person must have not only time but also space. Tillich asks if a new spatial bondage will arise out of the Zionist movement which will then manifest itself as nationalistic and polytheistic. For Tillich, Roman Catholicism also has the problem of space tending to swallow up time.[14]

Although time and space are bound to each other, they also stand in dialectical tension. Human history, to a large extent, is determined by the struggle between space and time.[15] In the realm of history, time is as much the dominant interpretive factor over space as space is over time in the inorganic realm. The common element which gives time its identity and distinctive characteristic is the element of "after-each-other-ness." The flow of time is thus one-way traffic. It cannot be reversed, for there is no such thing as an identical historical repetition. Time never goes backward but rather always runs toward the new. Since historical time is ontologically or essentially united with the dimension of the spirit, it is creative and aims toward a final fulfillment which is not relative. Man's conscious participation in history thus leads him to the question of the *goal* of history.

As indicated above, space must be included in any discussion of time, for there can be no time without space. This is true even though space in the historical dimension stands under the predominant characteristic of time. The distinguishing spatial quality is "beside-each-other-ness" where different groups co-exist in space. This spatial quality prompts one to seek fulfillment of space in a "kingdom" which unites all spaces and is a place above all places. This kingdom is, consequently, never for Tillich a spaceless spirituality.[16]

b. *Causality and substance.* Causality is the order of things according to which there is a conditioning precedence for everything. Substance is the underlying identity with respect to changing phenomena.

In the inorganic realm substance tends to be the dominant distinguishing characteristic. In the dimension of the human spirit, causality is more distinctive than substance. This, of course, does not mean that historical substance is not important. Historical names such as Hellenism, Renaissance, or Absolutism would be meaningless unless they pointed to a historical reality of substance. Causality is of primary significance, however, because creations of the spirit imply the new which is underived and is the product of freedom over against determination. Thus, a spirit-determined, centered person is not bound deterministically to substance. Rather he transcends substance and even affects the character of the substance.

Historical causality is thus future-directed and draws substance with it toward the new. Of course, every creation of the human spirit in some ways is "old" because it is tied to the past in some way. But historical consciousness looks toward the "new creation" and quests toward the possibility of an absolutely transcendent and universal continuum or substance. This means that all four categories—time, space, causality, and substance—under the dimensions of history, point to that which is beyond history, the kingdom of God.[17]

(3) *The dynamic movement of history.*

a. *The periodic rhythms of life.* In the area of history, Tillich continues to utilize the polarities of necessity and contingency. To avoid any concept of ironclad necessity, he speaks of historical necessity as "trend" rather than as immutable law. Trends point to regularities in history but not to that which could be predicted absolutely on the basis of scientific determinism. In addition to trends in every historical situation, there is also contingency or chance. The fact of chance denies all forms of historical determinism. Chances are occasions which provide an opportunity to change the determining power of a trend.

Tillich is willing to admit the place of dialectic, action and reaction, growth and decay in his interpretation of history. But these elements must be seen as flexible structures rather than as a fixed framework which determines history. As we have noted, he even affirms the dialectical movement (yes, no, synthesis) in the divine life itself in his doctrine of the Trinity. There is this historical yes, no, and synthesis wherever life comes into conflict with itself and moves toward a new stage beyond the conflict.

Despite the fact that Tillich was influenced by the dialectical method of Hegel, he insists that if dialectics is made into a fixed law in the manner of Hegel, life is distorted into a mechanized scheme and the use of the term "dialectics" cannot be justified by empirical means.

Even the use of characterization for historical periods (Victorian, feudalism, Renaissance) employs subjective elements and is dependent to some extent on the perspective of the viewer. There is much overlapping and many advances and delays in relation to these periods. But in a broad sense, there are discernible indicators of importance which mark the boundary line between qualitatively different series or epochs of historical time. The major example of this is the event of Jesus as the Christ which for 2,000 years has induced people, especially in the West, to see in this event the boundary between the two main periods of human history.

b. *History and the processes of life.* In addition to its movement in terms of the four ontological categories, Tillich points out that history moves in terms of the processes of life. In the section on "Ambiguous Life and the Quest for Unambiguous Life" we discussed these three processes of self-integration, self-creativity, and self-transcendence. In the historical dimension these three processes are united as a movement toward a single aim.

The self-integrating function of life moves historically toward "an unambiguous harmony" between groups and individuals expressed in power and justice. The self-creativity function moves historically toward a new, unambiguous balance between dynamics and form. The self-transcendent function of life moves in history toward the universal, unambiguous fulfillment of the potentiality of being. But history is like all of life and thus stands under the negativities of existence and therefore under the ambiguities of life. It can only ask the question of the meaning of history and cannot give the answer of the kingdom of God in its own wisdom and knowledge.[18]

c. *Historical progress.* In one sense, there can be progress in history. This may come when progress is seen as "a step beyond the given," of a movement toward the new. For example, there is intended, and sometimes actual, progress from the beginning to the end of a political action or a scientific inquiry. Even in these realms a nonprogressive element appears when one asks concerning the ends of political action or technology. Progress can also be made in methodological research, skill-training, and the conquest of spatial divisions. In art, there is progress in the technical use of materials. Science has helped in giving us insights into certain levels of our psychological make-up.[19]

In another sense, however, some interpreters of history have made of progress a symbol for the very meaning of history. For them, history progressively approaches its ultimate aim. In this sense, Tillich does not want to apply the word "progress" to the functions of life in history. He admits progress in ethical content, education, technology, and science. But at the core of man's spiritual functions there is no inevitable progress because freedom is at the core of man's being.

There is no necessary progress in the moral act because each individual makes his decision on his own. In every individual we have in a sense a new historical beginning and the necessity for new grace. The ethical act itself involves freedom and is always new. The same is true of art. There is progress within a stylistic tradition, but each work of art stands alone and is not the result of quantitative progress. There is no necessary progress, for example, in architecture from the Gothic to later styles. In humanity there may be a quantitative increase in breadth, refinement, and depth among peoples in succeeding generations. But the qualitative maturity and realized humanism of each person is independent of so-called cultural progress. In fact, often after human conditions are raised to a new high, other forms of estrangement occur at a more refined level.

Tillich also addresses the crucial question regarding the problem of progress in the area of religion. There is some truth in the idea of progress in the cultural side of every religion such as in its cognitive self-interpretation and in its aesthetic self-expression. But we must remember that each religion is based on a given revelatory and saving manifestation of the Spiritual Presence which remains constant in its ultimateness. In this respect there is no progress. On the other hand, progress could be possible as certain cultures *receive* the manifestation of the spiritual with more clarity and power.

For Tillich, there is one area in the field of religion which is unique and crucial, and that is the area of the conflict between the divine and the demonic. According to Christianity, the ultimate victory over the demonic has taken place in Jesus as the Christ. This event is not the result of a progressive approximation or the actualization of a religious potentiality. In history, there will always be conflict with the demonic as described in the Book of Revelation. But the event in Jesus as the Christ is the *uniting* and *judging fulfillment* of all potentialities which are implicitly present in one's encounter with the holy. This does not mean that Christianity as a *religion* is absolute. Rather the absolute is the event of Jesus as the Christ by which Christianity as a religion is created-and-judged just as any other religion. This view of the history of religions is thus not horizontal but vertical. Christianity claims to be based on the final, victoriously antidemonic, revelatory event of Jesus as the Christ. There is consequently no progressive scheme of the history of religions in this view.[20]

2. *The ambiguities of history.* This is an important theme for it is out

of the ambiguities of history that the question of history arises, which is answered correlatively by the kingdom of God. Essence provides the starting point of a quest or *telos*-thrust of history toward unambiguous fulfillment. But the historical dimension, like all dimensions of life, falls from essence to existence. History stands under the ambiguities of existence and therefore under the ambiguities of life. Tillich, therefore, describes historical ambiguity in both negative and positive terms. From the negative perspective, history is fraught with risks. Sometimes it leaps into the demonic rather than rising into a divine fulfillment. In more positive terms, history on occasion may actualize limited aims, and in so doing substitutes an immediate realization for its ultimate goal.[21]

(1) *The ambiguities of self-integration.* The self-integrating function of a historical group gives rise to the ambiguous drive toward the formation of an ever-enlarging empire in which power is exercised. Empires express not only will to power but also the vocational self-interpretation of a historical group such as Roman law, Soviet social justice, and American liberty. Such aims have some good aspects but, at the same time, may cause suffering and the loss of life and meaning. There is also the continual danger of that which Tillich calls the internal force of centeredness. In order for an empire to maintain rigid central control, it may suppress creative potencies which could move into the future and create the new.

(2) *The ambiguities of historical self-creativity.* In the historical dimension, the ambiguities of self-creativity in such areas as art, philosophy, and politics are expressed in revolution and reaction. If a system is not structured to allow the new to emerge, pressures and contradictions within the culture build to the point of revolution. *Revolution* obviously produces the new, but at the expense of destroying the values of the old. We see this in the conflict in every young generation which rightly seeks to make its own place, but fails to appreciate the accomplishments of the old which it sets aside. Tillich warns against the dangers of revolutionary purpose being betrayed by the dynamics of the revolutionary action.

Reaction preserves past creations, but is a stumbling block to advancement. This is reflected in older generations which refuse to give place to new creativity. Consequently, the question for an answer to historical self-creativity becomes urgent when a devastating struggle develops between revolution and reaction. The danger of utter chaos oftentimes leads to counterrevolution. Immense personal sacrifice and destruction are often the results.

(3) *The ambiguities of historical self-transcendence.* There is a danger that the finite may be raised to infinite value and meaning. Sometimes this is seen when either the old or new claims ultimacy for itself. By far the most demonic form of this ambiguity is found in religion. Theological totalitarianism has often resulted in physical as well as spiritual persecutions.

The claim for historical ultimacy is interpreted by Tillich as the "third" or final stage of history. (The first stage is the innocence of creation; the second is the fall.) This third stage can be considered as "given" which means that the present moment is absolutized by declaring that the ultimate has already appeared. Tillich's prime example in this area is the Roman Catholic Church which has a demonic tendency to identify the ultimate with its own symbols.

The third stage as "expected" is utopianism. For the Montanists and Joachim de Fiori, the third stage is the immanent age of the Spirit. In the secular realm the third stage is the "age of reason" or the "classless society." This "as expected" utopianism generates creativity by the enthusiasm it arouses. But it ambiguously leads to cynicism and despair when its expectations fail to materialize.[22]

(4) *The ambiguity of the individual in history.* In all realism, Tillich states that the individual in history is subordinate to the political group. Nevertheless, the individual constitutes the group and so has a significance in history. Even if we accept democracy as the "best yet" guarantee of protecting human freedom within an organized group, there are ambiguities present. Techniques of representations in democracy reduce the individual's place in government. Public communication developments can create mass conformity and reduce the freedom of creativity. Majority rule can be misused to deprive minorities of expression. Divisions within the democratic group can arise. This sometimes results in chaos and leads to dictatorship.

These ambiguities often lead to the giving up of political responsibility and resultant hopelessness and resignation. Some people look above history in resignation or become involved in mystical elevation. For many, history is negativity without hope.

The ambiguities of life under the dimension of history discussed above lead to a consideration of the interpretation of history which tries to answer the question of the significance of history for the meaning of existence universally.[23]

3. *Alternative interpretations of the meaning of history.*

(1) *The nature and the problem of an interpretation of history.* As already indicated, all history is interpreted history. This means that a detached approach to history is impossible. A person must plunge into the stream of history. But what type of historical activity or which historical group has the key? The answer is circular. Systematic theology moves within a theological circle. For Tillich, the Christian perspective and vocational consciousness affirm history in such a way that the ambiguities of life already discussed are answered in all dimensions through the kingdom of God.

Before presenting the kingdom of God as the answer to the question of the meaning of history, Tillich sets up a contrast by examining two competing types of interpretation. In the nonhistorical type, history is interpreted through nature, and space is predominant. In the historical type, history is interpreted through history and time is predominant.[24]

(2) *Negative, nonhistorical interpretations.* This view sees time as having no goal either within or above history. History is a circle or simply a series of happenings. It is merely the place in which individual beings live their lives without external *telos* or aim for their personal lives. Space is superior to time, and time is subordinate to, and incorporated into, space. This nonhistorical view appears in three versions: the tragic, the mystical, and the mechanistic.[25]

a. The *tragic* interpretation is best exemplified by the Greek view of history as an eternal cycle of genesis, greatness, decay, praise of great moments (the heroic), and forlornness about the destructive end of all things. The whole cycle is determined by fate, and there is no hope of either an immanent or a transcendent fulfillment in history. In other words, there is no forward-looking and dynamic philosophy of history in Greek thought. Time is swallowed by space.[26]

b. The *mystical* interpretation is found in the West in Neoplatonism and in the philosophy of Spinoza. But its most developed expression is in the East in Hinduism, Taoism, and Buddhism. This view grants that one must live in history, but history itself is seen as barren, its ambiguities unconquerable, and its motion aimless. In fact, true reality is dissociated from the temporal flux. There is little historical memory. It does have a recognition of and deep compassion for the universality of suffering. But it retreats from a reality which it feels powerless to transform. There is no impulse to channel history in the direction of universal humanity and justice. History is not progress but deterioration, decay, and corruption. By mystical union with the ultimate one overcomes not reality, but one's own involvement in reality.[27]

c. The third version of nonhistorical interpretation is the *mechanistic* view. This reductionist, naturalistic view is preoccupied with technical time. The question of the aim, purpose, and meaning of history is viewed with indifference and cynicism. Followers of this view oscillate between unrealistic optimism and profound pessimism. This oscillation has a catastrophic effect upon a person's historical consciousness and sense of responsibility.[28]

(3) *Positive, but inadequate historical interpretations.* This view sees history as running toward an end which is fulfilled within history itself. It also appears in three versions: the progressivistic, the utopian, and the transcendental.

a. The *progressivistic* view takes two forms. One form sees infinite progress itself as a process without end. Progress becomes a universal law. This view has had a great influence in the West and has given meaning for many people. But the world tragedies of our age and insights into the nonprogressive nature of freedom have almost negated the importance of this interpretation. After the first three atomic bombs were dropped, there arose a forceful reaction to the idea of an infinite progress through technology.[29]

b. The second form of progressivism believes in a final stage of fulfillment and is known as *utopianism*. This view holds that present revolutionary action will bring about the final transformation of reality which will be that stage of history in which the ambiguities of life are conquered. Utopianism was a child of the Renaissance, but it has been adopted by revolutionary movements up to the present day. For Tillich, the fatal error of this view is that it gives an idolatrous quality of ultimacy to something preliminary and conditioned (a particular historical situation).

c. A third type of positive historical interpretation is the *transcendental* model. Tillich finds this approach in the early church up to Augustine and in orthodox Lutheranism. History is the place where the Christ has appeared to save men from sin and guilt and make them members of a heavenly realm after death.

Tillich sees this view as separating the salvation of the individual from the salvation of the world in general and the group in particular. It denies the New Testament teaching that the kingdom of God is powerful in the world, transforming and saving it in the present. It severs nature, society, and culture from the fulfilling processes of history.[30]

4. *The kingdom of God as the answer to the quest for the meaning of history.*

(1) *Characteristics of the kingdom of God.* The irrelevancy of the nonhistorical interpretation of history and the inadequacies of the historical types led Tillich to develop his own interpretation of the symbol of "the kingdom of God" as Christianity's answer to the ambiguities of history. Braaten contends that Tillich did more than any of the other great theologians of his era to reinstate the kingdom of God as a living symbol. This is the third major symbol which Tillich uses to express unambiguous life, the other two being that of the Spiritual Presence and Eternal Life. Of the three symbols, the symbol of the kingdom of God is the most inclusive. It has both an inner-historical and a trans-historical dimension. As inner-historical it participates in the dynamics of history here and now (Spiritual Presence). As trans-historical it answers the questions implied in the ambiguities of the dynamics of history in furnishing transcendent unity and fulfillment of the meaning of our existence.

The kingdom of God provides the final meaning of history because it grants fulfillment to man in every area of his life. First, the kingdom of God has a *political* connotation which corresponds to the political character of history-bearing groups. Even though it is a cosmic symbol relating to a new reality, this political dimension is not lost.

Secondly, the kingdom of God has a *social* connotation of peace and justice. This meets legitimate utopian expectations. However, it is also "of God" so as to imply the impossibility of any merely earthly or solely human fulfillment.

Thirdly, the kingdom of God has a *personalistic* connotation. It gives eternal meaning to individuals. The fulfillment and unity of the kingdom does not destroy personality, but fulfills and unites it.

Fourthly, the kingdom of God connotes *universality*. It provides the possibility for the fulfillment not only of individuals but of all life under all dimensions.[31]

(2) *The kingdom of God as immanent and transcendent.* The most important characteristic of the kingdom of God is its double quality of being both immanent and transcendent at the same time. In opposition to the nonhistorical interpretation of history, the kingdom of God must be anchored in the temporal. God moves in history toward a final goal. The kingdom of God must be involved in historical events. But against the inadequate historical interpretation, it must not be overwhelmed or submerged in the temporal.

The Old Testament prophets stressed the "immanent-political" aspect of the kingdom. But the transcendent element was never absent since it is God who brings the kingdom to fulfillment.

In the New Testament the "transcendent-universal" aspect of the kingdom emerges more clearly as the political version is replaced by a cosmic vision which will be realized not by historical developments, but by divine power from above. But the immanent-historical element is not abandoned because of the historical appearance of Jesus as the Christ and because of the dynamic establishment of the church in the midst of the ambiguities of history.

Thus Tillich sees the kingdom of God as offering the balanced and meaningful interpretation of history as both realized in the present and fulfilled in the future, although unfortunately one side or another is usually theologically predominant. In the last section of his *Systematic Theology*, Tillich explains in detail how his interpretation of the kingdom of God answers the questions of man's historical existence.[32]

B.   *The Kingdom of God as the Answer within History*

1.   *The New Being and the dynamics of history.*

(1) *The idea of the history of salvation.* The manifestation of the Spiritual Presence in the individual human spirit and in the Spiritual Community was described in Chapter IX without reference to the historical dimension. The revelation of the Spirit, however, does take place in history. The kingdom of God means salvation for human history and so creates in history a special "history of salvation" or *Heilsgeschichte*. As described in Chapter VI, this history of salvation is identical with the history of revelation.

Because of the ambiguities of human history, the saving events of God are not to be seen as identical with human history, the history of religion, or the history of the churches. The saving event of God stands over against these histories to judge and to save. The "history of salvation" can be defined as "a sequence of events in which saving power breaks into historical processes." In one sense, therefore, one can speak of salvation as a part of universal history, for "it can be identified in terms of measured time, historical causality, a definite space, and a concrete situation." It is sacred and secular in the same series of events.

Thus salvation is manifest in history, but it is not a product of history. But because it does manifest itself in history, the salvation of the kingdom of God should not be spoken of as "supra-historical."[33]

(2) *The central manifestation of the kingdom of God in history.* For Tillich, the interpretation of history is a search for meaning. And it is in Jesus as the Christ that the source of this meaning is found. Therefore, Jesus as the Christ is declared to be the center of history where the meaning-giving principle of history is found. That history is to be interpreted Christologically and that Christology is to be interpreted historically forms the major thesis of Tillich's approach to history.[34]

As we have already seen, history possesses a subject-object structure and thus is not a purely objective, temporal process. This means that the center of history is not a point between a temporal beginning and end. It is also to be noted that the center of history is not the culmination point of some progressive development. Rather, the center of history is the source for the meaning of history.[35]

There does have to be progress in terms of a preparation for the reception of this center of meaning. Mankind had to mature to a certain point so that the center of history could appear and be received as the center. The Old Testament is the record of the maturing process which led to the final revelation in Jesus as the Christ.

It should be noted, however, that what happened once in the process of the original revelation happens again and again whenever the Christ is received as the center of history, regardless of time and place. The "central event" of Jesus as the Christ, while occurring only once, is actually repeated over and over again in his reception as the center of the meaning of history. In some way and on some level, every human being has a longing for a new reality to replace the distorted reality in which he is living.[36]

People are not *outside* of God. Rather they are *grasped* by God on the level in which they *can* be grasped even though the symbols in which God is expressed may seem extremely primitive and idolatrous. It may be a distorted religion, but it cannot be construed as nonreligion. One might call this preparation the "Old Testament" for these people. And yet this is not exactly right for the term "Old Testament" is properly used for the preparation of the coming of Christ as the center of history through the elected nation.[37]

Obviously there are other interpretations of history which make a claim for other central events. Thus, the center of history for the Jews is the exodus from Egypt; for the Persians, the appearance of Zarathustra; and for the Muslims, Mohammed's flight from Mecca to Medina.[38]

The center of national interpretations of history is the moment in which the nation's vocational consciousness arose in an event or in a legendary tradition. For world religions, such as Islam and Buddhism, the event of their foundation is the center of history.

How can Christianity justify its claim to be based in the universal center of the manifestations of the kingdom of God in history? The first answer is the positivistic answer of the daring courage of the Christian faith. But Christianity also has a *logos*-oriented explanation of faith. The questions implied in historical time and in the ambiguities of historical dynamics have been answered in none of the other assumed centers of history. Politically determined centers are too particularistic. Islam is a religion of the law and as such has only a function of educational progress toward maturity. The universality of Judaism has not been liberated from particularity. Buddha is not seen in a historical movement which leads to him and is derived from him, but he is seen primarily as a decisive example of the Spirit of Illumination.

For Tillich, such a survey as given above shows that the only historical event in which the universal center of the history of revelation and salvation *can* be seen is the event on which Christianity is based. This is not only a matter of daring faith, but this conviction is also based on a rational interpretation of this faith.

Tillich further affirms that this event of Jesus as the Christ is the only event in which the historical dimension is fully and universally affirmed and in which history becomes aware of itself and its meaning. There is no other event of which this *could* be affirmed. But the *actual* affirmation of this event is and remains a matter of daring faith.[39]

(3) *The concept of kairos.* In theological terms, the *kairos* idea is related to the center of history as God's action in Jesus as the Christ. But this action took place at the mature moment when history was able to receive this event. *Kairos* is thus "right time" in contrast to *chronos*, which is measured or clock time. In the New Testament *kairos* is used to indicate the occasion of the coming of Christ. The New Testament *kairos* indicates all that is distinctive in the Christian conception of time. This means that time has a direction and that it has a center and therefore can be divided into periods based upon qualitative differences.

Kairos, as Tillich uses it, has both a general and a unique sense. In its general sense it refers to every turning point in history in which the eternal judges and transforms the temporal. In its unique and universal sense for the Christian faith, it is the appearing of Jesus as the Christ.[40]

Thus the original appearance of Jesus as the Christ is the "great *kairos*," but his manifestation is re-experienced again and again in "*relative kairoi*." These secondary *kairoi* depend upon the great *kairos* as their criterion and source of power. *Kairoi* are rare, and the great *kairos* is unique, but, for Tillich, together they make up the dynamics of history. A period of history, ripe for a *kairos*, is characterized by an openness to the unconditional to permeate and guide all cultural functions and forms.[41]

It should be apparent that *kairos* is related to other key Tillichian concepts. The breakthrough of a *kairos* coincides with the establishment of a theonomous culture. The dialectic of autonomy-heteronomy-theonomy explains the waxing and waning of theonomous periods in the development of history. Thus history has its eras of progress and decline and its periods of creativity and conservative bondage.[42]

The concept of *kairos* is also in Tillich's Protestant principle. *Kairos* includes both a prophetic protest, which prepares for and accompanies the manifestation of the center of history, and an affirmation of the presence of the kingdom of God among us. Interpreted Christologically *kairos* thus unites criticism and creation.[43] It should, however, always be remembered that *kairoi* may be demonically distorted, as in the case of Hirsch and the Nazis as previously noted. There is also the danger of error about the calculation of time and detail in relationship to the *kairos*.[44]

As late as 1964, Tillich was calling for an analysis and denouncement of the cultural structure of industrial mass society as a way of preparing the prophetic spirit which hopefully would rise again and show the image of a new "theonomy."[45] Raymond Bulman, in 1976, suggested that Vietnam, Watergate, and the growing economic, political, and social crises reveal more powerfully than ever the demonic structures of technological society. He suggested that if Tillich were still with us, he might well discern within the depths of our anxiety and desolation the dawn of a new *kairos*.[46]

(4) *Historical providence.* In relation to the dynamics of history, Tillich refers again to the doctrine of providence which he developed in the section on "Being and God" under the title of God's directing creativity. In this section, Tillich seeks to emphasize even more the element of contingency in divine providence. There is no uncontrollable inevitability. But historical providence is creative and moves toward the new even though evil may interrupt this progress. The negative can never prevail against the temporal and eternal aims of the historical process as Paul suggested in Romans, chapter 8, where the demonic powers were overcome by the love of God as manifested in the Christ. There is a universal dominion of divine action present in historical creativity, judgment, and grace. Particular providential acts remain hidden in the mystery of the divine life.[47]

2. *The kingdom of God and the churches.*

(1) *The churches as the representatives of the kingdom.* In Chapter IX we saw that the churches represent the Spiritual Community. Now, in the terms of the more inclusive historical dimension, we see that the churches are representatives of the kingdom of God. But even as representatives of the kingdom, the churches are ambiguous and both reveal and hide. This is true because the churches live in a period between *kairoi,* between an "already" and a "not yet."

Under the power of the Spirit, the churches are to fight against demonization and profanization in history. This fight must first be directed against the demonic and profane in the church itself. This often calls for reformation movements. Another way for the churches to manifest New Being is through their liturgical life and through constantly pointing toward the expectation of the coming kingdom. It should be noted that the demonic cannot stand the immediate presence of the holy.

The latent church is also a vehicle of the kingdom. Before the New Being in Jesus as the Christ there were no manifest churches. But there was and is a latent Spiritual Community before and after Christ which also serves the kingdom.

(2) *The history of the churches in relation to the kingdom.* Tillich makes a distinction between the history of the true church, which is identical with the history of the kingdom of God, and the actual history of the churches. The actual, phenomenological history is not identical with the kingdom although it always contains some manifestations of the kingdom.

The ambiguous situation in church history is seen in the fact that the life of the churches is limited to certain sections of mankind. There are also many contradictory interpretations in the churches, and there is profanization by ritualization (Roman Catholic), and secularization (Protestantism), of the central event of Jesus as the Christ. Thus we must say that sacred and saving history is both hidden and revealed in church history.

Fortunately, the churches have within themselves the criterion for judgment which is the witness to the New Being in Jesus as the Christ. No other historical group can claim this. This does not mean that the churches are always ethically and spiritually better, but that they *are* elevated above other religious groups because they have a better *criterion* by which to judge themselves and other groups. Within this struggle in church history, there are actual, although fragmentary, victories.[48]

3. *Church history and world history.* The churches must also struggle against ambiguity in world history. The churches judge the world while judging themselves in the light of Jesus as the Christ. And the churches have had a transforming influence on world history. An example is the way in which Christianity has changed person-to-person relations in a fundamental manner.

4. *The kingdom of God and the ambiguities of history.* As a part of his correlation method, in each area Tillich describes how the existential questions are met by theological answers. In this section we see how the existential questions of man who is involved in the ambiguities of history are correlated with the revelation of the kingdom of God. These questions related to the ambiguities of history are related to the ambiguities of the three basic life processes discussed earlier in this section.

(1) *The answer to the ambiguities of historical self-integration.* The first life-function is self-integration which relates to the use of power. Man under existence turns this drive toward force and control which destroys identity and creativity.

The kingdom of God answers this ambiguity by expressing within history a power which allows its object freedom within the structure of force. Churches must be willing to recognize this manifestation of the kingdom of God wherever any political group handles properly the ambiguities of power. For example, pure pacifism or pure militarism are not the answers. There should be a middle way which judges the use of power in war and peace against the norm of the divine approach which integrates life in the context of freedom. When this is done the kingdom of God in history has conquered in a fragmentary way the ambiguities of control.

(2) *The answer to the ambiguities of historical self-creativity.* As was mentioned earlier, the function of life known as self-creativity as exercised by man in existence leads to the ambiguities of revolution or conservatism. Both revolution (for change and growth) and tradition (for identity) are needed. The kingdom of God reconciles this ambiguity by seeking to build revolution into tradition. This means that, despite tension, a creative solution can be found in community for the realization of the highest goals of history.

(3) *The answer to the ambiguities of historical self-transcendence.* The self-transcendent function of life under existence leads to the historical ambiguities related to the exaltation of fragmentary manifestations of the kingdom of God to the place of the final kingdom itself. Ultimate solutions are expected from finite institutions. This leads to impossible hopes from finite institutions (utopianism) and a resultant cynical despair. In the churches this leads to a conflict between an emphasis on man's future salvation and a prophetic preoccupation with social transformation.

The answer to this conflict is given by the kingdom of God. The kingdom furnishes a power and a vision which unites the vertical with the horizontal. This power enables a church to await the kingdom of God and seek at the same time to realize and augment its sovereignty in history. In other words, the sacramental church also recognizes its responsibility for social transformation. On the other hand, the activistic church emphasizes the vertical dimension of salvation as well as the horizontal thrust of historical activity.[49]

(4) *The answer to the ambiguities of the individual in history.* In this

section Tillich emphasizes that it is not a victory for the kingdom of God if the individual takes himself out of actual creative participation in history while pledging allegiance to the spiritual aspects of the kingdom of God. The kingdom actually works in and through the tangible-spiritual dialectics of history.

While people are thrown by life into actual participation and sacrifice in history, sacrifice without an aim is little more than self-annihilation. There are secondary aims that bring relative fulfillment, such as glory in classical Greece, honor in feudal cultures, mystical identification with a nation or party, truth in scientism, or human self-actualization in progressivism. But the symbol of the kingdom of God unites the cosmic, social, and personal elements. It unites the glory of God with the love of God. And it allows the individual to experience the divine transcendence in an unlimited manifoldness of creative potentialities.

The answer furnished by the kingdom of God given thus far in this section occurs within history, and through the medium of finite institutions. This means that the answers are only fragmentary and partial. This naturally leads to the conclusion of Tillich's system which is his description of the final answer of history which is not fragmentary or within history. This final answer occurs at the end of history and is Eternal Life.[50]

C. *The Kingdom of God as the Answer in Terms of Eternal Life or the End of History*

1. *The End of History or Eternal Life.*

(1) *The double meaning of the "End of History" and the permanent presence of the end.* We have noted the fragmentary nature of the victories of the kingdom of God within world history. These victories came through the proper use of political power, constructive social growth, and individual fulfillment through sacrifice. But what about the nonfragmentary, total realization of the kingdom of God at the end of history?

The word "end" can mean "finish" in terms of clock time. This means that at some time life on earth and the earth itself will cease to have existence in time and space. But "end" also means "aim" which is that toward which the temporal process points as its goal. The end or inner aim of history in this second sense is "eternal life."

Eternal Life, for Tillich, means the "transition" from the temporal to the eternal. This metaphor of "transition" reminds us of Tillich's basic idea which is essence (related to the transition from the eternal to the temporal in the doctrine of creation), existence (related to the transition from essence to existence in the doctrine of the fall), and essentialization (related to the transition from existence to essence in the doctrine of salvation).

For Tillich, the theological problem of eschatology is not related to the many things which happen in the last of all days as described in poetic and dramatic apocalyptic literature. This type of concern makes eschatology an appendix to a theological system. He believed that it is better to begin with the immediate existential significance of eternal life for the present history of man in the "now." The past and the future are important. God *has* created the world (we are dependent for creaturely existence on him) and God *will* bring the world to its end (there will be a fulfillment of creaturely existence in God.)

But in Tillich's view both past and present meet in the present and both are included in the eternal "now." With this approach, eternal life becomes a matter of present experience, urgency, and seriousness without losing its futuristic dimension. The historical catastrophes and the threat of man's self-annihilation in recent decades have aroused a passionate interest in the eschatological problem as it relates to the end of the universe, the end of history, and to the eternal destiny of the individual.[51]

Tillich believes that his approach encourages Christians to have courage to appropriate eternal resources for the here and now and not escape to false notions of "life after death." The "now" approach should lead a person to take both life and death seriously. For Tillich, the desire for self-preservation becomes evil if it excludes self-giving in community in the "now."[52]

(2) *The elevation of the temporal into eternity.* Tillich rejects the emphasis of some that the primary purpose of this earthly life is for a person to concern himself with how he can get into the heavenly kingdom. In this view, churches are seen as institutions to prepare individuals for the heavenly realm and are not seen as institutions to actualize New Being in the here and now. The answer of Tillich is that Eternal Life should be seen as the ever present end of history which elevates the positive in history (love, creativity, and so on) into eternity and into the kingdom of God. This means that creative life in human history which is positive, liberated from its negative distortions, and fulfilled in its potentialities, is significant for eternal life and for God. In contrast, the negative is excluded from participation in eternity.

(3) *Ultimate judgment as the exposure of the negative.* As we have seen, for Tillich, the positive in existence is elevated into eternal life. This implies that life in eternity is liberated from its involvement with the negative which characterizes life under the conditions of existence. This is the last, final, or ultimate judgment.

The negative (illness, death, falsehood, and so on) in existence has the appearance of a positive force. But in the presence of Being-itself, it is revealed as having no real ontological standing, and thus its terrifying threat is negated. The positive in existence is accordingly freed to participate in essential being in an unambiguous way. Eternal life is likened to eternal memory in which the positive is remembered and the negative forgotten, or acknowledged and rejected as nonbeing. It is important at this point for Tillich to emphasize that, unlike Hindu teaching, the new, positive and creative acts performed in time and space actually add something new to essential being. These positive acts and deeds make a contribution to the kingdom of God and contribute toward its fulfillment. This means that every decision and creation in time and space has infinite weight, and "ultimate judgment" is serious indeed.

Insofar as the negative has maintained possession of a person, the negative is exposed and excluded from eternal memory. But if the essential in a person has conquered existential distortion, he will have a greater participation in Eternal Life. In relation to participation in Eternal Life, what one has made of his temporal existence is crucial.[53]

Just as creation is not a *temporal event* for Tillich, neither is essentialization a *temporal event*. Both are beyond time in the eternity of God. To describe creation and eternity, Tillich uses poetic language such as "dreaming innocence" and "eternal memory." In both areas the use of such language presents difficulties for many theologians.[54]

(4) *The final conquest of the ambiguities of life as essentialization.* Since Eternal Life and the Kingdom of God are identical with regard to what they expect for fulfillment, Eternal Life also looks toward the complete conquest of the ambiguities of life. We have discussed the ambiguities that accompany the life processes of self-integration, self-creativity, and self-transcendence. They are overcome by the perfect balancing of the ontological polar elements: individualization-participation, dynamics-form, and freedom-destiny. This means that in the fulfilled kingdom of God the special functions of morality, culture, and religion disappear. There is no morality because there is no ought-to-be which is not. The work of the human spirit becomes the work of the Divine Spirit and so there is no culture. There is no religion because there is no estrangement. There is no temple because God is present as all in all.[55]

Proudfoot sees this mystical or monistic emphasis of Tillich as jeopardizing the integrity and distinctiveness of the individual in Eternal Life. God as the ground of being tends to transcend all personhood.[56]

(5) *The continuing and eternal conquest of the negative.* The exclusion of the negative from Eternal Life does not mean that eternal blessedness is a state of immovable perfection. God is a "living" God who is constantly moving away from and back to himself (as in the Trinity). He is also constantly involved in a conflict with and a victory over nonbeing. This means that a person's participation in eternal life does not eliminate the dynamics of his life. Negativity is present and is to be overcome.[57]

In this same connection, Tillich discusses the conflicts and sufferings of nature under the condition of existence. He suggests that nature's longing for salvation, of which Paul speaks (Romans 8), helps to serve the enrichment of essential being when the essentialization process is completed.

2. *The individual person and his eternal destiny.*

(1) *Universal and individual fulfillment.* In the earlier discussions, Eternal Life has been discussed in general terms. In this section there is a special treatment of the relation of the individual person to Eternal Life. Man is special for he alone is aware of his potential destiny and is free to reject it. Man as essence lives in existence which means that he turns away from Eternal Life even as he aspires to it. He can partially waste the potentialities given to him by destiny and partially fulfill them. In other words, there are "degrees of essentialization" which contradict the absolute symbols and concepts such as heaven and hell, and eternal death and eternal bliss.

Tillich rejects Origen's almost mechanistic doctrine of the "restitution of everything" as inadequate. God does have to express judgment and wrath against every negative thing. Tillich also rejects the doctrine of double predestination and a twofold eternal destiny. For Tillich, this predestinarian view contradicts the idea of God's permanent creation of the finite as something "very good." If being as being is good, then nothing that *is* can become completely evil.

According to Tillich, all men are composites of good and evil, being and nonbeing. No person is unambiguously good or bad, accepted or rejected. The so-called "damned soul" retains a positive element which required the sustaining creativity of God and which may be ultimately conserved in essentialization. However, despite the hope of essentialization, the seriousness of falling short is not diminished. Essentialization is not an automatic restitution. What is restored can either exceed or fall short of the original created essence. Falling short of total essentialization (not realizing possibilities that *should* have been realized) is a waste of potentialities that brings with it a corresponding measure of despair.

However, Tillich also rejects eternal damnation and its idea of the radical separation of person from person. For Tillich, a person's total being (conscious and unconscious) is largely determined by social conditions surrounding him as he enters existence. Furthermore, a person's spirit is closely related to the physical and biological factors of life. Thus it is hard to separate the eternal destiny of any person from the destiny of the whole race.

This view, from Tillich's perspective, helps to answer the question of distorted forms of life such as premature death, psychological disease, and morally destructive environments. In the essence of the least actualized person, the essences of other individuals are involved. According to Tillich, whoever condemns one of these to eternal death condemns himself for his essence cannot be absolutely separated from the one he condemns. On the other hand, one in despair can be told that he achieves some fulfillment because his essence participates in the essences of those who have attained lofty heights. This motif corresponds appropriately to Tillich's concept of vicarious fulfillment and gives new content to the concept of Spiritual Community.[58]

For Tillich, the response to Jesus who is the Christ in time and space is crucial. History has eternal significance because it is in history that the depth of all things became manifest to man through the one man in whom God found his image undistorted and who is thus called the Son and the Christ.[59]

(2) *Immortality of the soul and resurrection of the body.*

a. *Wrong approaches to individual participation in Eternal Life.* How should we describe the participation of the individual in Eternal Life? *First,* we should not use *immortality* if by this we mean the continuation of the *temporal* life of an individual after death without a body. For Tillich, participation in eternity is not merely the existence of life hereafter nor a natural quality of the human soul. Rather, participation in eternity is made possible through the creative act of God. On the other hand, the term immortality is acceptable if it is used to refer to a quality of life which transcends temporality (1 Tim. 6:16).

Second, Tillich states that we should not use the term "immortality of the soul." This phrase introduces a dualism between the soul and the body and is not in keeping with the New Testament concept of the "resurrection of the body."

Third, immortality can be used as a *symbol* if it refers to man's finiteness and to the infinite nature of the "immortal Gods." But immortality must not be used as a *concept* referring to a *naturally* immortal substance, the soul. The term "Eternal Life" is preferable.

b. *The positive approach of "resurrection of the body" and "spiritual body."* According to Tillich, man's participation in Eternal Life beyond death is most adequately expressed by the symbolic term "resurrection of the body." The Pauline phrase "spiritual body" is helpful if properly understood. It negates the "nakedness" of a merely spiritual existence. Moreover, the word "body" in this context is an affirmation of the goodness of creation. The phrase "spiritual body" prevents us from falling into primitive literalism. "Spiritual" also refers to God who is present to man's spirit, transforming it and elevating it. A "spiritual body" is thus a body which expresses the spiritually transformed total personality of man including all dimensions (psychological, spiritual, social).

Furthermore, the "resurrection body" also indicates the eternal significance of the individual person's uniqueness. The art of portrait-painting calls to mind that the molecules and cells can express the individuality of a person, especially in his face. An authentic portrait reproduces the condensation of many personal moments in an image of what this individual essentially has become through the experiences and decisions of his life process. In one sense, the Greek-Orthodox icons are essentialized portraits of Christ, the apostles, and the saints. This religious transparency makes understandable the belief that the icons participate mystically in the heavenly reality of those whom they represent. For Tillich, this development in visual arts mirrors what he calls "essentialization" through artistic anticipation.[60]

c. *Self-conscious life in eternity.* Tillich's strong emphasis on the fact that individual selfhood is related to temporality and the realm of existence, and his concern for reunion, raised doubts about his view of the presence of the self-conscious self in Eternal Life. In his Ingersoll Lecture at Harvard in 1962 on "Symbols of Eternal Life" Tillich clearly states that participation in eternity is not extinction of the self. But, he insists, there is a mystery. You can erect two signposts, but you cannot describe that which lies between them. Eternal Life is neither total continuation *nor* complete extinction of the conscious self.[61]

In his *Systematic Theology*, Tillich spells out the meaning of the two signposts mentioned above in the form of two negative statements. The first is that the self-conscious life cannot be excluded from Eternal Life or the crucial element of participation would disappear. Without personal centers there could be no participation. Neither the dimension of the spirit (in all its functions) in man, nor the biological dimension in man can be denied eternal fulfillment.

But Tillich states that he must make the opposite negation. The self-conscious self in Eternal Life is not what it is in temporal life. The self-consciousness of eternity transcends temporality and at least the kind of experienced self-consciousness known in time and space. In some way self-consciousness will be renewed and changed. Beyond these two negative statements Tillich will not go in his theological conceptualization. He states that to do so would be to depart into the realm of poetic imagination.[62]

(3) *Eternal Life and Eternal Death.*

a. *Tillich's rejection of options concerning "eternal death."* For Tillich, "eternal death" contradicts the truth that everything as created is rooted in the eternal Ground of Being and must continue to be in relation to Being. In most orthodox Christian churches the threat of "death away from eternity" is preached. Other groups, following Origen and Socinus, affirm the certainty of *man's* being rooted in eternity and believe that everything *temporal* continues to be in relation to the temporal.

The orthodox group believes that the universal restitution teaching would destroy the seriousness of religion and ethical decisions. Tillich affirms that *both* the threat of eternal death and the inevitability of man's return must be denied.

Tillich surveys and rejects, although he seeks to glean truthful insights from, three attempts both outside and inside Christianity, to overcome the polarity of eternal death and eternal return. All three of these attempts express the problem of making the moment of death decisive for man's ultimate destiny. This problem is acute in the case of infants, children, and undeveloped adults.

Reincarnation in the Asiatic world, which is a painful way of returning to the eternal, is based on the negative character of all life. For Tillich, reincarnation must be seen as a symbol of the way in which higher or lower forces, which are present in every person, fight with each other to determine the individual's higher or lower essentialization. One does not *become* an animal in the next incarnation, but animal-like qualities may determine the level of one's essentialization.

The Roman Catholic doctrine of *purgatory* teaches that suffering "purges" the soul from distorting elements of temporal existence. In response, Tillich suggests that transformation does not come from pain alone but from grace which gives blessedness within pain.

Protestantism, noting doctrinal inconsistencies (i.e. between the grace of salvation and the punishment of purgatory) and severe abuses in the ecclesiastical application of this doctrine, abolished purgatory. It made, however, a weak attempt to avoid these problems by positing the doctrine of the *intermediate state*.

According to Tillich, reincarnation, purgatory, and the intermediate state cannot perform the function for which they were created. This function is to discover a way to combine the vision of an eternal, positive destiny for every man with the obvious fact that most, or in some way, all men do not live within the physical, social, and psychological conditions which are conducive for attaining this destiny. Tillich rejects the strictly predestinarian doctrine which asserts that God does not care for the large majority of beings who were born as men but never reached the age or state of maturity. This contradicts the God who creates the world for the sake of the fulfillment of all created potentialities.[63]

b. *Tillich's positive solution.* Tillich seeks to reconcile the seriousness of man's negativity (partially determined by his own rebellion) with the universal and final power of God over negativity. He argues that time, change, and development are potentially present in depth for everyone who participates in Eternal Life. But this possibility of human development and the victory over nonbeing occur *within* the eternal unity of the Divine Life. This would imply that there is a continued development beyond death in which those who fall short of full actualization and fulfillment (presumably all of us) are able to move ever nearer toward fulfillment in an endless progress.[64]

Tillich also refers back to his earlier statement that no individual destiny is separated from the destiny of the universe. The Catholic doctrine of prayer and sacrifice for the deceased is seen as a powerful expression of this belief in the unity of individual and universal destiny in Eternal Life.

For Tillich, the symbols "heaven" and "hell" must be taken seriously as metaphors for the polar ultimates in man's experience of the divine. He points out, however, that they are symbols of states of blessedness and despair and not localities. They point to the objective basis of blessedness and despair which is the amount of fulfillment or nonfulfillment which goes into a person's essentialization.

Although the literal interpretation of heaven and hell often has negative psychological effects, one cannot "psychologize away" basic experiences of threat and despair about the ultimate meaning of existence. At best, psychology can only dissolve the neurotic consequences of the literalistic distortion of the two symbols. According to Tillich, a proper, realistic, nonsuperstitious preaching and teaching of these symbols of heaven and hell would be helpful morally and existentially in moving one toward essentialization.[65]

3. *The Kingdom of God, time and eternity.*

(1) *Eternity and the movement of time.* Tillich developed his own unique view of the relation of time to eternity. Eternity and the Divine Life contain movement, change, and development. This makes it possible for an individual to develop in Eternal Life.

Tillich's view is different from that of both Plato and Augustine. Plato saw time as circular, and called it the "moving image of eternity." As Plato's view developed in classical Greek thought, there was no aim toward which time is supposed to run and consequently there was a lack of symbols for the beginning and the end.

Augustine abandoned the Platonic view of time as circular and replaced it with a linear, durational model. This linear process begins with the creation of the temporal and ends with the transformation of everything temporal. This means that time has purpose and direction. Time not only moves with and mirrors eternity, but it contributes to Eternal Life in each of its moments.

Tillich, however, had difficulty with Augustine's view because it does not make clear the fact that time not only goes from beginning to end, but also comes from and remains in eternal correlation with the eternal. Without this eternal perspective, modern progressivism has denied a beginning and an end and thus has isolated time from the temporality and meaningfulness of the eternal.[66] For Tillich, eternity must transcend but also contain temporality. But this temporality must not be subject to the law of finite transitoriness and must unite, without negating, the past and the future.[67]

Tillich illustrates his model graphically with the diagram of a curve which comes from above (implying the creation of the temporal and the beginning of time), moves down as well as ahead, reaches the deepest point (the existential now), and climbs toward the elevated, transcendental level from which it came (implying the end of time). This means that the curve goes forward with real progression as well as ascending toward eternity.[68]

Tillich maintains, however, that his view keeps history running toward its end in the eternal while still allowing the eternal to participate in the moments of time by judging and elevating them to the eternal. In another context, Tillich states that "eternal fulfillment must be seen not only as . . . present but also as eternity which is future." In other words, "eternal now" implies "eternal yet-to-be." [69]

(2) *Eternal Life and Divine Life.* For Tillich, God is living and eternal. How is the eternal God related to Eternal Life, the receiving of which should be, and is to some extent, the inner aim of all men? Already we have noted that history and everything temporal comes from God and moves toward God. This means we are taken up into a life *in* God which corresponds to the Pauline vision that in ultimate fulfillment God shall be all in all. Tillich calls this an "eschatological pan-en-theism."

Tillich describes three different meanings or modes of being "in" God which closely relate to his basic thesis of essence-existence-essentialization. The *first* meaning of life "in" God, related to *essence*, is that man is eternally "in" God in that he is dependent upon God as the source of his creative origin. This is similar to Aristotle's concept of the essences which exist "in" the mind of God. The *second* meaning, related to *existence*, is that man is "in" God as his ontological supporting and sustaining power even when he is in a state of existential estrangement from God. The *third* meaning, related to *essentialization*, is that man is "in" God as ultimate fulfillment when he ascends to or is reconciled with essential being (which being God is).

Our life and individuality cannot *be* apart from an identity with God at any and every moment. The Trinitarian symbol of the *Logos* introduces the element of "otherness" into the Divine Life which portrays the divine individuality and sustains our personal freedom and uniqueness. In the *Logos* we find the immanence of creative potentiality in the divine Ground of Being. Creation into time produces the possibility of self-realization, estrangement, and reconciliation for man.

For Tillich, this basic thrust indicates that the world process means something for God. His eternal act of creation is motivated by a love which finds fulfillment only through the *other* one who has the freedom to reject and to accept love. Yet, God both in his Being and his actions moves toward the actualization and essentialization of everything that exists.

Tillich admits that these intricate theological formulations concerning the Divine Life and the destiny of man may seem to violate or trespass upon the divine mystery. The answer to this danger is threefold. *First*, theological language is to be seen as symbol, and this should prevent us from distorting God into an object which could be analyzed and described. *Second*, a proper theology flows from a serious and genuine interest in God who is close to each person in terms of his external and internal infinite concern for man and his creation. Theology is thus only the drawing out of the conceptual implications of this religious faith and certainty. *Third*, understood in this sense, theology expresses, in the final analysis, a reverent, God-centered vision of life and existence.

It is true that the symbols used in this God-centered view of theology were developed as answers to the questions implied in human existence. But even in a theology which builds on a theological correlation (which starts with an analysis of the human condition), the final consideration points toward that dialectical pole which speaks primarily of God and his relation to man and the world. Among other values, this God-centered approach prevents religious symbols such as "life hereafter" from being misunderstood as products of man's wishful imagination and projection. Moreover, this approach emphasizes the importance of considering man as being ontologically significant for the glory and blessedness of the Divine Life.[70]

4. *Summary and Evaluation.* One interpreter of Tillich states that "stimulating" is the best adjective to describe Tillich's view of history. The sweep and vigor of his thought presents a richly developed theology of history to those who accept it and a formidable challenge to those who criticize it.

But criticisms of Tillich's perspective are numerous. For Carl Armbruster and John MacQuarrie, Tillich is vague and imprecise about the goal of history.[71] For John Stumme, Tillich's view of last things does not do justice to the intentions of the biblical message. In fact, in Stumme's view, Tillich sees the end of history as standing equally close to and equally distant from each moment of history. In other words, the last days are defuturized, and history's relation to the ultimate is verticalized. The future evaporates into the eternal present.[72]

Armbruster sees Tillich's indifference to death as related to his focus on the transhistorical aspect of reality and his indifference to time itself. The "last day" is a symbol for the end of history, not the moment when the universe ceases to exist. For Armbruster, personal death is an awesome event as is the death of the universe. Time is very important for it is the stairway to Eternal Life. But Tillich's stress is upon essentialization which renders death no longer absolutely decisive for eternity.

Some critics also feel that Tillich does not have a clearly outlined and positive doctrine of individual self-conscious persistence in being after death. This is an existential problem which is too important to leave unsolved.[73]

Part Three

Tillich in Dialogue with Other Faiths

XI. Non-Judeo-Christian World Religions

A. *The Importance of the Contemporary Interest in the Study of Non-Judeo-Christian World Religions*

As we have noted in the biographical section, Tillich's interest in world religions dates back to 1910 and his Schelling dissertation on "The Construction of the History of Religion in Schelling's Positive Philosophy: Its Presuppositions and Principles." This early interest was heightened by his dialogues with Rudolf Otto at Marburg in 1924. The *Systematic Theology* also reveals significant interest in world religions. In the analysis of his systematic theology, we noted that his concepts of universal revelation, the *Logos* idea and latent Spiritual Community all show the high esteem Tillich had for the revealing and saving powers inherent in all religions.

As early as 1957 and 1958 Tillich was giving formal lectures on World Religions at Wesleyan University in Connecticut and at the University of North Carolina. In 1960, as we have reported, he spent ten weeks in Japan. For the first time he immersed himself in a living and varied religious milieu which was completely different from the Judeo-Christian tradition. He was impressed and moved by the Shintoist cosmic type of religion, and by the various Buddhist groups, including Zen. In 1961, he gave the Bampton lectures at Columbia University which were to be published in 1963 as *Christianity and the Encounter of the World Religions*. According

175

to Mircea Eliade, the chapter in this book on Christian-Buddhist dialogue signified the beginning of a new phase in Tillich's thought.[1]

In the introduction to Volume III of the *Systematic Theology*, also published in 1963, Tillich pointed out that Christian theology must enter into creative dialogue with the theological thought of other religions or it will miss a world-historical occasion and remain provincial.[2] This interest continued and increased in the winter and autumn quarters of 1964 as Tillich participated in a joint seminar on the history of religions with Mircea Eliade at the University of Chicago. He stated that this seminar provided him with new and fresh insights into the Christian message. He gave his final lecture at Chicago on 12 October 1965 on "The Significance of the History of Religions for a Systematic Theologian." In this lecture Tillich indicated that his *Systematic Theology* had primarily been oriented toward twentieth-century Western society which was involved in the secular world of science and technology. He further stated that had he time he would write a new *Systematic Theology* oriented toward, and in dialogue with, the whole history of religions.

Later Eliade was to state how highly significant it was that Tillich surmised before his death the decisive role of an encounter with primitive and oriental religions both for Christian theology and the world at large. Since Tillich's death in 1965, we are even more rapidly approaching a planetary culture. According to Eliade, in the near future even the most provincial philosopher or theologian will be compelled to think through his problems and formulate his beliefs in dialogue with colleagues from other continents and believers in other religions.

B. *The Approach to the History of Religion and Non-Christian Faiths*

1. *The orthodox-exclusive approach.* Tillich does not accept the so-called simplistic Barthian approach which says that non-Christian world religions are false, man-made efforts to reach God and that they contain no revelation at all.[3] He admits that this approach has been seen as necessary at various points of crisis in the history of Christianity (for example, opposing the Nazi paganizing of Christianity). On the other hand, this view has also resulted in a theological and ecclesiastical narrowness which has blinded many theological leaders to the new situation arising out of the encounters of world religions and quasi-religions. This approach, for Tillich, is now a barrier, and we need rather to build bridges.[4]

2. *The secular-rejective approach.* Tillich likewise does not accept the secularistic dismissal of religion as obsolete or passé in a world in which modern man has outgrown his adolescent myths about God. This view states that the sacred has been fully absorbed in the secular. The only thing which is left of the whole message of the Christ is that Christ makes an ethical call to secularity. For Tillich, this is a reductionistic view.

Some see a relationship between the secular view and Hegel's view of world religions. In any case, Tillich rejected the view of Hegel that world religions other than Christianity still exist but the World-Spirit is no longer creatively in them. These two views would make dialogue with the world religions impossible.[5]

3. *Presuppositions of a proper approach.* For Tillich, a person must be willing to accept five presuppositions before he can fully and seriously affirm the significance of the history of religions for theology.

(1) There is divine revelation in all religions. This view reflects the influence of Rudolf Otto.[6] (2) Revelation is received by estranged man in a limited and distorted way. (3) There is a revelatory process which subjects the history of religions to mystical, prophetic, and secular criticism. (4) There *may* be a central event in the history of religions which unites the positive results of critical developments and makes possible a concrete theology that has universal significance.[7]

The phrasing of this statement with the emphasis on "may" marks a considerable deflation of Tillich's previous emphasis on the "final revelation" which is the *finis* or *telos* of every revelation. For example, in the *Systematic Theology* he states that in Christ alone the absolutely universal and the absolutely concrete coincide. In another place we find the emphasis that all men participate in the healing power of New Being but the ultimate criterion of saving power is in Jesus as the Christ. Other statements in the *Systematic Theology* are: only in Jesus as the Christ is the Divine Spirit present without distortion; Jesus as the Christ is the keystone of the arch of spiritual manifestation in history; the only historical event in which the universal center of the history of revelation and salvation *can* be seen is in the event of Jesus as the Christ.[8]

(5) Religion is the creative ground and critic of the secular although the secular is a tool of religious self-criticism. Tillich grants that religion must use the secular as a critical tool against itself. But a theologian must see the lasting necessity of religion for even the most secularized culture. This is true because the Spirit requires embodiment in myths and rites to become real and effective. God-language and religious symbols and rites are necessary. The Holy is *in* the secular culture, but it is also *outside* of it. Without a genuine sacred ground or depth the secular becomes empty and often becomes the victim of demonic "quasi-religions." [9]

4. *The dynamic-typological, theological approach.* (1) Elements in the dynamic-typological approach. In all religions there are elements of the experience of the Holy: the sacramental, the mystical, and the prophetic. If a given element dominates the other two in a certain religion, it will create a particular religious type. The other two elements will be present but deemphasized.

a. *The sacramental element* is the fact that the Holy appears in a special way in the finite in a natural object, a human being, a historical event, or a sacred text. This means that despite the mysterious character of the Holy, it can be seen, dealt with, or heard. We have remnants of this in the sacraments or ordinances of the highest religions.

In certain religious cults the sacramental element dominates the other two elements. This means that a religion becomes demonic or oppressive or heteronomous in the name of the Holy. This leads to criticism by the mystical and prophetic elements.[10]

b. *The mystical element* devalues the concrete embodiment of the Holy and seeks to unite the soul directly to the Holy or the Ground of Being or the Ultimate itself. The sacramental embodiments of the Holy are accepted by mysticism but considered secondary. The Holy lies beyond any of its embodiments.[11]

It is this mystical element which dominates Indian-born religions including certain forms of Buddhism. For Tillich, while mysticism liberates from the demonic distortions of the sacramental sphere, it pays the price of removing any concrete character of revelation and making concern about the actual human situation largely irrelevant. The relationship to concrete history tends to be insignificant. History does not reveal anything.[12]

c. *The prophetic element* is the ethical element of what "ought to be." This element criticizes sacramental religion because it has denied justice in the name of the Holy. Decisive in prophetic Judaism, this element can be seen in Amos and Hosea. They cried out against the religious priestly system and the cultic practices of Israel. Christianity also has a strong ethical element.

These three elements—the sacramental, mystical and prophetic—combine in various ways in different religions, but all three elements are present in higher religions. Specific religions grow and die, but these type-determining elements belong to the nature of the revelatory self-manifestation of the Holy. Other religions will arise with these elements.[13]

(2) The three elements unite in "The Religion of the Concrete Spirit."

a. *The inner aim of the history of religions* (and the three elements) is to become a Religion of the Concrete Spirit (ROCS). In the ROCS there would be a balance and unity of the elements. Tillich states that in, with, and under all religions there are authentic elements that point to and fight for this Religion of the Concrete Spirit. Sometimes this fight takes mystical form (against too much sacramental concreteness). At other times the fight takes a prophetic form (against escapism and lack of ethical emphasis). Even the secular critique of religion can be seen at times as a struggle for the "Religion of the Concrete Spirit." [14]

b. *The appearance of the Religion of the Concrete Spirit.* In a study of the history of religions we can find this Religion of the Concrete Spirit appearing in a fragmentary way in many moments and places. This "fight of God" for the ROCS helps to provide a key for understanding the chaotic history of religions.

Tillich states that as Christians we see the appearance of Jesus as the Christ as fulfillment of the inner aim of all religion. This is true because the Christ event is a personal life which shows no break in his relation to God and makes no claim for himself in his particularity. He crucified the particular in himself for the sake of the universal. This liberates his image from bondage to a particular religion—the religion to which he belonged has thrown him out—and to the religious sphere in general. The principle of love in him embraces both the religious and the secular spheres. This image constitutes the criterion by which Christianity judges itself and also judges the other religions and quasi-religions.[15] The Religion of the Concrete Spirit has only appeared and will only appear fully in Jesus as the Christ at the cross. Nevertheless, according to Tillich, it can appear, has appeared, and will appear *fragmentarily* in other places and moments even though these appearances are not historically or empirically connected with the cross.[16]

C. *The Method of the Christian-World Religions Dialogue*

1. *The early Christian model.* According to Tillich, early Christianity did not consider itself as a radical-exclusive religion. Rather it saw itself as the all-inclusive religion in the sense of the saying that "All that is true anywhere in the world belongs to us, the Christians." The early church adapted basic concepts from pagan metaphysical thought and moral principles from the Stoics. It borrowed ritual structures from the mystery religions and used Roman legal forms. It transformed many other pagan motifs and symbols.

Since the situation today in Christian theology is much like the Hellenistic Age, Tillich feels that it is appropriate to adopt the *Logos* doctrine which was used by the church fathers as a principle for dialoguing with other religions. These early Christian leaders emphasized the universal presence of the *Logos*, the Word, the principle of divine self-manifestation, in all religions. This *Logos* is a preparation for the central appearance of the *Logos* in a historical person, the Christ. They tried to show the convergent lines between the Christian message and the intrinsic quests of the non-Christian religions. They used a large body of literature in which the pagans criticized their own religions (for example, the Greek philosophers), but they also made free use of the positive creations of the pagan religions.

2. *Background for developing a Buddhist-Christian dialogue model.*

(1) The impact of Buddhism on the West has come primarily through Schopenhauer, Rudolf Otto, Japanese Zen Buddhism and some Hindu and Japanese "New Religions."

(2) The impact of Christianity on Buddhism has come through the direct

missionary way, indirect cultural way and the personal-dialogical way. Direct mission influence has been limited among the educated classes of Buddhist nations. More influential has been the indirect influence of Christian humanism. The dialogical-personal approach has both quantitative and qualitative possibilities.

(3) The most significant opportunity for dialogue in the future will probably center on the common problems related to secularization and the attack of powerful quasi-religions (for example, Communism) on all religions proper.

3. *A systematic Buddhist-Christian model of dialogue (based on principles).*

(1) Comparison of the intrinsic aims of existence of all true religions.

a. Christianity: aim of every*one* and everything united in the kingdom of God. The kingdom of God is a social, political and personalistic symbol. It emphasizes a reign of justice and peace.

b. Buddhism: aim of every*thing* and everyone fulfilled in Nirvana. Nirvana is an ontological symbol. It emphasizes finitude, separation, blindness, and suffering. Its answer is the blessed oneness of everything in the ultimate Ground of Being.

c. Implications of differences. The ultimate in Christianity is seen in personal categories and man is responsible for the fall. Buddhism is seen in transpersonal categories and man is a finite creature bound to the wheel of life with self-affirmation, blindness, and suffering.

(2) The relation of man to man and man to society.

a. Christianity in its view of participation leads to *agape* love and accepting the unacceptable and transformation.

b. Buddhism and its view of identity leads to compassion and suffering by identification.

(3) The problem of history.

a. For Christianity and its content of the kingdom of God, history is the scene in which the destiny of individuals is decided. In history, the new is created and runs ahead. This view calls for revolutionary force directed toward *transformation.* In some Christian groups, however, the emphasis is more on mysticism.

b. For Buddhism and the concept of Nirvana, the emphasis is not on transformation of reality but on *salvation from reality.* This view can lead to affirmation of daily activities, but the ultimate principle is that of detachment. Nirvana does not emphasize the new in history nor call for the transformation of society. Social interest would be related to the principle of compassion.

(4) The problem of democracy.

a. Christianity sees each individual as a person with equal rights under God. For Christianity, *only* if each person has substance of his own is community possible.

b. History has driven Buddhism to take history seriously. Buddhist Japan is asking about the spiritual foundation of democracy. How can democracy work if the Christian estimation of every person has no roots in Buddhism or Shintoism? Basically, Buddhism calls for identity but not community.[17]

Tillich's own conclusion is that democracy is a fragile corrective of the tendency toward dehumanization and tyranny and is the best way to protect creativity. It appears only seldom in lands such as the United States which are influenced by Christianity. In the United States, for example, there is always the tendency toward a secular conformism. Tillich could not see democracy as continuing in a dynamic way in lands dominated by Buddhism or Islam. Democracy as a continuing factor is particularly threatened in Buddhist-dominated lands where the necessary spiritual foundation is lacking.

Ronald Stone points out that more recent scholarship on Buddhism has located support for democracy of which Tillich was unaware.[18] Victor Nuovo also indicates that there is strong evidence for the possibility of community in Buddhism. In fact, Nuovo details how Buddhism is deeply concerned with the social-ethical element in religion.[19]

D. *Christianity and the Future of "Religion"*

Historically, Christianity has tended to become a "religion" instead of remaining a center of crystallization for all positive religious elements after they have been subjected to the criteria seen in the image of Jesus as the Christ. To correct this tendency, according to Tillich, Christianity must begin by both judging itself and then judging other religions in the light of the criteria established by Jesus as the Christ. Such an attitude allows a sharing which opens up the possibility of change on both sides of the Christianity-world religions dialogue. The Islams, for example, have a growing sense of insecurity in face of the secular world. They may come to self-criticism in analogy to our own self-criticism and look anew at Jesus as the Christ. A similar result might come in relation to Hinduism, Buddhism, and Taoism.

Tillich further states that if Christianity denies itself as a religion and centers again on the event of Jesus as the Christ at the cross, the development of secularism might not be understood in a completely negative sense. Rather this secular development could be seen as the indirect way which historical destiny takes to unite mankind. This could prepare people formerly involved in largely distorted religions, who have now become communists, for religious transformation.

Tillich does not call for a synthesis of religions, the end of religion, or the victory of one religion if it remains a "religion." Synthesis would destroy the concreteness which gives each religion its dynamic power. Religion cannot come to an end. The question of the ultimate meaning of life cannot be silenced as long as men are men. A particular religion will be lasting to the degree in which it negates itself as a religion.[20]

E. *Conclusion*

Robert Young suggests that the absolute (ontological) principle in Tillich's thought tended to become more important than the concrete existence of Jesus.[21] This implies that Jesus represents the universal principle of intelligibility more than the intelligibility of a specific revelation. Does this tendency lead to the statement in Tillich's last Chicago lecture that "there *may* be a central event. . ."? Or does Tillich change his emphasis depending on the circle in which he is operating? As a philosopher or historian of universal religious experience, he operates in one circle. As a systematic theologian, he works in a theological circle.

The largest corpus of Tillich's work finds him working within the "theological circle." It has already been indicated that an emphasis on the finality of Jesus as the Christ dominates his most significant work, the *Systematic Theology*. An address published in 1961 on "Missions and World History" sums up the perspective toward world religions reflected in the majority of his writings. This address is more explicit than some of his more academic materials.

According to Christian conviction, Jesus as the Christ is *the* center of history. The moment in which the meaning of history becomes fully manifest is in Christ. This means that he is the uniting point in which all religions (including Christianity) can be united after they have been subjected to the criticism of the power of the New Being which is in the Christ. In this center the contradictions of historical existence are overcome in "being and power." Missions is the attempt to transform the latent church, which is present in the world religions and even in Christianity, into the New Reality in Jesus as the Christ.

The transformation of the state of latency into one of actualization is a necessary function of the church—both in formal mission activity and in personal contacts. Some say that other religions are of equal value and that Christianity belongs to the Western world and should not interfere with the religious developments of the Eastern world. According to Tillich, such statements deny that Jesus who brings the New Being is an absolute figure of an all-embracing character.

That Christ is universal and valid for *all* cultures and religions cannot be absolutely proved by a theoretical analysis because the criteria used are themselves taken from Christianity. However, in some of his writing and speaking Tillich does list criteria necessary for any acceptable absolute for World Religions. These reasons why Christianity is superior to other religions include the fact that it is an event and not a law, Christ sacrifices the finite in himself for that which is infinite, and Jesus presents the principle of reuniting love. But in his theological address on "Missions and World History" he stated that only missions, in the final analysis, can provide the proof needed. The action of missions day by day gives the pragmatic and continuous proof of power and Spirit. Missions show that Jesus as the Christ and the New Being in him have the power to conquer the world in its ambiguities.

It is also true that only missions can prove that the church is the agent through which the kingdom of God actualizes itself in history. In some way and on some level, every human being is longing for a new reality which is in contrast to the distorted reality in which he is living. People are not *outside* of God. Rather they are *grasped* by God on the level in which they *can* be grasped. They are grasped in the experience of the Divine in which they are educated and in which they have performed acts of faith and adoration and prayer and cult. This is a divine preparation for the coming of the manifest church even though some of the symbols through which the Holy is experienced may seem extremely primitive, idolatrous, and distorted. Missionaries open up and bring to manifestation and fulfillment what is potentially given in the different religions and cultures outside Christianity.

What Christianity has to offer is not Christianity as an organized historical reality—certainly not Western Christianity. The goal of missions is the mediation of the reality of Jesus as the Christ which is the criterion for *all* human history. This criterion not only stands critically against world religions, but it also stands critically against many of the developments in historical Christianity.

Christianity as it has developed in the Western world is only *one* of the preliminary and transitory expressions of the reality of the New Being in Christ. It is not the end. Perhaps the greatest triumph of Christian missions is that it has created new churches in another cultural orbit. In turn these churches have developed their independence and resisted the identification of the kingdom of God with any special form of Christianity. These new Christian churches provide another great proof that Jesus is the center of history.[22]

XII. Judaism

A. Tillich's Interest in Judaism

Paul Tillich was concerned about the relationship of Christianity and Judaism on personal (existential), sociological (historical), and theological levels.

1. *Personal or existential reasons.* In his Berlin lectures on Judaism in 1952, Tillich pointed out that for many years the Jews had belonged to his circle of most intimate friends. Many of his associates in the Institute for Social Research of the University of Frankfurt were Jewish. In fact, he was known as "Paul among the Jews." His long friendship with Jews and appreciation for Jewish philosophers conditioned him to become one of the best friends that Judaism had among Christian theologians. When he delivered the Founder's Day address at the University of Frankfurt a few days before Hitler came to power, he stressed the Jewish contribution to German culture from Spinoza to Marx. His defense of Jewish students contributed to his dismissal from Frankfurt University. Tillich's first speech in the United States against Hitler's regime dealt with its anti-Semitism. His first broadcast into Germany over the Voice of America in 1942 was on "The Jewish Question." He called on Christians to defend the Jews. Tillich also did a great deal to assist Jewish scholars who were exiled to the United States from Germany.

2. *Sociological or historical reasons.* A second reason for Tillich's interest was related to his German birth and to his witness of the rise of anti-Semitism under the Nazis. Some groups of Christians supported Hitler and the Nazis, and other Christians remained quiet. As has already been indicated, Tillich early stood against anti-Semitism, and this stand contributed to his forced emigration to the United States in 1933.

3. *Theological reasons.* As we will note, Tillich believed that Christians cannot surrender their Jewish origins without giving up their Christianity. In fact, in one of the Voice of America talks he noted that those who attacked Judaism were essentially giving up Christianity. The Old Testament is part of the Christian Bible, and the Protestant Reformation was founded in the spirit and name of the Jewish Paul. Based on the prophetic emphasis of the Old Testament, Tillich saw the Jews as having a crucial vocation in history in defending the just God of time over against the polytheism of the pagan gods of space.[1]

B. *The Definition of Judaism*

For Tillich, the essence of Judaism is religion. The existence of the Jewish people, quite unlike any other group, is determined through religion. Paradoxically, Judaism is both a society and *not* a society. The Jewish people are both a people and *not* a people. Although the Jews now have the land of Israel, for Tillich the true existence of the Jews is necessarily the Diaspora or scattered existence. As we will see, this means, for Tillich, that the Jews are primarily a people of time, not of space. The implication is that they should live necessarily in dispersion.

Tillich suggests that the majority of Jews who recognize the truth of this time and Diaspora-related existence attempt to evade it in two ways. One way is through assimilation, by which the Jew identifies himself with the space in which he lives, not only geographically but also psychologically, sociologically, and culturally. A Jew can assimilate without becoming a Christian. Whenever assimilation succeeds, Judaism gives up its religious mission.

The second way to evade this unique time and Diaspora-related existence is for a Jew to create for himself a new space which is his own called Israel. This means the end of the Diaspora existence for many Jews, and it has both sociological and spiritual consequences which will be noted.[2]

C. *The Significance of Judaism*

In terms of world history, Tillich sees the significance of Judaism in its calling to be a people of time. Abraham is the archetypical Jew. He was called into a time-oriented existence from bondage to closed cultic space in Ur of Chaldees. Many associate Abraham and his family with moon-god worship in Chaldea. Space as such is not denied to Abraham, but it remains undetermined and is spatially undefined. "A land that I will show you" (Gen. 12:1) is a floating concept that emphasizes how the spatial is replaced by the temporal, even though time finds a space once again. The end of history is identified by the prophets as the moment in which all peoples are loosed from their national bonds. It is true that this no-longer-spatial God does have a place, Mt. Zion. This indicates that the temporal, in the Old Testament, has not completely overcome the dominance of the spatial.[3]

The experience symbolized in Abraham's call has repeated itself over and over again in Jewish history. The root-experiences of Israel after Abraham (the Exodus, the Exile, the destruction of the second temple and the Diaspora) are all experiences of "going-out." The high point of Jewish history is the universal monotheism of the prophetic period in which God was freed from being the god of a particular people (the god of space) to be the God of all people (the God of time).[4]

It was a great turning point in the history of religion when Amos announced that Israel's God was not confined to blood and soil. God did not lose when the blood-and-soil base in Palestine was lost. The prophets witnessed to ethics and justice and monotheism in a world of barbarism and idolatry. They revealed that God would cut his ties, even with the elected nation, if it did not uphold justice.[5]

In his 1952 lectures on Judaism, Tillich stated that to be true to its mission, Israel must remain perpetually exiled in time. Even if most Jews betrayed their divine calling, a faithful remnant would remain. Israel is to constitute for all time a thorn in the flesh of every polytheistic nationalist or imperialist who absolutizes his particular space in the name of God and wants to conquer neighboring, and ultimately all spaces. This type of polytheism which Judaism must expose stands behind all social and political conflict and injustice. Later we will see that this vocation of Judaism has great significance for Christianity.[6]

D. The Place of Israel in the Mission of Judaism

1. *Early misgivings about Zionism.* The attempts of the Jews to create their own space was expressed in the Zionist movement. For Tillich, this meant that an important group of Jews was lost to the Diaspora mission.

From a religious point of view, the Old Testament indicates that every attempt to identify God's kingdom with a nation must fail. The covenant people in the original Israel were continually disobedient to God's ways. The chosen people constantly contradicted that to which they were called. They constantly failed their mission and broke the covenant on which their mission rested. The solution to which the Old Testament leaders were driven under God's guidance was the idea of the "holy remnant" composed of people who would be bearers of law and prophecy.[7]

Tillich has misgivings that the creation of Israel will end up with the same results as were noted in the Old Testament Israel. Prophetic attributes which characterized the Jews in the Diaspora have disappeared in some cases. In Israel, ideas and ideals have been produced which resemble those which the Jews struggled against in foreign lands. For example, social levels have developed which are similar to class distinctions in other countries.

2. *Later reconsiderations concerning Israel.* In 1959, Tillich spoke in Chicago before the Christian-Jewish Colloquy on Israel's rebirth in the Middle East. His subject was "My Changing Thoughts on Zionism." In this speech he noted how his position on Israel had changed and that he had accepted Zionism as a legitimate expression of Judaism.[8]

In justifying his change, Tillich recognized the reality of the failure of Europe to protect Jews. He acknowledged that he had come to feel that any historically relevant group had to make space for itself. Therefore, the Jews need a land.[9]

Tillich states that one can hardly expect the average Jew to be a suffering prophet and a member of the faithful remnant which is committed to a prophetic life in time. The average Jew needs the identity of a space such as the nation of Israel. Christians should not ask Jews to accept as a role that which they would not accept.

3. *Continuing qualifications and misgivings about Israel.* But despite this approval of Israel, Tillich warns that there are perils in Zionism, such as the loss of spiritual foundations and prophetic self-criticism.[10] On the other hand, Tillich was realistic in noting that Israel as a contemporary political reality participates in the historical ambiguities of justice and injustice. Support for Israel does not mean that one accepts the idea held by some that Israel is the fulfillment of the symbol of the Promised Land. It should be recognized that the prophetic minority or remnant is partially resident in Israel but is also resident in the Diaspora. Israel "as a nation" is not to be equated with the nature and destiny of God's unique prophetic people of time.[11]

Tillich notes with regret the reports of intolerance and other difficulties in Israel occasioned by the attempt of some orthodox groups in Israel to establish a theocracy. He questions whether it is possible to build a modern national state on a theocratic foundation.[12] It is noted that many Jewish people are apprehensive that a new spatial bondage will arise out of the Zionist movement. This spatial bondage tends to manifest itself in nationalistic and polytheistic trends. The Zionists respond to these charges by stating that to be a real being in time a person must have space. The tension between these two elements of time and space continues to be *the* problem of Judaism.[13]

4. *Practical suggestions relating to Israel.* By implication, Tillich's counsel to the Germans in his 1952 lectures, according to Ronald Stone, could serve as practical counsel to the Jews concerning Israel.

(1) Accept finite borders and develop vocational consciousness and security.

(2) In a negotiating process, borders should be sought which would recognize the vitalities of the parties to the dispute and promote relative, though never absolute, security.

(3) Do not seek to base Zionism upon biblical legalism regarding borders or absolute solutions.[14]

As early as in his 1952 German lectures on Judaism, Tillich suggests that it is possible that the space which Israel has found as its own space will lead to a new embodiment of the prophetic spirit. He sees the possibility that new prophetic impulses for Israel as well as for the Diaspora will come from this new space. There is an opportunity to fill this new space both psychologically and sociologically by a totally Jewish spirit. But Tillich emphasizes that history cannot be calculated. It is possible that the prophetic spirit will be lost.[15]

E.   *The Historical Background of the Dialogue between Christians and Jews*

1. *The early dialogue.* The dialogue between Christians and Jews has gone on since the time of Jesus. In the teachings of John the Baptist and Jesus, Christianity attacks the tendency of Judaism to be space-bound and nationalistic. Jesus stated that his teaching that God must be worshiped neither in a temple nor on a mountain, but in Spirit and truth, fulfills the prophetic message.[16] The early Christians believed that with Jesus, there came the full universality, monotheism, and justice anticipated in the prophets.[17]

In Paul's time the dialogue became quite intense. The converted Jews under the leadership of James, and partially Peter, attempted to consider Christianity as a Jewish sect within the Jewish law. For Tillich, Christianity was able to become a world religion because of Paul's leadership, breaking through the narrow limits of the particularistic Jewish group which was dominant. The dialogue was intensified by the use of the Old Testament by the Christians. In more general terms, Christianity separated from Judaism in the first-century situation, because Judaism made a decision for space in terms of its national law.

An exception is that Judaism produced the first thinker to develop the *Logos* doctrine—Philo of Alexandria. But Philonic Judaism was never accepted by the dominant Jewish tradition.

2. *The contemporary dialogue.* Many modern Jewish scholars, such as Martin Buber, contend that the law does not mean legalism for the Jews. Buber, as a mystically minded Jew, states that the commandments are like stars. They cannot be fulfilled but they show us the direction in which we should go.

Other Jews state that the law is a help and not a commanding power which presses them down and pushes them, as it did for Paul and Luther, into despair. On the other hand, Tillich states that the law seems to be taken literally by orthodox Judaism.

The Jews argue that Jesus cannot be the Christ because he did not bring in the new aeon. Furthermore, the kingdom of God did not appear visibly with his coming. The Christian faith responded that the new aeon had already arrived in a preliminary and proleptic way in Jesus. This means that the conditioned universalism of the Jews is replaced by an unconditional universalism. The Spirit is available to everybody and replaces the authoritarian law. The nationally and historically conditioned elements of the law have lost their validity. The unconditional elements in the law which are independent of the Jewish national vocation are restated and actualized in the new era of Christianity.

According to the Christian perspective, men are constantly beset by the problem of how we can experience a merciful God in the light of our guilt. For Tillich, the Jew has no basic answer. Judaism does have its Day of Reconciliation, but it is not elaborated in daily life.

Divine forgiveness is central in Christianity with its story of the cross which symbolizes that God is willing to forgive. This experience of forgiveness constitutes a gap between Tillich and his Jewish friends. There seems to be a danger among the Jews of self-justification by their good life or their personal obedience to the law. From the Christian perspective, we can be good only in the light of grace. In Church history, some forms of Catholicism and rigid moralistic Protestantism practice religious legalism in such a way that their spirit is almost indistinguishable from legalistic Judaism.[18]

F. *The Theological Basis of Jewish-Christian Relations*

For Tillich, the community of the Jewish nation and the community of the synagogue into which Jesus was born are preparatory stages for the coming of the center of history (Jesus as the Christ), the church, and the kingdom of God. But they remain preparatory. They anticipate in the prophets. They actualize in a fragmentary way and with many distortions in legalism. However, Judaism is not the manifest church but still the latent church.

It is a fact of history that when Christianity comes to Jews, more often than not, the Jews do not accept the transformation out of latency into manifestation. In some areas of the world, this acceptance of transformation is comparatively easy for non-Christian groups. But for many in Judaism it is almost impossible. This was true for Paul. Even after his break with Judaism, Paul was not anti-Jewish. In spite of his breaks and fights with the "Judaizers," Paul was deeply concerned about Judaism and its place in salvation history.

Tillich considers Paul's solution to the "Jewish question" in Romans 9-11 as a deeply meaningful contribution to the interpretation of history. According to this Pauline key, Judaism has a continuing function, even in the new era introduced by Jesus as the Christ. This function will not cease as long as there are pagans. An implication is that mission to the Jews would not succeed until the pagans would have become members of the manifest church.

Tillich sees this teaching of Paul creating a question in his mind and in the mind of other biblical theologians about whether Christianity should try to convert Judaism as a whole. Tillich and many others have the feeling, based on Romans 9-11, that it is by historical providence that the Jews have an everlasting function in history. "Ever" means as long as there is still history and, therefore, paganism.[19]

As already indicated, Tillich sees that the function of Judaism is to criticize, in the power of the prophetic spirit, tendencies in Christianity which drive toward idolatry and paganism. In summary, Tillich accepts Romans 9-11 as the Christian answer to the Jewish question in general. In any case, this answer contains nothing anti-Jewish. It is the "no" and the "yes" of Christianity to Judaism in the Christian world.

G. *The Christian Response to the Importance of Judaism*

1. It is important that Christianity affirm that the Old Testament, with its emphasis on time, is an integral part of Christian existence. This emphasis was made early in church history when the church rejected all forms of Marcionism and realized anew that the Old Testament functions to keep the Christian community from lapsing back into paganism. For Tillich, Nazism was a latter-day form of gnosticism. The Church's decision to stand against the Nazis is analogous to its crucial decision to stand against Marcion.

In the early Middle Ages the Roman Catholic Church made Rome the sacred center of space, from which the kingdom of God shines forth, is directed, and finds its place. Once again, the Old Testament emphasis was needed. The Protestant Reformation sought to negate this spatial bondage in the name of the prophetic teaching of the Old Testament on the primacy of time. Nonspatial groups and radical sects came into being under the power of the prophetic emphasis on time and fought against capitulation to space. There is a close relationship between the Protestant Reformation and Old Testament prophetism.[20]

Tillich notes that the world-wide ecumenical movement is creating a space emphasis once again at Geneva, Switzerland. Similar tendencies are seen in the Chinese civilization (Peking as the center of all being) and in the emphasis on Moscow as the spatial center for Soviet Communism. It is ironic that the communist movement, which arose with a time emphasis, should sink into a spatial bondage.[21]

It should be remembered that the Old Testament not only represents the "God of time" but the "God of justice" as well. By taking the Old Testament seriously (especially the prophets), the church raises its social conscience.

2. The church must understand Judaism as representing the prophetic critique of itself. The church is always in danger of identifying herself with a national church, or of leaving injustice, the will-to-power, and national and racial arrogance unchallenged. In other words, the church is always in danger of losing her prophetic spirit.[22]

Already in the Middle Ages, Tillich explains, the existence of Judaism was felt to be a warning against the paganization of Christendom. In the modern period, with such "pagan" movements as Nazism, the warning is even more necessary. The church must recognize that it belongs to the function of Judaism to hold up before Christianity the mirror of its own regression into paganism.[23]

3. The church must battle against its own anti-Judaism. Tillich notes that Christianity, as a Jewish renewal movement, contains polemical anti-Judaism in its sacred Scriptures. This was interpreted as blaming the Jews with the guilt of the crucifixion. He mentions that his background in a minister's home had bred anti-Judaic tendencies in his own mind, especially during Holy Week. Fortunately, this problem was discussed openly and anti-Semitism was rejected in his father's household.

At this point Tillich makes a distinction between historical Christian anti-Judaism and racial anti-Semitism. Anti-Judaism is related to the Jews' part in the crucifixion and to the theological resistance of the Jews to the universal claims of the gospel. This resentment and tension can be called "anti-Judaism."

Anti-Semitism is a different thing. It speaks of racial inferiority. Systematic anti-Semitism is an invention of naturalistic anthropology of the late nineteenth century. In varying degrees it tolerates discrimination or even persecution. Expressed in biological theories of race, anti-Semitism played into the hands of Nazism which had to create an enemy to further its own program. For Tillich, the mass psychosis related to anti-Semitism that gripped Germany under Nazism reduced the anti-Semites to something less than human.[24]

To counteract anti-Judaism Tillich suggests that Christians should be taught the historical background of the New Testament writings. They should learn that much of the negative imagery of the Jews in the Gospels was intended (and should be interpreted) typologically and symbolically.[25]

Tillich traces anti-Judaism from the church fathers down to the position of Innocent III and the Fourth Lateran Council. In practice, Tillich affirms, Catholic anti-Judaism could evolve into anti-Semitism, but in theory anti-Semitism was not the position of the Catholic Church. Luther's attack on Jews was deplored by Tillich. He praised official Protestant statements which condemn anti-Semitism.[26] He was afraid, however, that local Protestant congregations would disregard official statements and foster or allow anti-Semitism. He did state that there is less anti-Semitism in America than in Europe. This is because of religious pluralism and because of the sectarian emphasis on the presence of the Divine in every human soul.

Tillich urges Christians to investigate their church's instructional material. It is from this often unconscious anti-Judaism in the Christian churches that the conscious anti-Semitism of the last one hundred years has drawn its nourishment. From a theological perspective, everyone (who has an opportunity) in the first century and in every century would crucify Jesus. Tillich says that it is absurd to blame the Jews as a race for the death of Jesus.[27]

H.   Practical Suggestions for Jewish-Christian Relations

1. *Do not engage in an active Christian mission to believing Jews.* Tillich rejects an active missionary policy toward believing Jews. This policy is not for theological reasons, but for psychological and sociological reasons. Some of these reasons relate to the dynamics of Christian guilt expressed in anti-Semitism through the Christian centuries and especially in the Holocaust.

2. *Tillich considers as legitimate, and even necessary on theological grounds, a passive mission to those Jews alienated from their tradition.* What Tillich calls an "admission-preparedness" on the Christian side is possible where Jews raise questions about something beyond the boundaries of Judaism. In such cases, the Christian can attempt to show that the Christian symbols can give an answer to the inner conflicts of Judaism. Implicit in Tillich's argument is the fact that, theologically speaking, Christianity has something which Judaism simply lacks in fundamental respects.

Beyond this passive approach, Tillich states, he will not go. The experiences of the Bible and church history show that only in the most unusual cases is it meaningful and fruitful to go beyond this approach.

3. *Maintain theological dialogue with the Jews about the Messiah.* Tillich affirms that there is a point where Christianity and Judaism have basic differences—the Christian claim that Jesus is the Messiah and the Jewish denial of that claim. Even here there are some converging lines which constitute a basis for dialogue. For one thing, Tillich suggests that the Jews and Christians live under the same ultimate covenant. Both groups look for a Messiah—the Christians say he has come and is coming again. The Jews say that he is coming.[28]

The thrust of the Jewish argument is related to the fact that the world has seen little change for the good and for justice. For the Jews this is obvious proof that the Messiah has not yet come. This means that we must expect his coming in the indefinite future. In the meantime, the Torah, the teaching of God, as given to Moses, is valid through all history.[29]

The Christian response is that the fulfillment of the messianic kingdom is only fragmentary in time and space, but in full reality beyond time and space. The Torah is no longer seen as central since Christ is the end of the law.

Tillich suggests that the dialogue is easier with a nonorthodox Jew. Bondage to the ritual in orthodox Judaism makes a free approach much more difficult.[30] He further suggests that we not seek to dialogue "by subtraction" of basic theological convictions.

4. *Reflect "life witness" concerning the New Being in Jesus as the Christ.* In most discussions with Jews there comes a point where analysis and theological argument end and "life witness" begins. This witness would be to show that through the coming of Jesus as the Christ a new reality has actually appeared. It is fragmentary and ambiguous yet capable of overcoming the conflicts of human existence.[31]

5. *Engage in practical cooperation with the Jews in the prophetic struggle for the God of time against the gods of space.* Tillich suggests that in the area of prophetic witness Christians and Jews have a unique common responsibility and vocation. The time may come when the two groups will stand under persecution and be martyred for their witness.[32]

I. Conclusion

Glen Earley suggests that Tillich's theological understanding of Judaism was colored by his rather restricted Jewish exposure. His primary contact was with the Reformed Judaism which he knew—and with alienated Jewish intellectuals. His view of Judaism was further influenced primarily by modern German Protestant scholarship. Earley also comments that Tillich's preconceptions about Judaism were formed rather early in his life and tended to filter out new input from Jewish history. This caused him to miss new patterns and developments in Jewish theology. For example, Tillich's distinctively Protestant view of biblical history (priority of the prophets) influenced him to give little emphasis to other important Old Testament themes or emphases.

But there is much to be learned from Tillich in regard to Jewish-Christian dialogue. Considering the fact that he did much of his writing on Jewish-Christian relations in the 1950s, Earley states that the positive features of Tillich's view are quite advanced and continue to be helpful.[33]

Part Four

Evaluating Tillich's Life and Significance

XIII. Tillich's Lifestyle and View of Personal Ethics

Introduction

The biographical section of this book mentions Tillich's relationship to his mother and father and his vows of chastity in his Wingolf fraternity days. It was also pointed out that his first wife broke the marriage vows and had a child by Tillich's friend, Richard Wegener, while Tillich was away at war. Some description was given of the general breakdown of traditional morals during the Weimar Republic after World War I and the involvement of both Paul and Hannah Tillich in the Weimar scene. Some note was made of Tillich's relationship with women during his New York days.

The publication in 1973 of two books, one by his wife Hannah and another by Rollo May which discuss Tillich's lifestyle, especially his sexual life, has resulted in a "Tillich as Person" discussion. This development led to a reexamination of Tillich's writings on personal ethics.

The books referred to above are *From Time to Time* by Hannah Tillich and *Paulus* by Rollo May. A more limited discussion of Tillich's personal life is given in *Paul Tillich* by Wilhelm and Marion Pauck in 1976. Reflections on Tillich's personal lifestyle by a longtime friend, Seward Hiltner, and respected Tillich scholars John J. Carey and Alexander J. McKelway are also helpful. Rollo May expanded on his book in a 1974 interview with Elliott Wright published in *The Christian Century*. It will also be

helpful to take a second look at some of Tillich's ethical teachings in
Systematic Theology III, *Love, Power and Justice, Morality Beyond,* and in
his sermons.

A. *The Perspective of Hannah Tillich* [1]

The first book which discussed Tillich's sexual life and struggles in
some detail was *From Time to Time* by Hannah Tillich, published in 1973.
Earlier autobiographical works by Tillich himself largely dealt with his
intellectual development. Hannah's book is primarily a book about her
own life, including descriptions of her bi-sexuality and her liaisons both
before and after marriage.

In the course of her impressionistic book Hannah gives a bittersweet
account of various episodes in Tillich's life. She describes Tillich in a
negative way as a husband and family man. According to Hannah, from
the very first periods of their relationship he had liaisons with other women,
including an affair on their wedding night. She tells of his affair with a
secretary and of love letters sent and received and mementos received
from various women. Some of these indictments are explicit. In the thinly
veiled construction of the mythical narrative between the old man and
the old woman in her book, she says many things about Tillich which
she could not easily say directly.

Hannah's book reflects her own sense of being submerged, abstracted,
and neglected as the wife of a distinguished and famous man. Grace Cali,
Tillich's former secretary, states that Hannah was fighting for the survival
of her own personhood.[2] Some contend that she overreacted. Hannah reported the same spirit of abstraction in the relationship between Tillich
and his daughter and son.

As indicated above, Hannah's book also reveals her own deficiencies
and personal sexual deviations. In fact, there is the suggestion that she
had had more experiences and fewer inhibitions in the sexual realm than
Tillich at the time they met. She reports having had lovers until the later
years of her life, with some of her extramarital relationships lasting over
considerable periods of time.

B. *The Perspective of Rollo May* [3]

Paulus, by well-known psychoanalyst Rollo May, was also published
in 1973. May was known to have been Tillich's closest friend for the
thirty-year period while Tillich was in the United States. He was Tillich's
student at Union Seminary. May's portrait is filled with personal reminiscences, flashbacks of Tillichian biography and psychoanalytical insights.
He expresses appreciation for Tillich's ecstatic reason and personal presence.

He also discusses Tillich's agony of doubt, his view of God, and his concern about death.

May places Tillich's erotic life in a less derogatory light. He theorizes that Tillich channeled his *eros* and libido in his first seventeen years around a quest for knowledge. May also interprets much of Tillich's personality and lifestyle as a consequence of having lost his mother while he was a young man of seventeen. Tillich first married an older woman who became pregnant by another man while he was at war. Grace Cali, his secretary for seven years, claims that Tillich never quite recovered from his first wife's unfaithfulness.[4] For several years Tillich was a bachelor. The social conditions in Berlin were decadent. He became involved with a number of women. For May, Tillich was trying to live out a delayed adolescence and to seek his lost mother.[5] He also had very strong sexual drives and "attracted women like flies." [6]

Tillich is also described as an emotionally sensitive person—an emotional, open book who was characterized by periods of melancholy, loneliness, and anxiety. There was a dark, depressing, and irrational side to Tillich's life as pictured by May.[7] Tillich was an adult who could be "psychiatrist to the psychiatrist," but nevertheless remained in some respects emotionally "at the twelve-year-old level."

Although May primarily describes Tillich's life between his fifty-fifth and seventy-ninth years, he does discuss Tillich's lifelong interest in the erotic as mentioned above. For many years Tillich was involved in and even sustained by relationships with numerous women. He stated that he could not write a book without having a woman in mind to write it for. However, there was never a hint of any homosexual activity or visitation of prostitutes for the purpose of explicit sexual experience. He disliked dirty or sexual jokes, although he did like "good" pornography.[8]

According to May, Tillich was more "sensuous than sexual" in his relationships to women. This "sensuous" interest in women related to companionship, presence, letters, and shared moments. May states that Tillich had a deep appreciation of and need for the feminine qualities of warmth, tenderness and acceptance. In fact, his way of relating to women evoked love and tenderness. May states that despite his devotion to "women in general" Tillich seems to have been psychologically incapable of investing his love openly and completely in the woman whom he married.[9]

In an interview with Eliott Wright published in *The Christian Century* six months after the publication of *Paulus*, May reacts openly to Hannah's book. He states that he does not think that Hannah's book presents an accurate picture of Tillich. He contends that Tillich's admiration of women should be called a spiritual seduction that had little to do with sexual intercourse. He further points out that Tillich came from a Lutheran background, not the Puritan background of the United States. He was physically robust and loved food and drink and nightclubs. Joy for him was being with people, and his relation to women was the epitome of that joy. Tillich thought that every woman was beautiful and thus was loving and tender with them. Women responded and many felt that his friendship was a great moment in their lives. Intimate sexual relations were seldom involved, and if so, they were only after he had known the women over a considerable period of time. In fact, some women would have liked to have gone further than Tillich desired. Tillich's motivation was the glory of loving and appreciating women, not intercourse. In contrast, Hannah leaves the impression that Tillich was seeking to seduce as many women as possible. For May, this is a distortion of fact and of Tillich's character.[10]

The Tillich Society in Germany agrees with May that Hannah's book contains "weighty distortions" and "misrepresentations" of Tillich. May further suggests that Hannah capitalized on the antihero mood and the spiritual and psychological decadence of Western society. This decadence takes delight in scandalizing and gloating over the foibles of important figures and cutting giants down to ordinary size.

After reading the manuscript prepared by Hannah, May urged her not to publish it. She refused his request, and May decided to finish his own book to provide a second version of Tillich. For May, Hannah is an emotional German woman who was made jealous many times by Tillich. She used this book to take revenge.

May agrees that Tillich was a product of the old authoritarian Germany and some of this authoritarianism carried over to his marriage. Hannah's book, however, is not just an exercise in woman's liberation, according to May.[11]

C. *The Perspective of the Paucks* [12]

In *Paul Tillich: His Life and Thought, Volume I: Life,* by Wilhelm and Marion Pauck, we have a richly documented life story by two people who had known Tillich for many years. Here Tillich's erotic life is set in a larger context. He was reared in a home with a deeply ingrained sexual moralism implanted by his father and enhanced by his membership in the Wingolf Society with its vows of chastity. His was a Lutheran minister's home marked by the early death of his mother and an unusual relationship with his first sister. At the beginning of World War I, Tillich was a shy, grown boy and a "dreaming innocent."

When Tillich returned to Berlin four years later, after the war, he was utterly transformed. The orthodox Christian believer had become a cultural pessimist and the repressed puritanical boy a "wild man." In the "wide-openness" of the German Weimar Republic, Tillich became unconventional with respect to heterosexual relations as well as in other areas. This attitude was doubtless encouraged by the fact that his first wife engaged in an illicit affair, giving birth to a child while Tillich was away at war.

It is now generally accepted that at the end of World War I Berlin became the entertainment capital of Europe. Walter Laqueur reports that a sex wave swept Berlin ranging from sex research institutes to nude shows and hard-core pornography. Periodicals were published such as *Free Love* and *Woman Without Man*. Books representing a new genre of literature which dealt with nights in a harem, women with whips and exotic methods of sexual intercourse were widely distributed. Nude "beauty dances" were popular. The climate was more permissive than in any other country. Trial marriage was widely discussed.[13] This situation obviously influenced both Paul and Hannah Tillich in the early 1920s and helped to establish some of their attitudes toward sexuality.

The Paucks give a restrained account of Tillich's relationships with women, drawing some of their material from Hannah Tillich's book, some from Rollo May, and some from personal interviews with Tillich and others. No general evaluation is given of the writings of either May or Hannah.

It is pointed out that Tillich mentioned often that he feared that his own salvation was uncertain and that he was a sinner who would be excommunicated from the kingdom of God. The Paucks quote Tillich as saying that his friendships with women, especially since he was a theologian, presented a particular agony as well as a keen pleasure. He feared the world would hold a candle to his shame.

According to the Paucks, Tillich's overriding fear was that his relationships to women might one day be made public and bring ruin on his work if these relationships were misunderstood or misrepresented. He thus seldom wrote directly about his conception of marriage or about sex, but he dropped hints which can be discovered throughout his work.[14] For example, in *Love, Power, and Justice* he states that the breaking of conventional laws regarding sex are evil if they are not under the ultimate criterion of the *agape* quality of love.[15] But *agape* love liberates us from bondage to absolute ethical traditions and conventional morals.[16]

All of this means, for the Paucks, that Tillich alternated between the Christian and the pagan and between law and grace. This way of life produced in him a burden of tragic guilt which is reflected in one of his sermons where he states that "We must risk tragic guilt in being free from father and mother. . . ." And this means "carrying scars in a person's soul for his whole life." [17]

Tillich justified his sexual behavior in the name of the "infinite possibilities of life which provide vital fulfillment." According to the Paucks, he refused to regard his wife as the absolute law which would imprison him once more. An absolute vow would make the moment in which we make it infinite or absolute. Other moments come which reveal the relativity of the moment in which the decision was made. According to the Paucks, Tillich's obsession with other women was as real as Hannah's jealousy and distrust. They suffered together. Toward the end of their life, there was more calm.[18]

The Paucks also defend Tillich by noting that he had a genuis for friendship, and fidelity to and concern for hundreds of people. In her review of the Pauck volume, Ursula Niebuhr comments that Tillich not only needed friends and students but women friends in particular. His lasting friendships were with women who were intellectually stimulating, interesting, unusual, open to him, and with whom he felt comfortable himself. His letters and conversations comforted, sympathized, celebrated, advised, and encouraged his women friends. He urged them to remain open, even as he was, to the infinite experiences of life. Tillich maintains that this desire for affectional relations with beautiful and intelligent women was motivated more by *agape* love than *eros* love.[19]

The Paucks suggest that Tillich's unconventional erotic pattern with its weaknesses helped to make him elusive, fascinating, and believable as a productive thinker and human being. But Tillich paid for this way of life with self-doubt and conflicts which lasted until his dying day. In his old age, Tillich concluded that love was tragic and marriage sad. But in one of his sermons, "You Are Accepted," he contends that he claims God's forgiveness.[20]

D. *The Perspective of Seward Hiltner* [21]

Seward Hiltner, formerly of Princeton Seminary, presents a somewhat different perspective in a *Theology Today* review article of the books by Rollo May and Hannah Tillich. Hiltner was closely associated with both May and the Tillichs from the late 1930s. He thinks that May is right in most of his discussion of Tillich's erotic life. More important, for Hiltner, is the fact that Tillich approached women "ontologically," as he did everything. Tillich was attracted by the "generality" or "archetypical" in women and could genuinely give more depths of himself in even a brief relationship than most men could in a whole married life. One of Tillich's women friends said that Tillich had "enough *eros* for all." But at the same time, there was very little concretely particularistic in any woman that was actually being attended to. It was the "universal potential" more than the particularism that Tillich saw in people.[22] This last idea of Hiltner's seems to be contradicted by the Pauck description of his particularistic communications with many women through the years.[23]

Hiltner comments that both of the Tillichs had a form of narcissism which means that things and people and institutions could be ignored if they do not point toward a person's own centered interest. For Tillich, that meant something archetypical, ultimate, and ontological which in turn can rule out many particular concerns and institutions important to most people. Hannah was impatient with the church, and indeed most institutions, from the time of her adolescence.

For Hiltner, concreteness and ultimacy are *both* indispensable. The implication is that Tillich tended to ignore or even oppose on a practical or day-by-day level the inherent need for structure through human institutions. He failed to balance the need for concrete churches, universities, seminaries (even the institution of marriage) with the need for ultimate categories in thinking and researching, writing and living.

Hiltner quotes Tillich as asking in his later life, "Was my erotic life a failure, or was it a daring way of opening up new possibilities?" May opts for the latter. Hiltner states that he is a little less sure that a fresh flower, even in a crannied wall, every day, is an effective way to break the legalistic bonds of our theological past.[24]

E. *New Perspectives on Tillich's Life and Work*

Alexander J. McKelway, author of a major work on Tillich, claims that the knowledge of Tillich's personal life suggests new perspectives on his life and thought.[25] He refers to the statement by the Paucks and May that Tillich's attachment to women was an expression of a general passion for life—the sea, trees, the dance, painting, and music. This may cause us to give more attention to the romantic element of Tillich's thought, especially the influence of Schelling and Schleiermacher.

McKelway also suggests that Tillich's struggle with the erotic may help to explain his basically negative attitude toward a more traditional approach to Christian dogmatics. For McKelway, given the correlation of rigid morality in Tillich's childhood, the repression of his sexuality, and the continuation of theological and ethical orthodoxy in the Wingolf Society, it is not strange that, when Tillich did revolt, his rejection of conventional behavior also involved a rejection of the orthodox statement of the theological tradition with which it was associated. According to McKelway, Tillich viewed the dogmatic tradition as a heteronomous imposition upon modern man, and was generally blind to its liberating and life-affirming dimensions.

For McKelway, our knowledge of Tillich's personal life cannot mean invalidation of Tillich's theology. If the moral rectitude of a theologian is the standard for judging his work, who then would survive? What about Augustine with his treatment of his child's mother, Luther with his hatred for the revolutionaries, and Calvin with his agreement to the condemnation of Servetus? There are also the Psalms and the personal life of King David.

F. *Tillich's View of Personal Ethics*

In the section on "Ambiguous Life and the Quest for Unambiguous Life" we discussed Tillich's view of ethics under the heading of individualization and participation and Spiritual Presence and morality. In *Love, Power, and Justice* Tillich showed the relationship between ethical categories and theology. The one published volume which is specifically related to ethics is *Morality and Beyond*. John J. Carey points out that in these writings Tillich consistently rejected any model of a divine command ethic. On theological grounds, such an approach places too much weight on prior revelation and becomes too legalistic. On personal grounds, the divine command approach cannot deal with the individual's yearning for personal wholeness and fulfillment.

In view of our new understanding of Tillich as a person, it is understandable why he so consistently resisted a divine command ethic. According to Carey, this view does not fit in with the personal complexities and ambiguities which Tillich knew and was living.[26] He thereby resisted all attempts to wed Christian ethics with the divine command approach, which he saw as related to middle class convention and morality. In some of his sermons, Tillich condemns those who in pulpit, schools, or families call the natural sexual strivings of the body sinful. The person open to the Spirit has to resist making ultimates of our traditional codes.[27] In *Morality and Beyond*, Tillich states that *agape* love breaks the prison of any absolute moral laws in a unique moment even when the laws are vested with the authority of sacred tradition.[28] Perhaps without breaking the rules one may have missed his own fulfillment as a person. In summary, moral acts, for Tillich, are those in which we actualize our potentiality as persons.

Tillich does force traditional Christian moralists to realize that marriage is a complicated social institution and marital relationships are complex and subtle. Carey suggests that the Tillichs had a devitalized marriage. Both partners found their basic human and professional satisfaction apart from the marriage. For Carey, the question of morality in such a marriage takes on a different focus than in a vital or nuclear marriage. Tillich, however, did not want a divorce, since it would impair his professional career and undermine the security of his children.

Carey also raises the question of whether or not Tillich's self-realization ethic can be called a Christian ethic. One looks in vain in Tillich's work on ethics for an explicit treatment of the Judaeo-Christian themes of responsibility and covenant. Tillich was never enamored of the institutional church and evidently felt that its ethics were too intertwined with white middle class convention and ideology. In this connection, Tillich's approach has some relation to recent Christian feminist thought, as well as black and liberation theology.[29]

In *Systematic Theology* III, as we have noted, Tillich states that ethics should be the task of philosophy and not theology. This is because theology is always in danger of placing heteronomous authority (divine command) over ethical analysis. When philosophy is free and objective in its analysis it may, when grasped by Spiritual Presence, provide theonomous ethics. It should be noted, however, that Tillich's principles of justice, love, and wisdom outlined in the section on "Ambiguous Life and the Quest for Unambiguous Life" have some relationship to the Judeo-Christian tradition. Here, as in so many areas, Tillich is seen as a boundary thinker, at the point of the intersection of Christian and humanist concerns.

McKelway suggests that it is one of the great strengths of Tillich's thought that morality and ethics are seen to be matters of the gracious presence of the Spirit. Ethics have to do with grace and not law. But in contrast to the more autonomous emphasis of Tillich, McKelway contends that the divine command approach is not oppressive or legalistic when the command of God takes a gracious and saving form in Jesus Christ. When the Spirit, which is the basis of morality and ethics, is the Spirit of Jesus Christ, there could be no thought of oppressiveness or heteronomy in theological ethics. Rather, ethics would find in the loving claim of God in Jesus Christ authentic liberation within fulfilling guidelines. For McKelway, philosophical ethics can help in bringing out the applications and implications of this gracious command of God in Jesus Christ but it cannot be the ultimate basis for ethics.[30]

XIV. Representative Criticisms, Strengths and Contributions

Introduction

Before giving a summary evaluation of Tillich's significance, it should be helpful to remind ourselves again of the purpose of this book. The basic purpose is descriptive. It is primarily intended for theological students, pastors, and interested laypersons. To accomplish this purpose it was suggested that there should be a willful suspension of disbelief in relation to Tillich's approach until there had been an exposition of his life and system.

It is also important to remember that Tillich is an existential or participational theologian. Therefore, it is helpful to see his writings in the context of his life. Ian Thompson contends that the proper interpretation of Tillich requires one to see his pre-war and World War I experiences as definitive in providing the impulse toward a systematic formulation of his ideas. His true greatness and his limitations cannot be appreciated except against that background.[1] We should also evaluate his writings in light of his basic purpose and his basic idea or ontology.

To complete a secondary purpose of this book, however, it is important to summarize representative evaluations of Tillich's significance, both negative and positive. In certain sections of the book evaluations were given as a particular doctrine or concept was presented. This section, therefore, constitutes in some instances a brief summary of what has already been presented.

It should be noted that in certain areas what some consider as Tillich's weaknesses are considered by others as his strengths. In other areas scholars say both yes and no to Tillich's ideas. Some disagree with him but praise his intellectual courage and his stimulus to discussion in crucial areas. Others applaud his attempt to present Christian theology for contemporary, educated audiences. Perhaps no theologian in this century has created more controversy in regard to his ideas and his life. He is seen as a bridge person—a bridge between continents and between centuries. Some say that he is the greatest theologian of the twentieth century, and others say that he is a great deceiver or the twentieth century's most dangerous theologian.

A. Representative Criticisms

1. Philosophical criticisms.

(1) *Philosophical eclecticism.* Adrian Thatcher suggests that a major criticism is related to Tillich's philosophical eclecticism. Different ontological concepts and ideas have become almost indistinguishably merged in his writings. He often uses ontological concepts carelessly and inconsistently. The term "nonbeing" is seen to operate in half a dozen different ways. The term "essence" has a number of different meanings. Even if allowances are made for the evolution of the meaning of key terms during the long development of Tillich's philosophical thought, the inconsistencies remain.[2]

Ian Thompson agrees that Tillich's loose, discursive pattern of argumentation has puzzled philosophical critics. His thought is eclectic and syncretistic in a manner that makes it difficult to identify him with any particular school. Thomists find his ontology a curious mixture of existentialist themes and idealist jargon. Philosophers of an idealist bent find him disturbingly unorthodox in terms of traditional Idealism. Existentialist critics find his thought too essentialist. British philosophers are puzzled by his ontological speculation and lack of analytical rigor in the exposition and defense of his views.[3] John Clayton states that Tillich's failure to use the dominant philosophical tools of the twentieth century, which for Clayton is the analytical tradition of philosophical analysis, is one of the most severe limitations on his lasting influence within the Anglo-American world.[4]

(2) *Lack of systematic rigor and technical scholarship.* No one would dispute the fact of Tillich's erudition which is revealed in the catholic scope of his knowledge and interests and in the massiveness of his literary output. Specialists, however, are invariably critical of his lack of systematic rigor and his disregard for the appropriate conventions of technical scholarship, whether in the theological disciplines or in philosophy, psychology, art history, the history of ideas, sociology, or politics. He could command respect and attention by what he had to say on any of these subjects, yet this recognition is not in any unambiguous sense recognized to be great in any field but theology. Even theologians find Tillich difficult to accommodate within their familiar categories.[5]

A part of the secret of Tillich's popularity was that he adopted the rhetorical style of a scholarly popularist, but this was also the reason for the feeling of uneasiness with which he left more careful or technical scholars. His rhetoric is more impressive than the dialectical analysis offered in its support. The fact that his system is primarily a work of theological rhetoric is a measure of his greatness and the source of his chief weaknesses.[6]

The less ambitious and more narrow concern of British philosophers with logic, semantics, epistemology, metaethics, and the attempt to develop a neutral and objective analytical method reflects the role of philosophy in a highly conformist society. In contrast, Tillich lived in the period of Continental history which was characterized by social and cultural upheaval and the radical questioning of traditional values. He belonged to a generation that set out to change the world rather than contemplate it. He stood in the idealist tradition and was inspired by its romantic utopianism and its enthusiasm for a revolutionary transformation of Europe spearheaded by Germany. Like his idealist predecessors, he was concerned to reinterpret the cultural history and destiny of Europe and on this basis to develop a credible and persuasive system of belief that would express the spirit of the times. He did not try to make sense of ordinary semantic problems. Therefore, his talk of symbols, myths, and paradox invites the charge of mystification and obscurantism.

The fact is that Tillich belonged to the age of ideology and his thought has the rhetorical style of the types of "life philosophy" which were popular earlier in the twentieth century. He does not have the rigorous coherence of certain types of philosophical systems. Rather, his approach is the expression of a conviction that a Christian realist philosophy of being could be developed out of a synthesis of Idealism, Marxism, and Existentialism. For Ian Thompson, Tillich's *Systematic Theology* has the aesthetic coherence of a vision but lacks the support of a developed theory to sustain and justify that vision.[7]

Ronald Stone answers the philosophical critics by stating that Tillich wrote in continuity with one approach to the Christian tradition and philosophical theology. Many of his critics simply stem from different traditions and criticize him for using the tradition he does. A more profound criticism would be to show that he misused his own tradition or that the tradition was flawed in its essential components.[8] Clayton even goes so far as to state that Tillich sought to use Idealism to transcend and go beyond Idealism.[9]

Tillich admitted that there are types of ontology other than his which are more personalistic, moral, and prophetic, but he believes that his mystical type of ontology is important because it stresses participation. He thinks that faith, experience, and inwardness are in danger of being overlooked. In other days he would have perhaps emphasized the more personal, moral, and prophetic approach. To achieve balance, Tillich affirms that he is perhaps overemphasizing the mystical side, which has been neglected. Tillich himself states that, whether good or bad, his imaginative tendency plus certain other circumstances prevented his becoming a technical scholar in the accepted sense of the word.[10]

(3) *Intentional deception and naturalistic humanism?* Leonard F. Wheat attributes to Tillich an intentional plan of deception and presents him as the great theological imposter of our times. By clever hoax, Tillich has managed to undermine the Christian faith from within. Beneath the protective covering of the traditional symbols, Tillich's authentic message (utilizing a clever mixture of idealist, existentialist, and psychoanalytic terms) is essentially a kind of ecstatic, naturalistic humanism that is quite irreconcilable with Christian belief.[11]

Raymond Bulman suggests that, leaving aside the question of Tillich's inner motives and intentions, a legitimate question raised by Wheat is whether the structure of Tillich's theology of culture leads by an inner logical necessity to the espousal of a purely secular humanism. Bulman contends that Tillich did not promote secular humanism as an alternative to the biblical faith nor secretly promulgate humanist ideals under the protective camouflage of Christian symbols. In fact, his doctrine of estrangement constitutes an important apologetic element against a purely secular view of man. This estrangement can only be overcome by the creation of the New Being through openness to the Spiritual Presence. Tillich puts stress on the divine action. Religion is the state of being grasped by an ultimate concern. As finite beings, we cannot come to God unless he chooses to manifest his presence to us. For Tillich, God has tremendous depth and infinitely transcends the finite being of which he is the ultimate source and power.[12]

2. *Theological criticisms.* There have been criticisms from a wide spectrum of writers concerning Tillich's approach to various theological doctrines. For David Kelsey, the main difficulty is not that Tillich's *Systematic Theology* makes use of ontological analysis or a philosophical description of religious experience or too little use of historical findings. Actually, any theology must use a philosophical base in some way, and Tillich at least has the virtue of developing a theological approach in a clearly labeled way. Rather, for Kelsey, the major question which must be put to Tillich's entire theological enterprise is the way in which he shifts the center of importance in his theology from the proposal of *belief* to the proposal of *attitude.*[13]

(1) *View of Scripture.* Tillich construes Scripture on an aesthetic model. Scripture is "authority" for theology only insofar as it is understood as a verbal icon or a "picture." He sees value in this approach because it seems to him to be a way of maintaining the importance of Scripture for theology even after historical-critical study has revealed the errors in facts of the Bible and the cultural parochialism of its world-view and ethics.[14]

According to Alan Richardson, Tillich decided that the facts upon which

Christianity is built are too dubious as acceptable foundations. So he decided to prove that Christ is the center of history by showing that he gives meaning to existence. He replaces the Jesus of history with the Christ principle. Christ is a *gnosis* from the ontological realm and is thus above historical criticism. The foundation of Christianity is the biblical picture of Christ and ecclesiastical belief and experience. Participation, not historical argument, is the guarantee of the reality of the event on which Christianity is based.[15]

For both Kelsey and Richardson, this approach creates difficulties. They see Tillich as claiming that Scripture is to be interpreted on the model of a picture like any important aesthetic object and it must be understood not to make any claims. The content of a work of art such as the Bible is simply the work itself. It does not inform us of anything. The most it can do is give us new insights, new attitudes, and new perspectives on "the way things are."

According to Kelsey, in contrast to Tillich, the biblical view stresses beliefs over attitudes. The striking characteristic of New Testament proclamation, despite all of its inner diversity, is that it does make truth claims. According to Ed Miller, the Christ event can only have significance if it is rooted in history. Of course, the New Testament also proposes policies for action in the adoption of an attitude toward life as a whole. But fundamental to both of these is the proposal that this state of affairs and the appropriateness of apologies for action are based on the particular fact of Jesus Christ's life, ministry, death, and resurrection.[16] This critical judgment, expressed by Kelsey, is agreed upon both from the Barthian-Protestant perspective of Alexander McKelway and from the Roman Catholic perspective of George Tavard.[17]

Conservative scholars such as Carl Henry and Ronald H. Nash criticize Tillich because he does not emphasize that biblical propositions have revelatory power in themselves. Both Henry and Nash would agree that the personal dimension of revelation through the action of the Holy Spirit is important. But for Nash, *belief* in a personal revelation establishes the *belief* that God has revealed himself in the written Word of God as a necessary condition. Without belief that revealed truth is inscripturated in the Bible, a balanced view of revelation becomes impossible. According to Henry, conservatives need to protest Tillich's relinquishment of the cognitive knowledge of God which is to be found in the inspired Bible.[18]

(2) *View of Christology.* Perhaps there is no section of Tillich's thought which is more controversial than his section on Christology. Adrian Thatcher points out that the wide diversity of judgments about Tillich's Christology demonstrates how difficult it is to judge a largely ontological vocabulary according to traditional theological norms. He further describes some of the problems for Tillich's Christology which largely arise from Tillich's

basic idea or ontology of essence-existence-essentialization. If Jesus was "Essential Manhood," how could he become actualized in existence without distortion and estrangement? If existence is estrangement, then Christ's existence and unbroken unity with God are presumably impossible without his being estranged. Here it appears that Tillich's ontology has distorted his Christology.

Another criticism leveled by Thatcher is related to the fact that the essence of Christ, for Tillich, does not fulfill existence but negates it. The divinity of Christ causes him to negate his humanity. Furthermore, Jesus as an individual sacrifices himself completely to the divine Ground of Being which is manifest in him. This destroys the harmony of individualization and participation. This is contrary to the Christian experience of salvation where the individual is reaffirmed as he participates in divine grace.[19]

Robert Cushman contends that Tillich's Christology is inherently docetic with a tendency toward gnosticism. He points out that Tillich revolts against the idea that the miracle of the divine act of redemption was a supranatural incursion into the ordinary course of nature and events. For Tillich this idea is absurd and irrelevant. His chief concern relates to man and his freedom and fallenness. The world, for Tillich, is almost completely dependent on man and has almost no independent ontological status. With such a phenomenological dissolution of the world the incarnation would no longer need to be seen as an incursion into nature, but rather would remain a spiritual (ecstatic) event in the life of the Christian community. There would not need to be any constellation of natural factors exceptional to the ordinary course of events. The New Being has a home in a tradition and community that lives by faith in the New Being. The incarnation is not in the objective order of history but only in "existential" history, as the sphere of existential estrangement. This means that the incarnation hovers insubstantially in the air without actualization, particularity, or uniqueness. For Cushman, this type of Christianity verges upon gnosticism.

In contrast to Tillich's thought, Cushman sees history as so grounded in nature that the shock of the divine incursion could, by extending its traumatic influence, leave traces and evidences in the nature in which Jesus' personal history is embedded. The divine initiative entails a transformation of nature and the realm of objectifiable history embedded in it.

In opposition to Tillich's incipient gnosticism, Cushman suggests that classical Christian theology was not content to locate the incarnation in subjective, individual, "existential" history. Rather the incarnation entailed nature as its temporal matrix, which gave it actuality, identifiability, and efficacy. The incarnation was not just a "sign event" but a miracle related to the incursion of God's power. In the incarnation the divine power evoked the response of both nature and history as embedded in nature.[20]

For Osborne, there is a problem in Tillich's view of Christ in that Tillich tends to interpret the participation of Jesus in the New Being in such a way as to eliminate his individualized features. The individuation-pole is overbalanced by the participation-pole. Osborne is also concerned to know when Jesus became or received this "New Being." Did he receive it at his conception, at his baptism, or on the cross when he totally surrendered himself to Jesus as the Christ? For Osborne, Tillich's restatement of Christology raises problems related to the mode of union between the personal centered self of Jesus and the substance of New Being created by the Spirit which shines transparently through Jesus to make him the Christ.

Osborne points out that Tillich, in saying that Essential Manhood appeared in Jesus as the Christ, is saying that "what-man-is" and "what-man-should-be" (Tillich's twofold content of essence) has appeared. In other words, it is man's essence rather than the incarnation of God's Son that has appeared. In one sense, we do not differ from Jesus as the Christ because his essence and our essence (the "what" and the "what-should-be") are identical. However, Jesus differs from other men in that he did not use his freedom to fall from essence to existence. Thus, for Osborne, Tillich holds an adoptionist theory of Christ's nature to explain the question, Why was Jesus chosen and we were not? [21]

(3) *View of the Trinity.* Tillich is criticized for his doctrine of the Trinity because the third person of the Trinity, the Spirit, tends to dominate Christology in Part IV, "Life and the Spirit," of the *Systematic Theology.*

McKelway sees Tillich, in his Trinitarian teaching, placing himself on the side of the Eastern church which taught that the procession of the Spirit came from God alone and not from God and the Son. McKelway asks the question: "If God the Father is not seen as he reveals himself in himself as God the Son through his presence as God the Spirit, how can we speak of the Trinity?" [22]

(4) *Views of the resurrection, faith, and God.* Tillich's doctrine of the resurrection is criticized because it is built on the idea of restitution and lacks biblical references. Tillich also has no doctrine of the virgin birth.

For Donald Bloesch, Tillich's idea of faith is to be seen more in terms of participation *in* God rather than in terms of a personal fellowship *with* God.[23] For Carl Henry, Tillich is to be criticized because he states that the metaphysical element alone and not history is the basis of theology.[24]

Tillich is further criticized for his tendency toward pantheism in his doctrine of God. God is seen as more immanent than transcendent. There are few moral attributes mentioned in regard to God. The personality of God is not brought out in the way which is in accord with the classical Christian tradition.[25]

(5) *Views of creation and the fall.* There is considerable dispute about Tillich's identification of the fall with creation. Tillich tries to protect himself in this regard because of his emphasis upon man's freedom. There is also

the problem of the idea that nature fell with man. For Thatcher, Tillich has difficulties when he relates too closely man's "fall" to the "fall" of the world. What about nature before the appearance and fall of man? Was it not fallen long before mankind had a place in it? Is the world fallen only from the point of view of man's distorted relationship to it, or is it also fallen in itself? Do not flaws, suffering, and disorder in the natural world show us that estrangement from essence is an indelible characteristic of the very existence of the natural world?

Another problem for Tillich, according to Thatcher, is that the essential goodness of creation never extends beyond pure potentiality. Whatever God creates is not *actual*. Thus creation, in Tillich's view, seems to be some sort of realm "in-between" the Creator and the creation which exists. God creates in "essential goodness." But this is not the same as existence. As existence, creation is not good but estranged. This does not seem to be consistent with the classical Christian doctrine that creation, at least initially, existed and was good.

A further question raised by Thatcher relates to *how*, for Tillich, essences "fall." Can they fall if they do not exist? Moreover, if God is Being-itself, he creates essence, and if essences are related to finitude, does God participate in finitude? How does God participate in estrangement if estrangement is evil and involves separation from God? These basic problems arise from the fact that existence, for Tillich, is not the object of God's creative activity and is therefore not essentially good.[26]

(6) *View of salvation.* In relation to Tillich's doctrine of salvation, there is too much emphasis upon man's *essential* relationship to God and not enough on the grace that is related to the objective work of Jesus Christ. There is a danger that Tillich confuses the Spirit of Jesus Christ with the spirit of man. McKelway states that Tillich confuses man's essential creative being with the New Being. For Osborne, Tillich teaches that the gift of grace is little different from the gift of creation. This tends toward a monistic view. Man in essence is given all possibilities.[27]

(7) *View of the demonic.* Tillich's idea of the demonic and the Devil is rooted in Luther's view of the ontological polarities in the depth of the divine life. Eric Rust claims that the more traditional concept of Satan as a personal form of rebellion against God avoids both monism and dualism and some of the problems created by Tillich's view.[28] Dale Moody thinks that it is better to affirm that the Devil belongs neither to the nature of God nor man and that he is both subjective and objective. The final victory over the Devil is found in the victorious Christ of the biblical faith. Locating the Devil in the nature of God or man makes this victory impossible.[29]

(8) *Views of history and the kingdom of God.* In regard to Tillich's view of history and the kingdom of God, a number of criticisms have been voiced. Carl Braaten finds a problem with his interpretation of the kingdom.

When Tillich turned to the transhistorical side of the kingdom, he applied a concept of transcendence that is too close to Platonic mysticism. According to Braaten, at the transhistorical level the symbol of the kingdom of God merges and passes over into the symbol of Eternal Life. The eschatological image of the end of history is elevated into the permanently present "eternal now." This is a door which lets in a transcendental mysticism that deprives the mode of the future of its meaning.

For Braaten, Tillich was right in stressing transcendence. But Tillich had conceptual difficulties in handling the idea of the future end of history. He sought to ease these difficulties by switching to the space-controlled thinking of mysticism. But by so doing Tillich loses real transcendence since this space-controlled mysticism passes over into the immanence of the "eternal now" or the permanent present. According to Braaten, transcendence can be better symbolized by the "future before us." This approach emphasizes the mystery of the power of the future in relation to the past and the present.

Braaten further criticizes Tillich's view of Christ as the center of history by maintaining that Tillich never attained a truly eschatological conception of history. For Braaten, history can be interpreted as a whole and its meaning can be disclosed only from the end. Christ should be seen as the *end* of history. To call Christ the *center* of history means that the center of gravity lies in the past. The real presence of Christ in the church is thus understood as "the presence of the past in the present." This view betrays Tillich's noneschatological conception of the reality of Christ in the world today, according to Braaten.[30]

A similar criticism of Tillich is expressed by John R. Stumme. He maintains that Tillich's basic Christological category of "center" is essentially dictated by his ontology. The symbol of center not only lacks New Testament support but also fails to express the forward direction of eschatology.[31]

McKelway sees Tillich moving in the development of his *Systematic Theology* (from Volume II to Volume III) toward a concentration on Christ as the beginning and end of all God's ways and works. As a Barthian, McKelway states that this development of Tillich's thought should have made it clear to Tillich that the task of theology is not to discover what the kingdom of God means in terms of *our* history, but to proclaim what our history means in the light of the kingdom of God.[32]

(9) *Views of life beyond death, and Eternal Life.* One of the more controversial areas in Tillich's thought relates to his view of life beyond death, and of Eternal Life. Russell Aldwinckle points out Tillich's ambiguity in reference to the relation of the temporal to Eternal Life. He has difficulty with Tillich's statement that "eternity transcends temporality and with it the experienced character of self-consciousness." Tillich also states that without time and change in time, subject and object would merge into

each other and this would be similar to a state of stupor. Tillich uses this analogy to state that self-conscious life in Eternal Life is not what it is in temporal life.[33] Ferré is worried by this analogy for he thinks that the "stupor" concept might imply that man has some participation in being which does not have the full sense of personal persistence and fellowship.[34]

In all fairness it should be stated that Tillich does leave room for mystery in this area. He implies that in some way self-consciousness will be continued in eternity in a renewed and changed manner.

Aldwinckle suggests that the present limitations of space and time could be overcome without our being taken completely and altogether out of some space-time framework which would be necessary to our continued existence as real and distinct individuals. This could be true no matter how profound our communion is with each other through the indwelling of the divine love in us. Heaven would be a created sphere in which the distinctions between Creator and creature would remain real and significant, however profound the communion of love may be. Heaven could be a created space-time of a dimension which would avoid the incautious talk about a heaven which could be reached by an astronaut.

At the very least, affirms Aldwinckle, we cannot abandon the Christian hope that we exist after death as real persons, and that we have communion with God, and with each other, without losing our individuality. The Christian hope also affirms that our relationship with God and one another depends on the basic fact of being "in Christ." If we are assured of these truths, says Aldwinckle, then we can be content to be agnostic about details. However, if the agnosticism is total, then the Christian hope has evaporated and in the words of Paul "we are of all men most to be pitied." [35]

David Roberts points out that there is a problem in relation to the way in which Tillich's universalism can be combined with his concept of freedom.[36] Aldwinckle also points out that freedom assumes the real responsibility of men, and therefore the genuine possibility of their final repudiation of God. For Aldwinckle, the correlate of man's freedom and consequent responsibility is the Christian's responsibility to remind men, as he reminds himself, that it is man's divinely given prerogative to shape his own destiny for good or bad, even though God has gone to the uttermost limits of sacrificial love to lead him to a decision for abundant and eternal life rather than death.[37]

B. *Representative Strengths*

1. Tillich's approach to questions of meaning and truth is *practical* and *existential*. He was concerned with man's problems in existence and with the answer to these problems which is found in God as Being-itself, the New Being, and the Spirit overcoming the split between essence and existence. His thought had an urgent, practical, and existential character. As

a thinker, he was more concerned with the existential problems of individuals and the dynamics of alienation in society than with the theoretical analysis of being.[38]

2. His idea of the latent and manifest church provided him with a *positive approach to world religions* and to quasi-religions. He saw a fundamental *a priori* kinship between the finite and the infinite without which religious response would be impossible. He saw a finality in Christianity and yet saw its continuity with other religions. He found religious responses in different types of groups such as secular quasi-religion and atheistic Hinayana Buddhism.

3. One of Tillich's strengths was his ability to *express the traditional teachings of Christianity in new ways* which appealed to many people, especially to intellectuals. He spoke and wrote in a self-consciously sophisticated and academic language which was very appropriate because he lived in and largely ministered to an academic community or to those with academic backgrounds. He sought to address himself primarily to the cultured despisers of religion.

Tillich stood in a theological tradition that emphasizes that preaching and communication of the Word are of primary importance. He sought to reach the religiously illiterate and alienated. He tried to forge a new language for the communication of the Christian faith in the modern world. To achieve these purposes, he developed a profoundly skillful and articulate system of theological rhetoric.[39]

As a communicator, Tillich realized that in religious knowledge, imagination is central.[40] He understood intuitively that if one wishes to influence mass attitudes and behavior, symbols are more important than rational discourse. He saw that the clash between ideologies is the clash between different symbols and their adequacy to express man's deepest longings and desires. As the chief "ideologue" of the Religious Socialist movement and later as a theologian, Tillich was concerned with propaganda. The difficulty that academic philosophers and theologians have had in understanding Tillich's work is partly because he was a propagandist, both in the sense of creating and circulating new symbols such as *kairos,* the demonic, and the New Being, and in the sense of being an important opinion-maker and molder of people's ideas.[41]

A helpful book by Laswell, Casey, and Smith on propaganda and promotional activities states that the task of the propagandist is to redefine the responses toward certain objects by the management of the available supply of symbols. A high degree of generality is essential to popular appeal. Symbols must be sufficiently vague to enable the individual to transfer his private loves and hates, hopes and fears to the slogans and catchwords of the new movement being presented.[42]

Tillich had limited access to the mass media and was not concerned

with the deliberate manipulation of people's attitudes, but there is no doubt
that he was seriously concerned to persuade people to change their attitudes
and behavior. The vagueness, generality, and element of deliberate mystification that characterizes Tillich's doctrine of symbolism is not accidental.
His primary concern was to promote a new understanding of the Christian
world-view or philosophy of life. He thus sought to bring new life to Christian
symbols and to create new symbols. He wanted to reexpress Christianity
in ways more understandable to groups which had not been reached in
our culture. He sought new ways to talk of God. It is obvious that Tillich's
new vision of being and meaning appealed to many people and seemed
to help to sustain and reconstruct the psychological and moral structure
of their inner world.[43]

4. Tillich developed a number of special doctrines such as the Protestant
Principle as instruments for the *critique of human culture*. He derived the
Protestant Principle from the classic Pauline and Lutheran doctrine of justification through faith. This principle rejected forms of heteronomy represented by the doctrines of papal infallibility and certain forms of
fundamentalism as well as by the self-complacent autonomy represented
by secular humanism. This principle is applied as a protest against the
identification of our ultimate concern with any creation of the church, such
as the biblical writings and the liturgical and theological traditions of the
church and church history. The Protestant Principle called for a theonomy
which transcends both autonomy and heteronomy.[44]

C. *Representative Contributions*

1. *The positive relationship between religion and culture.* Ian Thompson
indicates that he first became interested in Paul Tillich because he read
his writings as an undergraduate student while wrestling with the problem
of how to achieve an integrated vision in relation to science, religion, art,
and philosophy. Tillich's faith in the ultimate significance and possible
synthesis of all forms of the human quest for meaning in personal cultural
life excited Thompson and encouraged him to explore Tillich's work further.
For Thompson, it became apparent that Tillich's thought had continuing
relevance for our times and, in spite of its difficulty, warranted careful reexamination.[45]

Raymond Bulman contends that Tillich's overall theology of culture,
his critique of secular humanism, and his outlines for a theonomous cultural
situation are essentially positive, profound, and filled with rich insights.
Theonomy, for example, is a fertile, philosophical concept. Tillich sees
the theonomous approach as the foundation for the struggle for a truly
human society. Theonomy presents an alternative to the humanistic, secular-
minded person, who cannot accept the alternatives of an authoritarian religion or a shallow secularism.[46] Paul Lehmann states that no Protestant

theologian addressed himself with greater passion to religion and culture.[47]

2. *Constructive approach to theological method.* John Clayton and Carl Heinz Ratschow agree that Tillich's greatest contribution to the constructive work of theology is involved in his methodology rather than in his dogmatics proper.[48] There was a celebrated debate between Barth and Tillich on the nature of theology, which centers on the question of whether it is kerygmatic or apologetic. In the broadest sense this debate is about the nature of the communication of the Christian faith to the contemporary world. In the narrow sense, it is a debate about the relative merits of two different kinds of theological rhetoric. For Barth it is either/or. For Tillich it is both/and. Tillich wants to have it both ways, and in a sense gets it both ways. This is the genius of his system.

Tillich's concern for correlation and the theology of culture reflects the common Protestant preoccupation with preaching, apologetics, and communication. Actually the kerygmatic and apologetic methods in theology could be described as two styles of preaching or two sides of apologetics. Tillich states that apologetic theology is answering theology. It answers the questions implied in the situation in the power of the eternal message and with the means provided by the situation whose questions it answers. This is a paraphrase of what he later calls the method of correlation on which the structure of his theology is built. However, it could equally well be taken as a description of his sermons.[49]

It has been suggested that Tillich's concept of correlation was strongly influenced by Luther's idea of law and gospel. Man is under the law. Law is similar to the question, and philosophy is analogous to the law. Then man is under the gospel which is the answer to the questions raised when man is under the law.[50]

3. *Dynamic approach to history.* James Luther Adams affirms that Tillich's interpretation of history is the most elaborate and substantial interpretation to be worked out in the history of Protestant philosophical theology.[51] Tillich shares with nineteenth-century Idealism the concern to transform history and reality by revolutionary ideals. He identifies himself with a philosophy of history and a theory of alienation derived from Christian existentialist and Marxist sources.[52]

Langdon Gilkey sees in Tillich's philosophy of history the contribution of hope that is latent in his theological vision of history and its divine ground. Tillich has a vision of the unconditioned and living divine power and meaning permeating and renewing as well as judging all creatures, life, and historical existence.[53]

4. *Realistic view of social theology.* Ronald Stone sees Tillich's basic vision of radical social thought as a springboard for a theory of social reality that finds meaning in the Christian faith as correlated with social

welfare capitalism. Tillich was correct in stating that social philosophy could neither consent to Marx nor ignore him. Tillich saw social welfare capitalism as a stage on the way to a society in which human creativity is given more opportunity for fulfillment than in any alternative we in the West have yet seen.

It is true that his American writings on social theology fought primarily against the dehumanizing forces in the society rather than advocating a restructuring of society. Stone conjectures that if the seminaries in Tillich's time had contained more Third World students who were conscious revolutionaries, more blacks, or more radical feminists, his theology would have been written with them more in mind. In the latter years of his life he remained a theologian of the Northern hemisphere wrestling with the questions of skepticism. However, writings from his earlier German period when he had the proletarian view in mind should be helpful to North Americans who want to enter into dialogue with Third World theologians.[54]

5. *Comprehensiveness and power as an apologist.* The apologetic power of Tillich's system is impressive, especially to those inclined toward the mystical side of Protestant theology but who also desire a realistic ethic. Stone suggests that there are other theological traditions, and it is proper for theologians in those traditions to write their own apologetics. They may produce systems that have a higher Christology or that rely more on biblical terminology. But, for Stone, it is doubtful that they can articulate a more powerful presentation of God as "Being-itself" or as "Spiritual Presence" than has Tillich.[55]

The fact that Tillich was a "participation" theologian means that his work has a "period piece" quality of a planned obsolescence. His writings were very much part and parcel of his times. He interpreted his time and contributed to the formation of his time. He constantly rethought his basic concepts, making it somewhat difficult to comprehend his thought. This is both a strength and a limitation.[56]

For Stone and many others Tillich's system stands at this point as the most adequate expression of twentieth-century systematic theological work. Despite particular problems, the beauty and power of the system are evident. From Stone's perspective, beneath the structure of Tillich's system stands a Christian who is grasped by the question and reality of God but who will not let go of the modern situation.[57] A similar evaluation is given by John Macquarrie. For Macquarrie, Tillich's statement of the Christian faith surpasses any other Protestant theologian of our time for its comprehensiveness, illuminating power, and its openness to the contemporary world.[58]

Ian Thompson states that if Tillich's *Systematic Theology* is a masterpiece, it is so because of the questions that it provokes and the stimulus it gives to new lines of research and discovery rather than because of any definitive answers which it gives. Ratschow contends that Tillich went beyond the questions of his time toward their solution. Tillich is dead, but his system remains. Whether or not it will finally be regarded as a masterpiece, we cannot ignore it, for it is surely one of the most significant contributions to Christian thought in this century.[59]

Appendix:
Special Topics

Introduction

As indicated in the biographical section, Tillich created or at least developed and elaborated a number of distinctive concepts. In addition, there are certain topics related to Tillich's life and thought which need special attention. In most cases these topics have been referred to and discussed in some detail in the biographical and systematic sections. In this part certain aspects of these topics which call for particular attention will be discussed.

Kairos, Religious Socialism, the Demonic, Theonomy, Belief-ful Realism, Culture, and the Arts

A. Kairos

Although a systematic discussion of *kairos* in its theoretical aspects is found in the section on "History and the Quest for the Kingdom of God," it should be helpful to see this concept in historical perspective.

Tillich saw the period in Germany and Europe after World War I as a time to develop new forms. Thus, he began to develop his famous *"kairos"* concept between 1919–1926. The concept of *kairos* comes from the New Testament where it means "right time" in contrast to *chronos*, or "formal time." The moments of absolute demand and opportunity are the moments of *kairos*. In these years which Tillich considered as *kairos* years he lived with ecstatic intensity. For Tillich, the *kairos* period was a time when the political and cultural world and Christianity could be transformed simultaneously into something effective and vigorous. He saw socialism and Christianity as spiritual streams moving to unite in a new wave of destiny in this *kairos* time. This vision was widely circulated with his publication in 1926 of *The Religious Situation*. But even by 1926 the early urgency of the *kairos* had given way to the resolution to see change over a longer period.

Tillich viewed the ruin of the European world by World War I as a *kairos*, creating a time of eschatological tension.[1] At stake is rescue before the ruin. Just as the Protestant principle is grace as well as judgment, so the *kairos* represents the emergence of new forms of meaning and life amidst the death of the old. *Kairos* is a turning. The old is abandoned or transformed. There are new possibilities in all areas.[2]

In these years Tillich battled against everything in bourgeois society—science, technics, economy, esthetics, and religion.[3] The *kairos* principle denied to the old bourgeois structures and forms all claims of absoluteness. These old forms which have come into crisis are to be replaced by new theonomous structures of meaning.[4] One student called Tillich an "idealist anarchist" in the early days of the Weimar Republic. He was also known as a "Red Socialist" in those days.[5] Tillich was caught between the conservative Christian traditions of the nineteenth century and the new radical creativity. His idea of theonomy beyond autonomy and heteronomy would not let him side with either autonomy (freedom and rebellion) or heteronomy (giving absolute devotion to a limited cause). He must transcend both.[6]

From 1926 on, the urgency of the *kairos* of this time declined somewhat. The proletariat did not prove to have the creative vitality which belonged to *kairos*. Tillich did not, however, give up the idea of *kairos*. It continued to have a place to the end in his systematic thought. Moments of *kairos* are rare. Some theologians and philosophers saw the Nazis as a part of the *kairos*. Against them Tillich argued that the cross of Christ was and is the absolute criterion of *kairos*. The Nazis were demonic, not theonomous.

Even though men must be alert to await periods of *kairos*, Tillich wants to avoid a dualism of the profane and the sacred. Such a dualism results in a profanation of cultural life and a primitivizing of religious life. Instead, as indicated above, Tillich wants a theonomous autonomy or an immanent dynamism. God must be seen as the ultimate source of both the "yes" and the "no" of historical development and as seeking to lead men to a transcending synthesis.

B. *Religious Socialism*

It was around the idea of *kairos* that the Religious-Socialist movement developed. Tillich and his colleagues believed that a *kairos* was at hand in the post-World War I situation of central Europe. Tillich saw positive religious possibilities in the midst of a situation of political and social chaos. He and his colleagues worked for a theonomous (God-centered) culture in which the breach between the religious and secular order would be closed.[7]

Religious Socialism as a movement is identified with neither the church nor a political party. It affirms religion to socialism and expresses religious reservations about socialism. It is an attempt to reunite the sacramental basis of society with a historical-critical consciousness.[8] Tillich wanted a future social order structured according to the socialist principles and empowered with the meaning-giving import of Christianity. Tillich saw socialism as the only hope for Europe.[9]

In economics, Tillich was close to the young Marx in his desire to overcome the alienation of the worker from technology or the product. On the other hand, he never considered Marxist-Socialism as a live option for the Christian faith because of its dogmatic rigidity and religious pretensions. Another criticism of Marxist-Socialism was that this view ended the dialectics of history with the communist revolution. For Tillich, Russia was not a model for the Germans.[10]

Yet, Tillich did not want to neglect the class struggle, for he saw it as the only hope for the isolated and hopeless workers. He thought that the system of production which was fundamental to capitalism was a threat to human meaning. But he criticized the Marxists, who deduced all aspects of culture from the system of production. The workers needed hope, and a plan to act against the demonic forces that enslaved them.

In this connection we must remember that Tillich was influenced in his socialist position by the Institute for Social Research at the University of Frankfurt. The Institute was humanist-Marxist. When Tillich moved to the United States, he was to follow Eric Fromm, an institute member, in incorporating more of the Freudian perspective while playing down the Marxist element. Tillich found little interest in America in Marxist terminology and social revolution.

Tillich's most important book written during the German period was probably *The Socialist Decision*. This book gives expression to his deep political commitments and was a response to the political situation of 1932. In this book Tillich attacks the roots of Nazism and proposes a reformulation of socialism. Nazism is grounded in the myth of origin. The alternative is a view based on the prophetic criticism of the myth of origin. Western capitalism is not an adequate attack on the Nazi myth of origin. The answer for Tillich is Religious Socialism which is the inheritor of a prophetic criticism rooted in Judaism, the New Testament, and the Reformation.

The goal of Religious Socialism is the rational utilization of the earthly possibilities for human development—first on a national basis and eventually on a global basis. Unfortunately, Hitler reached the masses of workers before the socialists and translated their dissatisfaction, frustration, and misery into his vision of the thousand-year Reich.

For Tillich, unrestrained capitalism as he knew it in Germany encouraged war, produced sterility of human character, ruthless pursuit of rationalized profit-taking, and social dislocation in the exploited classes.[11]

C. The Demonic

The concept of "demonic" became an important emphasis in Tillich's thought. This concept was originally developed in a 1926 essay which was included in his book, *The Interpretation of History*. The demonic is the form-destroying eruption of the creative basis of things. There is no independent eruption of the abyss such as a personal Satan. Rather, there is a unity of the form-creating and form-destroying qualities of life in Being-itself. Everything that comes into being takes on a form. But in everything there is also the tendency to break out of a being's own form to realize infinity and make a prideful assertion. Being-itself is not static but active, uniting form-creation and form-destruction in the Divine Life. Tillich is indebted to Jakob Böhme and Friedrich Schelling for many parts of this concept.

In the 1926 essay on the demonic, Tillich portrays capitalism and nationalism as the major demonic movements of that time. Both capitalism and nationalism express the vitality of creative life that produces helpful forms of existence. However, they both contain also the drive to destroy form and to deprive people of their essential humanity. Total resistance to the demonic is required with the assurance that the demonic will only be vanquished ultimately.[12]

D. Theonomy, Belief-ful Realism, Culture, and the Arts

1. *Definition of theonomy.* Although Tillich did not originate the term theonomy, it became a crucial idea in his thought and permeated his entire theological inquiry.[13]

(1) *Theonomy as compared to autonomy and heteronomy.* a. In autonomy there are two elements. One element is *"nomos,"* law or structured form which should be related to its *unconditional* depth. The second element is *"autos,"* the self-assertion of the *conditioned,* which in its emphasis on form loses its unconditional depth. Thus autonomy can be defined as both obedience to and revolt against the "unconditional." Autonomy tends to emphasize form to the exclusion of import or depth.[14]

The difficulty with a self-sufficient or purely secular autonomy is that it creates a void. This void will eventually be filled by something finite and limited which is the essence of idolatry.[15] Religious heteronomy provoked the autonomy of the Renaissance and the Enlightenment. This Enlightenment type of autonomy later led to naturalism and revolutionary movements.[16]

b. Heteronomy imposes a strange (*heteros*) law (*nomos*) upon the intellect by issuing commands from "outside" as to how reason should grasp and shape reality. It affirms that man is unable to act according to universal human reason and must be subjected to a law which is superior to him. Heteronomy is thus the authority claimed or exercised by a finite being in the name of the infinite. An example would be the attempt of religion to dominate autonomous cultural activity from the outside. Such a religious heteronomy was developed by the Catholicism of the late Middle Ages and later by Protestant Orthodoxy. Sometimes absolute churches or absolute states even exercised terror.[17]

(2) *Theonomy as the union of the truth in autonomy and heteronomy.* Theonomy recognized God (*theos*) as the law (*nomos*) for both the structure and ground. This means that autonomous reason is united with its own depth. Theonomy overcomes the contradiction between empty autonomy and imposed totalitarian heteronomy. Theonomy constitutes the higher unity of the two. Theonomy is autonomy driven to its depths.[18]

Theonomy is the balanced concern for import or ultimate meaning that never destroys the form of content. The challenge of theonomy is to struggle through the problem of autonomy toward a culture and society that is filled with transcendent import. If Spiritual Community is made manifest in its midst, the church is a primary place where theonomy becomes actual.[19]

2. *Theonomy as related to artistic experience and the artistic model.*

(1) *The origin of Tillich's concept of theonomy.* Tillich speaks frequently of the influence of his artistic or aesthetic experience in molding his concept of theonomy. In this artistic emphasis he was no doubt influenced by Schelling who had developed a very intricate philosophy of aesthetics. In this philosophy Schelling considered art to be the door to reality. But Tillich explicitly states that what he says about theonomy was primarily derived from his own experience in the area of the arts.[20]

(2) *Art as expression of ultimate meaning.* In Tillich's experience, the enjoyment of art was not merely an aesthetic experience in the narrow sense of the term. Rather, for Tillich, art had the force of expressing meaning. Art reveals pure being or unconditioned import in the particular form of things. The eternal meaning of paintings, for example, is not just to be identified with the subject matter or content of the pictures but with the dimension of depth which shines through the paintings.[21]

According to Tillich, art without import is without style. It is either abstract formalism or formless arbitrariness. The material used by the given artist is of no special significance. A picture of an apple by Cézanne or a tree by Van Gogh may convey theonomy and sacredness. On the other hand, a picture of Jesus by Uhde or Hoffman, Raphael or Rubens may have nothing but distance from sacred import or religious depth.[22]

For Tillich, it is the task of a theology of culture to investigate and describe the process whereby meaning or an ultimate religious import is expressed in spheres and creations of culture. The concern of theology is not primarily with form but with import. The import, however, is expressed through forms, though it may have to burst or shatter the form. The theologian is to indicate the presence or absence of import in the actual expressions of art and point to possible fulfillments. The theologian must also seek to set forth a normative, systematic outline of a religiously imbued culture or a theonomous society. The high Middle Ages had some approximation to this idea.

(3) *Examples of theonomy in relation to representative art forms.*

a. *Domestic architecture.* An example of this theology of culture is Tillich's interpretation of domestic architecture at the dedication of a house in 1933. In the dwelling house man creates for himself the space that is *his* space. Through the house a part of existence is made homelike and rendered familiar. This space thus demands to be intellectually apprehended and organized in its proper context of reference.

The space of the animal sphere is the nest or den or cave. Man can overcome the limited movement space of the animal. In creating his space, man takes into it the images of plant and animal existence in the forms and colors of furniture and walls. But he also opens himself to the space of the world through light. For example, the window encloses a space but also lets in infinite space. The limitation of the cave and den is mitigated through a relation to infinite space represented by the window, the balcony, the tower, the court, and the garden. A person's outlook on life will determine whether the limited or unlimited dimension will dominate.[23]

In Dresden, the Tillichs secured the services of a professional at the Academy of Arts and Crafts to help them remodel their apartment. The remodeled apartment was characterized by light colors, a style of lightness in furniture and an extensive use of lamps. A similar approach was made in remodeling their apartment in Frankfurt.[24]

b. *Religious dance.* Another example of theology of culture is the development of the art of the dance. Tillich cites the Laban school of dance which developed ritual and group dances. The expressive gestures of the dancers revealed metaphysical meanings.[25]

c. *Secular art.* In an address at the opening of an art exhibition in Berlin in 1930, Tillich lamented the fact that in the exhibition the secular art objects (in contrast to the religious art) were penetrating and impressive. He noted that the Art Association had taken up the struggle for a new, contemporary, real art form that had the power of witness. Religion, in its institutional expression, had become a sort of cultural residue and had not maintained a vital relation to the driving tendencies of the age. At best the religious art depicted an ideal, finite reality. The reference to the eternal was seldom successfully expressed.[26]

d. *Religious art.* As already mentioned, in the 1920s in Germany, authentic religious art for Tillich took the form of art which expressed ultimate concern. This was in contrast to religious art which used particular Christian symbols related to Christ, Mary, and the saints, but which did not express ultimate concern. For Tillich, a religious style is one that is characterized by something always breaking out of the depths to the surface. Whenever this happens the style is religious even if it does not depict religious content.

Tillich does emphasize that there are some pictures of explicit religious subjects which do have depth and what he calls religious style. There were pictures of this type long before modern time. He refers to El Greco's

"Crucifixion" and Grünewald's famous "Crucifixion." In more modern times he mentions Sutherland's "Crucifixion" and the religious paintings of Nolde and Roualt.[27]

Architecture and liturgical art. Protestantism has had difficulty in expressing theonomy through explicit Christian symbols in the area of visual arts, including church architecture. The predominance of the "ear" over against the "eye" in Protestant thought has resulted in more emphasis on expressing theonomy through music and poetry than through architecture, painting, or sculpture.

In the period of the Reformation the existing Catholic churches were taken over and subjected to more or less radical purges of sculptural and pictorial symbols to make them more congenial to Protestant thought. Tensions arose over the style of these acquired buildings (Romanesque, Gothic, Renaissance, and Baroque) and the symbolic needs of the Protestant churches.

Protestantism, as with Christianity in general, is not bound to a special house. In certain situations a house must be used for Christian purposes when its architecture is not appropriate. But if a new church house is built, sensitive Protestant leaders, such as Tillich, urge that the style should be appropriate to the Protestant understanding of Christianity. Symbols such as the cross are present in every period in Christian history, but the style used to display these symbols should change.[28]

According to Tillich, the principles of creativity and ethics demand that new church buildings should be stylistically contemporary (although related to the past), and honest in self-expression. To be "real" art, church architecture needs fresh, imaginative creativity. Gothic was once artistically vital but now belongs to another historical epoch. Each age *must* develop its own style and idiom. Contemporary artists must have the courage not to retreat into empty formalism, traditional conventionalism, or dishonest, saccharine prettiness.[29] An artistic style is honest only if it expresses the real situation of the artists and the cultural period to which it belongs. Of course, we can participate in the artistic style of the past insofar as the people of that time were honestly expressing the encounter which they had with God, man, and the world.[30]

Tillich suggests two fundamental elements which distinguish a Protestant church service. One is the predominance of the Word over the sacrament. The second element is the predominance of the congregation over the liturgical leader or leaders. These concepts will receive greater or less emphasis depending upon the denomination.

In the architectural realm, the Protestant perspective abolishes any kind of hierarchical dualism between laymen and clergy because of the Protestant doctrine of the priesthood of all believers. It is essentially un-Protestant to retain a central aisle leading to a removed altar as the holy place. The members of the congregation ideally should look at each other and the minister should be in the midst of the congregation for preaching and leading the liturgy. The altar should preserve the character of a table for the sacramental meal in which, ideally, all members participate.

Tillich points out that the quality of the church building is more than the appropriate arrangement of seating and liturgical furnishings. The architect must deal with the conflict of two religious principles. One principle is to convey the idea of the distance between a Holy God and finite man. This is the Protestant principle. The other is the principle that God has revealed himself in a personal life, at a definite time, in a definite place. This principle of incarnation justifies the expression of God through finite objects. For Tillich, the latter principle is called catholic substance.

In employing these principles, Protestantism must follow definite criteria. First, nothing can be admitted that furthers idolatry or ideas and attitudes of magic. The vigorous opposition of the Reformers to the transubstantiation theory of the Lord's Supper was the belief that it was a regression into the magical identification of the Divine with the bearer of the Divine. Individual, figurative pieces are too indicative of ancient idol worship. On the liturgical level, all kinds of signs (objects, gestures, garb) are often elevated into ultimate significance. Murals are more appropriate than statues because murals are elements of architecture rather than objects of veneration. A sculptural organization of a wall or door might also be used in a Protestant church.

Tillich suggests that it is inadvisable to open the building too widely toward surrounding nature. Opaque glass or glass brick might be acceptable. Stained glass, seen as an architectural element, sheds a deeper and more mystical or numinal illumination upon the interior of the church.

If representation is used, a naturalistic or sentimental style should not be employed. Great expressiveness can be achieved by means of lines that indicate bodily reality without showing this reality in an overly elaborate detail. According to Tillich, the expressionistic style of the early twentieth century is in many ways still contemporary.[31]

Liturgical art which is traditionalistic and manneristic is "bad" art. In contrast, the handling of "religious" material by such contemporary painters as Rouault, Rattner, and Chagall is authentic and explicitly expressive art. Tillich calls for as full and rich a symbolization as possible without lapsing into idolatry. Symbols cannot be taken literally but are accepted as that which points beyond the symbolical material.[32]

For Tillich, the cross is the most powerful and meaningful symbol of the Christian church. But when it is used, the simple, nonnaturalistic cross in an expressive rather than a realistic style is preferable.

Today, a genuine Protestant church architecture is possible, perhaps for the first time in history. Tillich insists that *only* by the creation of new forms can Protestant churches achieve an honest expression of their faith. This expression should be made real, even if many experiments are necessary.[33]

(4) *Theonomy and technology.* As a theologian of culture, Tillich points out that technology is neutral. The inmost drive of the true technician is his awareness of the fact that through him new forms of creative possibilities come into existence. But technology can also bring a new emptiness of meaning and harmfulness to nature. Technology must be redeemed.

The possibilities and danger of technology can be seen in the modern city. In the beginning the technological city was seen as a liberation by man into a new utopia. But the technological city has also become a symbol of new threats. It has become rigid. It has removed us from the soil and vital forces and thus has brought on emptiness. Naturalism and Impressionism, for Tillich, with their self-sufficient finitude, were the products of the capitalist temper of a technological society.[34]

3. *The significance of Expressionism.*

(1) *Expressionism in painting.* Expressionism in painting was a revolution against the realism of the nineteenth century. It was a rebellion against the naturalistic-critical, as well as against the idealistic-conventional wing of realism. Expressionism went beyond the limits of the subjective-impressionistic realism from which it came.[35]

Impressionism is the style of the individualistic middle classes of the nineteenth century. Monet and Degas see every individual subordinated to the primacy of nature in its surfaces—not in its depth. Impressionism uses light to unite men and things. This light illumines the surface. The form is primary.[36]

In philosophy, Expressionism was represented by Nietzsche and in social thought by Karl Marx. In painting, Expressionism brought a new depth, a new inner experience of things, a new import, and thus a new style. The main emphasis was on depth.

Tillich sees this expressionistic revolt in the painting of such artists as Cézanne and Van Gogh. Cézanne battled with the form that depicted self-sufficient finitude and restored to things their real metaphysical meaning. Van Gogh revealed the creative dynamics in light and color. The Scandinavian Munch showed the cosmic dread present in nature and mankind. Picasso's "Guernica" is also an important painting in this regard. The individual forms of things were dissolved in favor of objective, metaphysical expression. The Abyss of Being was evoked in lines, colors, and plastic forms.

Some of the artists turned back to older, primitive and exotic forms in which the inner expressive force of reality was still to be found untamed. For Cubism and Futurism the dissolution of the natural form of things took on a geometric character. The planes, lines, and cubes acquired an almost mystical quality.[37] The picture by Braque entitled "Table" is an example of this cubist development. Tillich includes pictures such as Chagall's "River without Edges" and Chirico's "Toys of a Prince" in this category.

Tillich also notes that many painters of earlier centuries had a religious style of depth even though they are not expressionists in the modern sense.[38] For example, he found metaphysical import in the mosaics of Ravenna, Michelangelo's paintings in the Sistine Chapel, and in the portraits of the older Rembrandt. Even though these works have conditioned meaning in themselves, they reveal unconditional meaning. Any painting will have form and subject matter, but if it has "greatness" it will point beyond itself to an eternal meaning or import which is called religion.[39]

(2) *Expressionism and disruption of form.* As early as a 1919 address, Tillich stresses the way expressionistic painters have distorted natural "form" (he seems to mean line, color, shape, composition) to express more intensely the inner and largely hidden "meaning" of the object represented. For Tillich, this is done most perfectly in Expressionism. The aim of these Expressionists may be positive and affirmative, but in Tillich's view the form-destroying aspect of their work tends to dominate the form-creating aspect. Content or outward appearance is regarded as a barrier to be broken through. Beauty is not central. An example is Munch's "Scream."

For Tillich, in the depths of all existence dwells horror, and this horror seizes us in the paintings of the expressionists. They seem to have a sense of cosmic guilt which is a guilt of sheer existence. Expressionism seems to raise problems of existence, but it is not capable of answering these problems. It must be stated, however, that Expressionism is struggling for the answer and this gives to these paintings a religious quality.

It is not the subject matter of a work which makes it religious art; rather it is the import which is brought to expression in it.[40] At this point it is well to remember that Tillich defines religion as "the experience of being grasped unconditionally and inescapably by that which is the supporting ground and the consuming abyss of our existence." A religious experience is a shattering, transforming eruption of that which is more than our existence and which is, therefore, alone able to give to our existence depth, seriousness, import, and meaning.[41]

Cubism, Surrealism and Abstractionism are honest forms of art since modern technical society does tend to swallow up the individual human person as an object among objects. For this reason, Tillich sees importance for these types of art.[42]

(3) *Expressionism in poetry and literature.* Tillich also points out that Rilke's late poetry had depth meaning for him. He speaks of the poetry

of Rilke as having psychoanalytic realism, mystical fullness and a form
charged with metaphysical import. Something of this same metaphysical
import is seen by Tillich in the novels of Franz Kafka.[43]

4. *The significance of "Belief-ful Realism."*

(1) *The rise of Belief-ful Realism.* Expressionism as a specific movement
was short-lived. Its energies began to lag. By the end of the 1920s it
had divided into two main directions. Expressionism's initial restraint gave
way to excess and loss of control, and it yielded to styles of painting in
which there was greater and greater independence from the natural objects
portrayed. These styles became increasingly abstract and nonrepresenta-
tional, although highly disciplined in the use of line, color, and composition.
This development is seen in the work of Kandinsky, Klee, and Albers.

The other direction of Expressionism was toward a more tightly controlled
"realism." This group of realistic artists tried both to recover something
of earlier sorts of Realism and also to fulfill the basic aims of Expressionism.
It is a postexpressionistic and not a preexpressionistic style. There was
no return to an idealizing naturalism. The movement or new style in German
art which most clearly exhibits this twofold approach is called "the new
objectivity." Its proponents included Grosz, Dix, and Max Beckmann. This
approach had some cynicism and resignation, but its positive side expressed
enthusiasm for looking objectively at the immediate reality before looking
for deeper implications. This cynical tendency gradually disappeared, and
there arose a demand for a single, unsophisticated awareness of things.[44]

Tillich maintains that the "new realism" was not interested in the natural
form of things for their own sake. Rather, these forms were seen as exhibiting
power in expressing the profounder levels and the universal significance
of things. This type of art is driving toward a self-transcending realism.
It has a genuinely Protestant character.[45] This course of development in
painting between Expressionism and the New Realism became for Tillich
the symbol of his own development toward what he called "Belief-ful
Realism." [46]

This new approach was to influence Tillich and be used by him. By
1925 he realized that his own earlier efforts had been naively utopian.
This new realization led him, not to despair, but toward this new sense
of realism. With the term, "Belief-ful Realism," Tillich intended to express
his growing concern for the concrete and actual, rather than merely the
abstract and ideal. He stated that he needed a fresh and direct approach
to reality.[47]

(2) *The superiority of Belief-ful Realism to mystical realism and technological realism.* Belief-ful Realism is seen by Tillich to be in sharp opposition
to mystical realism. Mystical realism looks for the "really real" in the
eternal essences which transcend time and empirical reality. It tends to
have unconcern for the significance of the present moment. Tillich was

attracted to the mystical approach in his own emotional structure. It was World War I and the social revolution that followed that freed him from this mystical approach and pointed him toward historical realism.

Tillich also reacted against technological realism which identified the "really real" with the practical utility of finite things. What he sought and found was a realism which was at the same time "belief-ful" or "self-transcending" as well as contemporaneous and concrete. Belief-ful Realism unites both realism and faith. In this perspective, culture must give due attention to the seriousness of the historical process and situation, while at the same time remaining open to the eternal meaning which it contains.[48] There is to be religious depth in historical realism.[49] This approach calls for passion and involvement in the historical situation of the present. It is related to Tillich's concept of the *kairos* which has been discussed in earlier sections of this study. To be aware and responsive to the *kairos* moment is to express "Belief-ful Realism." [50] "Belief-ful Realism" is also to be seen as another expression of Tillich's concept of theonomy.[51]

Abbreviations for Works by Tillich

BR   Biblical Religion and the Search for Ultimate Reality (Chicago: University of Chicago Press, 1955)

CE   Christianity and the Encounter of the World Religions (New York: Columbia University Press, 1963)

CTB   The Courage to Be (New Haven: Yale University Press, 1952)

DF   Dynamics of Faith (New York: Harper and Row, 1957)

EN   The Eternal Now (New York: Charles Scribner's Sons, 1963)

FR   The Future of Religions, ed. by Jerald C. Brauer (New York: Harper & Row, 1966)

HCT   A History of Christian Thought: From Its Judaic and Hellenistic Origins to Existentialism, ed. by Carl E. Braaten (New York: Simon and Schuster, 1967)

IH   The Interpretation of History (New York: Charles Scribner's Sons, 1936)

LPJ   Love, Power and Justice (New York: Oxford University Press, 1954)

MB   Morality and Beyond (New York: Charles Scribner's Sons, 1963)

MSA My Search for Absolutes (New York: Simon and Schuster, 1967)

MTD My Travel Diary: 1936—Between Two Worlds, ed. by Jerald C. Brauer (New York: Harper & Row, 1970)

NB The New Being (New York: Charles Scribner's Sons, 1955)

OB On the Boundary: An Autobiographical Sketch (New York: Charles Scribner's Sons, 1966)

P Perspectives on 19th and 20th Century Protestant Theology, ed. by Carl E. Braaten (New York: Harper & Row, 1967)

PE The Protestant Era (Chicago: University of Chicago Press, 1948)

PolEx Political Expectation, ed., by James Luther Adams (New York: Harper & Row, 1971)

RS The Religious Situation (New York: Meridian Books, 1956)

SD The Socialist Decision (New York: Harper & Row, 1977)

ST Systematic Theology, 3 vols. (Chicago: University of Chicago Press, 1951, 1957, 1963)

TC Theology of Culture, ed. by Robert C. Kimball (New York: Oxford University Press, 1959, 1965)

Other Abbreviations

NAPTS North American Paul Tillich Society

Notes

INTRODUCTION

1. Kenan B. Osborne, *New Being: A Study of the Relationship Between Conditioned and Unconditioned Being According to Paul Tillich* (The Hague: Martinus Nijhoff, 1967), pp. 187, 205.
2. Rollo May, *Paulus: Reminiscences of a Friendship* (New York: Harper and Row, 1973).
3. Hannah Tillich, *From Time to Time* (New York: Stein and Day, 1973).
4. Wilhelm Pauck and Marion Pauck, *Paul Tillich: His Life and Thought* (New York: Harper and Row, 1976).
5. John J. Carey, "Tillich Archives: A Bibliographical and Research Report," *Theology Today* 32 (1975):46.
6. Ibid., p. 55.
7. Ibid., pp. 48, 46; *Newsletter of the NAPTS*, November 1983, p. 5.
8. *Newsletter of the NAPTS*, October 1978, p. 15.
9. Thor Hall, *Systematic Theology Today: State of the Art in North America* (Washington, D.C.: University Press of America, 1978), p. 94.
10. *Newsletter of the NAPTS*, October 1978, pp. 14–15.
11. John R. Stumme, *Socialism in Theological Perspective: A Study of Paul Tillich, 1918–1933*, American Academy of Religion Dissertation Series, no. 21 (Missoula, MT: Scholars Press, 1978), pp. 11, 241, 249, 265.
12. Ronald E. Modras, *Paul Tillich's Theology of the Church* (Detroit: Wayne State University Press, 1976), p. 167–168.

PART ONE: PAUL TILLICH'S LIFE AND PERSPECTIVE

CHAPTER I

1. See *OB, IH, MSA, PE,* and Charles W. Kegley and Robert W. Bretall, eds., *The Theology of Paul Tillich* (New York: McMillan, 1952, 1961, 1964; Revised edition, New York: Pilgrim Press, 1982).

2. David Hopper, *Tillich: A Theological Portrait* (New York: J. B. Lippincott Co., 1968), p. 19, *MSA*, p. 24.

3. May, pp. 39–40.

4. Ronald H. Stone, *Paul Tillich's Radical Social Thought* (Atlanta: John Knox Press, 1980), p. 20.

5. Carl Heinz Ratschow, *Paul Tillich*, trans. by Robert P. Scharlemann (Iowa City, IO: NAPTS, 1980), p. 14.

6. *MSA*, pp. 34–35; Hopper, p. 22.

7. Ratschow, p. 14.

8. *MSA*, p. 29; Hopper, p. 21.

9. *MSA*, p. 29, 30.

10. *MSA*, p. 33; Stone, p. 22; James R. Lyons, ed. *The Intellectual Legacy of Paul Tillich* (Detroit: Wayne State Press, 1969), pp. 101–107.

11. Hopper, p. 29.

12. Stone, p. 20.

13. *MSA*, pp. 37, 38; Stone, p. 23.

14. Stone, pp. 22, 24.

15. Wilhelm Pauck, "To Be or Not to Be: Paul Tillich on the Meaning of Life," *The American Academy of Arts and Sciences Bulletin* XXXIII (November 1979):13; *PE*, XIII, XIV, XV.

16. Ratschow, pp. 15–16, 38.

17. Pauck, "To Be or Not to Be," p. 13.

18. Pauck and Pauck, p. 296.

19. Ibid., pp. 43–46.

20. Stone, p. 35.

21. Pauck and Pauck, pp. 49, 51.

22. Stone, p. 34.

23. Pauck and Pauck, p. 49.

24. Stone, p. 35.

25. Pauck and Pauck, pp. 52–53.

26. Stone, p. 37.

27. Pauck and Pauck, p. 55.

28. Stumme, p. 21.

29. Pauck, "To Be or Not to Be," p. 18.

30. Stone, p. 36.

31. Ratschow, p. 17.

32. Stone, pp. 36–37.

33. Stumme, pp. 20, 56.

34. Ratschow, pp. 18, 20.

35. Pauck and Pauck, pp. 79–80.

36. Stone, p. 36.

37. James Luther Adams, "Words for Paul Tillich," *Harvard Divinity Bulletin* 30 (1966):8.

38. Pauck and Pauck, p. 52.

39. Stone, p. 36.

40. Pauck and Pauck, pp. 75–77.

41. Ratschow, p. 21.

42. Pauck and Pauck, p. 56.

43. Stumme, pp. 56 fn. 43, 21.

44. Pauck and Pauck, pp. 56, 48.

45. Ratschow, p. 21.

46. Stumme, pp. 57, fn. 55, 21.

47. Stone, p. 37.

48. Ibid., pp. 45, 51, *PolEx*, pp. 58–88.

49. Hopper, p. 39.
50. Pauck and Pauck, pp. 80–81.
51. Ratschow, pp. 23–24.
52. Pauck and Pauck, pp. 81–91.
53. Ibid., pp. 95, 98; *MSA*, p. 42.
54. Hopper, p. 66; *MSA*, p. 42.
55. Pauck and Pauck, pp. 96, 97, 98.
56. Ibid., pp. 99, 105, 108.
57. *SD*, p. xvii.
58. Pauck and Pauck, pp. 109, 110.
59. Ibid., pp. 117–18, 120.
60. *SD*, p. xviii.
61. Stumme, p. 46.
62. Stone, pp. 84–85.
63. *SD*, p. xviii.
64. Stone, pp. 63, 67.
65. *SD*, p. xxiii.
66. Stumme, p. 49.
67. Stone, p. 73.
68. Pauck and Pauck, pp. 127–28.
69. Stone, p. 65.
70. Pauck and Pauck, p. 130.
71. Stone, p. 84.
72. Pauck and Pauck, pp. 133–34, 137.
73. Kegley and Bretall, pp. 16, 17.
74. H. Tillich, *From Time to Time*, p. 171.
75. Leslie Gordon Tait, *The Promise of Paul Tillich* (New York: J. B. Lippincott, 1971), p. 20.
76. Pauck and Pauck, pp. 143.
77. Ibid., pp. 150–52, 186.
78. Stone, pp. 109–10.
79. Pauck and Pauck, pp. 152–53.
80. Stone, pp. 88–90.
81. Pauck and Pauck, p. 155.
82. Stone, p. 86.
83. Pauck and Pauck, pp. 158–61.
84. Notes from address given by Wilhelm Pauck, "Paul Tillich: Autobiographical Thinker," NAPTS meeting, Chicago, Illinois, 31 October 1975.
85. Pauck and Pauck, p. 160.
86. H. Tillich, *From Time to Time*, pp. 182–83, 189.
87. Pauck and Pauck, pp. 163, 171, 173–74, 181.
88. Pauck, "Paul Tillich: Autobiographical Thinker."
89. Pauck and Pauck, p. 313, fn. 93.
90. *MTD*.
91. Stone, pp. 90, 92.
92. Pauck and Pauck, p. 191.
93. Stone, p. 91.
94. Pauck and Pauck, p. 192.
95. Stumme, p. 251.
96. Pauck and Pauck, p. 194.
97. Stumme, p. 153 fn. 3.
98. Pauck and Pauck, pp. 194–95, 315 fn. 2.
99. Stone, pp. 96–98.

100. Pauck and Pauck, pp. 184, 185, 186.
101. Ibid., p. 197.
102. Ibid., Stone, p. 99.
103. Pauck and Pauck, p. 197.
104. Stone, p. 99.
105. Pauck and Pauck, pp. 163, 320, fn. 64.
106. Stumme, p. 251.
107. Pauck and Pauck, pp. 198, 199.
108. Stumme, p. 251.
109. Stone pp. 107, 108.
110. Pauck and Pauck, pp. 202, 203, 204.
111. Stone, p. 108.
112. Pauck and Pauck, p. 204.
113. Stone, p. 112.
114. Pauck and Pauck, pp. 206–207.
115. H. Tillich, *From Time to Time*, pp. 235–43.
116. Stone, p. 112.
117. Stumme, p. 252.
118. Pauck and Pauck, pp. 208–10, 218.
119. Stone, p. 113.
120. Pauck and Pauck, pp. 210–218.
121. Ibid., pp. 229–231.
122. Ibid., pp. 237–238; Stone, p. 135.
123. Ibid., pp. 225–227.
124. Stone, pp. 148, 149.
125. Stone, pp. 117, 122–23.
126. Stumme, p. 254.
127. Pauck and Pauck, pp. 248–49, 174.
128. Ibid., p. 247.
129. H. Tillich, *From Time to Time*, pp. 197, 199, 202.
130. Pauck and Pauck, pp. 250–55, 264–65.
131. Stone, pp. 137, 138.
132. Eberhard Busch, *Karl Barth*, trans. by John Bowden (Philadelphia: Fortress Press, 1975), pp. 457–58.
133. Pauck and Pauck, pp. 268–69, 265, 326, fn. 57.
134. *FR*, p. 31.
135. Pauck and Pauck, pp. 258–59.
136. Stone, p. 151.
137. Pauck and Pauck, p. 259.
138. Stone, pp. 151–52.
139. H. Tillich, *From Place to Place* (New York: Stein and Day, 1976), pp. 99–106.
140. Pauck and Pauck, p. 257.
141. Tait, p. 23.
142. Pauck and Pauck, p. 256.
143. *FR*, p. 32.
144. Pauck and Pauck, pp. 271–72.
145. Paul Tillich, "Words by Paul Tillich," *Harvard Divinity Bulletin* 30 (1966):27–28.
146. H. Tillich, *From Time to Time*, pp. 217–18.
147. Pauck and Pauck, pp. 265–67.
148. *FR*, p. 9.
149. Pauck and Pauck, pp. 273–74.
150. Tait, p. 24.

151. Pauck and Pauck, pp. 276–78.
152. May, p. 106.
153. Pauck and Pauck, pp. 261–62; H. Tillich, *From Place to Place,* pp. 47, 48; 57–63.
154. Pauck and Pauck, p. 263.
155. Busch, pp. 470, 476.
156. Stone, p. 139.
157. Stone, pp. 142, 143.
158. Jerald C. Brauer, "Tillich According to the Paucks," *Christian Century* 93 (17 November 1976) :1019.
159. D. MacKenzie Brown, ed., *Ultimate Concern: Tillich in Dialogue* (New York: Evanston, 1956), p. xii.
160. Pauck and Pauck, pp. 278, 280.
161. *FR,* pp. 32–33, 35.
162. Pauck and Pauck, p. 257; Tait, p. 24.
163. Stone, p. 128.
164. Pauck and Pauck, pp. 280, 281.
165. H. Tillich, *From Time to Time,* p. 219.
166. Stone, p. 152.
167. *FR,* p. 7.
168. Pauck and Pauck, pp. 282–83.
169. H. Tillich, *From Time to Time,* pp. 219–22, 224; May, p. 105.
170. Pauck and Pauck, pp. 283–84; May, p. 107.
171. Ratschow, pp. 28–29, 31.
172. Pauck and Pauck, p. 168.
173. Ratschow, pp. 29–30.
174. *FR,* pp. 18–20.
175. Ibid., p. 20; Ratschow, p. 30; Carl E. Braaten, *Christ and Counter-Christ* (Philadelphia: Fortress Press, 1972), p. 57.
176. Stumme, pp. 252–53.
177. Stumme, pp. 254–55.
178. Pauck, "To Be or Not to Be," p. 19.

CHAPTER II
1. Raymond F. Bulman, *A Blueprint for Humanity: Paul Tillich's Theology of Culture* (East Brunswick, NJ: Associated University Presses, 1981), pp. 92, 97, 49, 69, 75, 78, 85.
2. Robert W. Schrader, *The Nature of Theological Argument: A Study of Paul Tillich,* Harvard Dissertations in Religion (Missoula, MT: Scholars Press, 1975), pp. 73–74.
3. Stone, p. 134.
4. Modras, p. 167.
5. Pauck, "To Be or Not to Be," p. 22.
6. John Powell Clayton, *The Concept of Correlation: Paul Tillich and the Possibility of a Mediating Theology* (Berlin: Walter de Gruyter, 1980), p. 5.
7. Pauck, "To Be or Not to Be," p. 23.
8. Schrader, pp. 73, 74.
9. Stone, p. 132.
10. Schrader, pp. 78–79.
11. *FR,* pp. 16–17.
12. Schrader, pp. 19, 23.
13. *HCT,* pp. xxvii–xxviii.
14. Schrader, pp. 25–26, 28, 41–43, 47–78, 52–53, 56, 58, 61, 65–70, 123–24, 138, 146.

CHAPTER III

1. Wayne Proudfoot, *God and the Self* (Cranbury, NJ: Associated University Presses, Inc., 1976), p. 23; Anders Nygren, *Meaning and Method* (Philadelphia: Fortress Press, 1972), p. 33.

2. *ST*, I:202–204.

3. John P. Dourley, *Paul Tillich and Bonaventure* (Leiden: E. J. Brill, 1975), pp. 4, 50–51, 54.

4. *ST*, I:225.

5. Ibid., pp. 3, 51; Adrian Thatcher, *The Ontology of Paul Tillich* (Oxford: Oxford University Press, 1978), pp. 102–103, 106, 111, 116.

6. *ST*, I:157–159, II:251.

7. Dourley, *Paul Tillich and Bonaventure*, pp. 59–61, 51–52.

8. Guyton B. Hammond, *Man in Estrangement: A Comparison of the Thought of Paul Tillich and Erich Fromm* (Nashville: Vanderbilt University Press, 1965), pp. 97–109.

9. Dourley, *Paul Tillich and Bonaventure*, pp. 3–4, 49, 55–57.

10. Thatcher, pp. 117–34.

11. Dourley, *Paul Tillich and Bonaventure*, pp. 1–4, 114, 165, 70, 67–68; Tillich, *ST*, III:395, 400–401, 422, II:118–19.

12. Thatcher, pp. 139–40; Hopper, p. 159.

13. Thatcher, pp. 140–41, 143, 146–47.

14. Hopper, p. 157.

15. Osborne, p. 193.

CHAPTER IV

1. *HCT*, pp. xvi–xvii, *ST*, III:301; I:104.

2. John P. Dourley, "Tillich's Evaluation of the Development of Western Christian Thought: Ontologism or Schizophrenia," *Tillich Studies: 1975*, ed. by John J. Carey (Tallahassee, FL: NAPTS, 1975), pp. 2–3.

3. Thatcher, pp. v, 158, 70, 94.

4. Tillich, *HCT*, pp. xiv.

5. Pauck, "To Be or Not to Be," p. 16.

6. James R. Lyons, ed., *The Intellectual Legacy of Paul Tillich* (Detroit: Wayne State Press, 1969), pp. 72, 73.

7. Walter Leibrecht, "The Life and Mind of Paul Tillich," in *Religion and Culture: Essays in Honor of Paul Tillich* (New York: Harper and Brothers, 1959), p. 7.

8. May, pp. 14, 15.

9. Thatcher, pp. 28, 45, 100.

10. *HCT*, p. xix.

11. Leibrecht, p. 7; Thatcher, pp. 85, 95; Bulman, p. 106.

12. *HCT*, pp. 31f.

13. *HCT*, pp. xix, xxi.

14. *HCT*, p. 112.

15. *HCT*, pp. 103–133, 185.

16. *HCT*, p. xxiii.

17. Ibid., pp. 158–165.

18. *HCT*, pp. 181–182; Dourley, *Paul Tillich and Bonaventure*, p. 30.

19. *HCT*, pp. 201–203; Thatcher, pp. 33, 85, 59.

20. *HCT*, pp. xxvii; 245–247.

21. Dourley, "Tillich's Evaluation," pp. 6–7; *HCT*, pp. 188, 201, 247, 248, 259.

22. Wayne G. Johnson, *Theological Method in Luther and Tillich* (Washington, D.C.: University Press of America, 1981).

23. *IH*, pp. 80–84; *HCT*, pp. 246, 480.

24. *HCT*, pp. xxvi–xix.
25. Nels F. S. Ferré, "Tillich and the Nature of Transcendence," in *Paul Tillich: Retrospect and Future* (Nashville: Abingdon Press, 1966), p. 11.
26. James Luther Adams, *Paul Tillich's Philosophy of Culture, Science and Religion* (New York: Harper and Row, 1965), p. 154.
27. Thatcher, pp. 59–60, 95, 54–55.
28. *HCT*, pp. 276–284.
29. *HCT*, pp. 284, 286.
30. *HCT*, pp. 286–287.
31. *HCT*, pp. 320–323; Clayton, pp. 34–35.
32. Osborne, pp. 52–53.
33. *PE*, p. xii.
34. *P*, p. 70.
35. Osborne, pp. 55–56.
36. Clayton, p. 42.
37. *P*, pp. 75, 94; Dourley, "Tillich's Evaluation," p. 8.
38. *HCT*, pp. xxx–xxxi.
39. *HCT*, pp. 390–402; *PE*, p. 105, *ST*, I:42.
40. Clayton, pp. 109, 42, 249.
41. Dourley, "Tillich's Evaluation," pp. 8–9.
42. *HCT*, pp. 410–429; Osborne, p. 78.
43. Clayton, pp. 132–34, 198; *HCT*, pp. 419–424.
44. *ST*, II:107; Clayton, pp. 229–30.
45. *P*, p. 142; *HCT*, p. 438.
46. Pauck, "To Be or Not to Be," p. 17.
47. Clayton, p. 92.
48. *HCT*, pp. 444–448; *P*, pp. 148–152.
49. John J. Carey, ed., *Kairos and Logos: Studies in the Roots and Implications of Tillich's Theology* (Cambridge, MA: NAPTS, 1978), pp. 23–24, 26.
50. Ibid., p. 23.
51. *Kairos and Logos*, pp. 31–33.
52. *Kairos and Logos*, pp. 32–33, 35–39.
53. *HCT*, pp. 473, 474; Osborne, pp. 39, 44.
54. *P*, p. 107; *ST*, II:34.
55. Osborne, pp. 42, 44–45.
56. *MSA*, p. 40.
57. Clayton, p. 135; *P*, pp. 142, 145; Stone, pp. 70f.
58. *MSA*, p. 40.
59. Bulman, pp. 52–53.
60. *MSA*, p. 40; *PE*, p. 85.
61. Bulman, pp. 53–54; Clayton, p. 138.
62. Clayton, pp. 137–38.
63. *HCT*, pp. 486–487; *P*, p. 180f. Bulman, pp. 52–53.
64. *P*, pp. 197f.
65. *LPJ*, pp. 36f., *ST*, II:63; *CTB*, pp. 156–177.
66. Guyton B. Hammond, *Man in Estrangement* (Nashville: Vanderbilt University Press, 1965), pp. 96, 102.
67. *MSA*, pp. 28–29.
68. Thatcher, pp. 57–58, *ST*, I:239; 172f.
69. Ibid., pp. 2, 3.
70. *OB*, pp. 42.
71. Clayton, p. 171.
72. Ibid., pp. 170–73; *Kairos and Logos*, pp. 149–52.

73. Thatcher, pp. 2–5, 17–18, 22–23.

74. Charles W. Kegley and Robert W. Bretall, eds., *The Theology of Paul Tillich* (New York: The Pilgrim Press, 1982), p. 14.

PART TWO:
TILLICH'S BASIC METHOD AND ITS OUTWORKING IN HIS SYSTEM

1. *ST*, I:3–6.
2. Ibid., pp. 6–8.; Pauck and Pauck, pp. 234–35.
3. Pauck, "To Be or Not to Be," p. 20.

CHAPTER V

1. John Dillenberger, "Paul Tillich: Theologian of Culture," in *Paul Tillich: Retrospect and Future*, p. 36.
2. May, p. 73.
3. Dillenberger, p. 36.
4. *FR*, pp. 29, 33.
5. *MSA*, pp. 45–46.
6. Dillenberger, pp. 37–38.
7. George F. Thomas, "The Method and Structure of Tillich's Theology," in Kegley and Bretall (1952), p. 88.
8. Dourley, *Paul Tillich and Bonaventure*, pp. 71, 187–88.
9. *TC*, pp. 45, 46, 49.
10. *MSA*, pp. 127, 130–32.
11. Osborne, p. 5.
12. Robert P. Scharlemann, *Reflection and Doubt in the Thought of Paul Tillich* (New Haven: Yale University Press, 1969), p. 155.
13. *ST*, III:201; Clayton, p. 68.
14. G. Thomas in Kegley and Bretall (1952), pp. 99–103.
15. Stone, pp. 143–44.

CHAPTER VI

1. *ST*, I:66–68.
2. Osborne, pp. 87–89.
3. *ST*, I: 72; Dourley, *Paul Tillich and Bonaventure*, pp. 73–74.
4. Ibid., pp. 75–76; Stone, p. 135; ST, I: 73f.
5. PE, 63–64
6. *ST*, I:76, 100.
7. *ST*, I: 94–98
8. *ST*, I: 79f.
9. *ST*, I: 80
10. Ibid., 240; DF, p. 41
11. Ibid., 239.
12. Ibid., 83–86.
13. Ibid., 86–89.
14. Ibid., 89–94 Dourley, *Paul Tillich and Bonaventure*, pp. 77–79; Stone, p. 136.
15. HCT, 186; Dourley, *Paul Tillich and Bonaventure*, p. 45.
16. Osborne, pp. 90, 92–94, 89–90.
17. *ST*, I:108–111.
18. Ibid., 111–115.
19. Ibid., 115–118.
20. Ibid., 118–126.

21. Ibid., 135–137.
22. *ST*, 1:137–43. Dourley, *Paul Tillich and Bonaventure*, pp. 97–98.
23. *ST*, 1:143–44.
24. Ibid., 147–150.
25. Ibid., 150–153.
26. Ibid., 153–155.
27. Ibid., 156–157.
28. *ST*, 1:157–59.
29. Ibid., 174–186.

CHAPTER VII
1. Osborne, p. 94.
2. Ibid., p. 95; *ST*, 1:176.
3. Osborne, p. 95; *ST*, 1:182.
4. *ST*, 1:168–171.
5. Ibid., 174–186.
6. Ibid., 186–192.
7. Ibid., 192–198.
8. Ibid., 198–201.
9. Ibid., 202–204.
10. *ST*, 1:163, 166, 168, 170, 175–76, 180, 184–85, 188–89, 191–93, 196, 198–200, 203–204; George Thomas, *Religious Philosophy of the West* (New York: Charles Scribner's Sons, 1965), pp. 389–403.
11. Thatcher, pp. 75–76.
12. *ST*, 1:205–208; *TC*, p. 23.
13. *ST*, 1:208–210; G. Thomas, pp. 404ff.
14. Ibid., 211–235.
15. Ibid., 235–249.
16. G. Thomas, pp. 405–407, 409–10, 421; *ST*, 1:209–11, 216, 233–39, 243–46.
17. *ST*, 1:249–52; G. Thomas, p. 411; Thatcher, p. 91.
18. *ST*, 1:253, 255.
19. *ST*, 11:6–7; G. Thomas, p. 411.
20. G. Thomas, pp. 412, 418; Dourley, *Paul Tillich and Bonaventure*, pp. 61–62; *ST*, 1:237.
21. *ST*, 1:261–270.
22. Ibid., 271–278.
23. Ibid., 278f.
24. *ST*, 1:279–89; G. Thomas, pp. 413–14.

CHAPTER VIII
1. Modras, p. 40.
2. Alexander J. McKelway, *The Systematic Theology of Paul Tillich: A Review and Analysis* (Richmond, VA: John Knox Press, 1964), p. 145.
3. Osborne, p. 109.
4. Scharlemann, pp. 150–51.
5. McKelway, pp. 145–46.
6. Thatcher, pp. 100–102.
7. *ST*, 11:23, 44; Robert E. Cushman, "The Christology of Paul Tillich," in *The Heritage of Christian Thought*, ed. by Robert E. Cushman and Egil Grislis (New York: Harper and Row, 1965), p. 168.
8. *ST*, 11:29, 37–38, 41, 50; Thatcher, p. 117; "Interrogation of Paul Tillich," conducted by William I. Reese, in *Philosophical Interrogations*, ed. by Sydney Rome and Beatrice Rome (New York: Holt, Rinehart and Winston, 1964), p. 400.

9. *ST,* II:37, 33, 40.
10. Bulman, p. 62.
11. *ST,* II:33, 35–39; Thatcher, p. 119.
12. *ST,* II:34–39.
13. *ST,* II:35–38, 40–43, 45.
14. Thatcher, pp. 119, 129–32.
15. Brown, pp. 184–85.
16. McKelway, p. 157.
17. *ST,* II:39f. Dourley, *Paul Tillich and Bonaventure,* p. 65.
18. *ST,* II:44, 91.
19. *ST,* I:255–56; II:43–44; Dourley, *Paul Tillich and Bonaventure,* p. 67; McKelway, p. 150.
20. *ST,* II:39–41; Cushman, pp. 179–80.
21. *ST,* II:34, 40, 50, 56; McKelway, pp. 151–52.
22. *ST,* II:44–78, 68; McKelway, pp. 152–55.
23. Osborne, p. 122.
24. *ST,* II:80–86
25. *ST,* II:86–88; McKelway, p. 157.
26. *ST,* II:89; Modras, p. 41.
27. *ST,* II:92; Modras, p. 42; Bulman, p. 88.
28. *ST,* II:125; Osborne, p. 164.
29. *ST,* II:97–99.
30. A. T. Mollegen, "Christology and Biblical Criticism in Tillich," in Kegley and Bretall (1952), pp. 231–234; "Interrogation of Paul Tillich," pp. 364, 367; *ST,* II:100–107.
31. *ST,* II:97, 99, 113–117.
32. Cushman, pp. 176–77.
33. Brown, pp. 143, 146–47, 155.
34. "Interrogation of Paul Tillich," pp. 364–67.
35. Brown, pp. 216–19.
36. *ST,* II:118–19, 121, 123–24, 126, 130, 133, 136; McKelway, pp. 161–63.
37. Osborne, p. 169.
38. *ST,* II:119.
39. Brown, pp. 214–15.
40. *ST,* II:141–42, 144–45; McKelway, pp. 163–64.
41. Brown, pp. 137–39.
42. *ST,* II:147–79, 94–95; McKelway, pp. 164–68.
43. McKelway, p. 168.
44. Thatcher, pp. 147–48.
45. *ST,* II:151–58.
46. Brown, p. 213.
47. McKelway, p. 171.
48. Ibid., p. 169; *ST,* II:159–65.
49. Osborne, pp. 177–78.
50. *ST,* II:165–168.
51. *ST,* II:168–76.
52. Osborne, pp. 180–81.
53. *ST,* II:176–80.

CHAPTER IX
1. *ST,* II:11–12; Osborne, p. 125.
2. McKelway, pp. 190–91.
3. *ST,* III:12–26; McKelway, p. 191; Osborne, p. 126.
4. Lyons, p. 50.

5. Bulman, pp. 174–75.
6. *ST*, III:22–28.
7. Bulman, p. 177.
8. McKelway, p. 192.
9. *ST*, III:26ff.; Bulman, p. 178.
10. Modras, pp. 59–60.
11. *ST*, III:32–50.
12. *ST*, III:69–70; McKelway, pp. 192–95.
13. *ST*, III:50–86; Osborne, pp. 131–32.
14. *ST*, III:86ff.; McKelway, p. 196.
15. *ST*, III:88–106; Osborne, p. 132.
16. *ST*, III:107; McKelway, p. 197.
17. *ST*, III:107–110.
18. *HCT*, pp. 230–31; Modras, p. 61.
19. *ST*, III:111–120; Modras, pp. 62–63.
20. *OB*, pp. 17–18; Paul Tillich, "Autobiographical Reflections," in Kegley and Bretall (1952), pp. 4–6.
21. *ST*, III:120–124; Modras, p. 109.
22. *ST*, III:122ff.; *PE*, p. 218.
23. Modras, p. 126.
24. *ST*, III:122; Modras, pp. 111–12; *PE*, pp. 112, 218.
25. Modras, p. 126; *ST*, III:123; *PE*, pp. 95–98.
26. *ST*, III:126f.
27. *ST*, III:124–28.
28. *ST*, III:129–138; McKelway, p. 202.
29. *ST*, III:138; Modras, p. 63.
30. *ST*, III:138–40.
31. Modras, p. 64.
32. *ST*, III:144–149; McKelway, pp. 202–203.
33. *ST*, III:149–152.
34. *ST*, III:152–155.
35. *HCT*, pp. 55, 133, 252–53.
36. *OB*, p. 67; *ST*, III:154f.
37. *ST*, III:162–172.
38. *ST*, III:172–182.
39. *ST*, III:182–216.
40. Paul Tillich, "Missions and World History," in *The Theology of Christian Mission*, ed. by Gerald H. Anderson (New York: McGraw and Hill, 1961), pp. 281–82.
41. *ST*, III:217–243.
42. *ST*, III:243–245
43. *PE*, p. 163.
44. *ST*, III:245–48.
45. Dillenberger, p. 32.
46. *ST*, III:249–65.
47. McKelway, p. 211.
48. *LPJ*, p. 76.
49. *ST*, III:267–68.
50. McKelway, pp. 217–18.
51. *ST*, III:269–75.
52. John J. Carey, "Morality and Beyond: Tillich's Ethics in Life and Death," in *Tillich Studies: 1975*, ed. by John J. Carey (Tallahassee: NAPTS, 1975), p. 107.
53. *MB*, p. 40.
54. Carey, pp. 109–110.

55. McKelway, p. 219.
56. *ST*, III:266–75; Dourley, *Paul Tillich and Bonaventure*, pp. 58–59.
57. *ST*, III:275–82.
58. Dourley, *Paul Tillich and Bonaventure*, p. 169.
59. Ibid., pp. 112–118; *ST*, III:283–94.
60. *LPJ*, p. 122; Dourley, *Paul Tillich and Bonaventure*, p. 113.

CHAPTER X
1. *ST*, III:297–299.
2. Hopper, p. 101.
3. *PE*, p. xvii.
4. Hopper, p. 101.
5. McKelway, p. 223.
6. *ST*, III:422; Osborne, p. 140.
7. Proudfoot, p. 78.
8. *ST*, III:300–11.
9. *PE*, p. 239; *IH*, pp. 194–96.
10. *ST*, III:311f., 341; Carl J. Armbruster, *The Vision of Paul Tillich* (New York: Sheed and Ward, 1967), pp. 247–78.
11. *ST*, III:311–13.
12. McKelway, pp. 226–27.
13. Ibid., p. 227; *ST*, III:315–18.
14. *PolEx*, pp. 150–51.
15. *TC*, p. 111.
16. *ST*, III:319–21; McKelway, p. 227.
17. *ST*, III:321–26; McKelway, p. 228.
18. *ST*, III:326–32.
19. Ibid., III:333f.; Brown, p. 121.
20. *ST*, III:334–39; McKelway, pp. 230–32.
21. *IH*, p. 282; *ST*, III:332.
22. *ST*, III:339–46; Armbruster, p. 251.
23. *ST*, III:346–48; McKelway, p. 233.
24. *ST*, III:348–50; Braaten, *Christ and Counter-Christ*, p. 56.
25. *ST*, III:350.
26. *TC*, p. 34.
27. *PolEx*, pp. 142–44; *ST*, III:351ff.
28. *ST*, III:352; McKelway, pp. 233–34.
29. *ST*, III:353; *PolEx*, p. 160.
30. *ST*, III:355–56; McKelway, p. 234.
31. *ST*, III:357–359; Armbruster, p. 357.
32. *ST*, III:359–61.
33. Ibid., III:362–64; McKelway, p. 237.
34. *IH*, pp. 242–65.
35. Armbruster, p. 256.
36. *ST*, III:365.
37. Tillich, "Missions and World History," pp. 286–87.
38. *IH*, p. 258.
39. *ST*, III:367–69.
40. *PE*, pp. 46–47.
41. *ST*, III:370–72; *PE*, p. 43.
42. Armbruster, p. 259; *ST*, III:371.
43. Armbruster, p. 259; *PE*, p. xvi.

44. *ST*, III:371–72.
45. "Interrogation of Paul Tillich," p. 406.
46. *Kairos and Logos*, p. 255.
47. *ST*, III:372–374.
48. *ST*, III:374–382.
49. *ST*, III:382–393.
50. McKelway, p. 242.
51. *ST*, III:394–96.
52. *EN*, pp. 125, 131.
53. *ST*, III:397–401.
54. Osborne, p. 115.
55. Armbruster, p. 264; *ST*, III:401–402.
56. Proudfoot, pp. 84–85.
57. *ST*, III:401–406; McKelway, p. 244.
58. *ST*, III:406–409.
59. *EN*, p. 76.
60. *ST*, III:409–13.
61. Paul Tillich, "Symbols of Eternal Life," *Harvard Divinity Bulletin* 26 (April 1962):9.
61a. *ST*, III:413f.
62. *ST*, III:415–19.
63. *ST*, III:418.
64. C. W. Christian, "Paul Tillich and the Life after Death," paper presented at the Southwestern Baptist Bible Teachers' Association, Fort Worth, TX, 12 March 1965, p. 8.
65a. *ST*, III:418f.
66. *ST*, III:419–20.
67. *BR*, pp. 77–78.
68. *ST*, III:420.
69. *BR*, p. 78; *NB*, p. 151.
70. *ST*, III:420–23.
71. Armbruster, p. 270.
72. Stumme, pp. 237, 238.
73. Armbruster, pp. 273–75.

PART THREE: TILLICH IN DIALOGUE WITH OTHER FAITHS

CHAPTER XI

1. *FR*, p. 32.
2. *ST*, III:6.
3. *FR*, pp. 91, 92, 80, 83.
4. *CE*, pp. 45–46.
5. Ibid., p. 56; *FR*, pp. 80–83.
6. *ST*, I:110–13.
7. *FR*, pp. 81–82.
8. *ST*, I:132–135; *ST*, II:120; *ST*, III:144, 364, 367f.
9. *CE*, 12f.
10. *FR*, pp. 86, 87; *ST*, I:139–40.
11. *ST*, I:140; *FR*, p. 87.
12. *ST*, I:40; Brown, p. 142.
13. *CE*, pp. 31–32, 57; *FR*, p. 87.
14. *FR*, pp. 87–89; Carl Braaten, *The Flaming Center: A Theology of the Christian Mission* (Philadelphia: Fortress Press, 1977), p. 111.

15. *CE*, pp. 81–82.
16. *FR*, p. 89.
17. *CE*, pp. 34–35, 59–61, 64–75.
18. Stone, pp. 152, 171 (fn. 58).
19. Paul Tillich, *The Construction of the History of Religion in Schelling's Positive Philosophy: Its Presuppositions and Principles* (Lewisburg, PA: Bucknell University Press, 1974), p. 31.
20. *CE*, pp. 94–97, 81, 84.
21. Robert Young, *Encounter with World Religions* (Philadelphia: Westminster Press, 1970), p. 142.
22. "Missions and World History," pp. 282–89.

CHAPTER XII

1. Stone, pp. 148; 101–102.
2. Glenn D. Earley, "An Analysis of 'Die Judenfrage—ein Christliches und ein Deutsches Problem,' Four Lectures Delivered by Paul Tillich in Berlin during 1952," paper written as preliminary work toward doctoral dissertation, pp. 15–16; cf also "Tillich and Judaism: An Analysis of the 'Jewish Question' " by Glen Earley in *Theonomy and Autonomy: Studies in Paul Tillich's Engagements with Modern Culture*, ed. by John Carey (Macon, Ga.: Mercer University Press, 1984).
3. *PolEx*, p. 152.
4. Earley, pp. 13–14.
5. Brown, p. 105.
6. Earley, pp. 13–14.
7. Earley, p. 16; Paul Tillich, "Nation of Time, Nation of Space," *Land Reborn* 8 (April–May 1957):5.
8. Ibid., p. 5.
9. Stone, p. 149.
10. Earley, pp. 16, 21.
11. Stone, p. 149.
12. "Nation," p. 5.
13. *PolEx*, pp. 150–51.
14. Stone, p. 149.
15. "Nation," p. 5.
16. *TC*, p. 36.
17. Earley, p. 14.
18. Brown, pp. 103–104, 107–109, 113–16.
19. "Missions and World History," p. 287.
20. Earley, pp. 18, 14; *PolEx*, p. 151.
21. *PolEx*, p. 151.
22. *TC*, p. 39.
23. Earley, p. 18.
24. Stone, p. 104, 148.
25. Earley, p. 18.
26. Stone, pp. 103–104.
27. Ibid., p. 147; Earley, pp. 7–8.
28. Earley, pp. 8–9, 21, 18–19; Brown, p. 105.
29. Paul Tillich, "Is There a Judeo-Christian Tradition?" *Judaism* 1 (April 1952):108.
30. Brown, pp. 105–106.
31. Earley, p. 19.
32. *TC*, p. 39.
33. Earley, pp. 19–20.

PART FOUR: EVALUATING TILLICH'S LIFE AND SIGNIFICANCE

CHAPTER XIII
1. See H. Tillich, *From Time to Time.*
2. Charlene Warnken, "Reflections on Paul Tillich," *The Houston Post* (29 September 1974), p. 2/AA.
3. See May, *Paulus.*
4. Warnken, p. 2/AA.
5. May, p. 56.
6. Seward Hiltner, "Tillich the Person: A Review Article," *Theology Today* XXX (1974):386.
7. Carey, "Morality and Beyond," p. 104.
8. May, pp. 57, 63.
9. Carey, "Morality and Beyond," pp. 104–105; May, p. 58.
10. Elliott Wright, "Paul Tillich as Hero: An Interview with Rollo May," *Christian Century* 91 (15 May 1974):530–33; May, pp. 53–54.
11. Wright, pp. 530–32.
12. See Pauck and Pauck, *Paul Tillich: His Life and Thought.*
13. Walter Laqueur, *Weimar: A Cultural History* (New York: G. P. Putnam's Sons, 1980), pp. 225–26.
14. Pauck and Pauck, pp. 275, 89–90.
15. *LPJ,* p. 117.
16. *MB,* p. 43.
17. Pauck and Pauck, p. 91; *NB,* p. 108.
18. Pauck and Pauck, pp. 87–89, 92; *LPJ,* p. 27.
19. Pauck and Pauck, pp. 275, 89; James Luther Adams, review of *Paul Tillich: His Life and Thought: Vol. 1: Life,* by Wilhelm and Marion Pauck, in *Union Seminary Quarterly Review* 32 (1976):45.
20. Paul Tillich, *The Shaking of the Foundations* (New York: Charles Scribner's Sons, 1948); pp. 153–163; Pauck and Pauck, pp. 93, 303 (fn. 74).
21. See Hiltner, "Tillich the Person," pp. 386–87.
22. Ibid., p. 385.
23. Pauck and Pauck, p. 89.
24. Hiltner, pp. 387–88.
25. Alexander J. McKelway, "New Perspectives on Paul Tillich," *Perspectives in Religious Studies* 4 (1977):178–79.
26. Carey, "Morality and Beyond," p. 109.
27. *EN,* pp. 139–40, 140.
28. *MB,* p. 43.
29. Carey, "Morality and Beyond," p. 109–11.
30. McKelway, *Systematic Theology of Paul Tillich,* pp. 217–19.

CHAPTER XIV
1. Ian Thompson, *Being and Meaning: Paul Tillich's Theory of Meaning, Truth and Logic* (Edinburgh: Edinburgh University Press, 1981), p. ix.
2. Thatcher, pp. 158, 160–61.
3. Thompson, pp. 16–17.
4. Clayton, p. 10.
5. Thompson, p. 8.
6. Ibid., p. 10.
7. Ibid., pp. 17–18.
8. Stone, p. 132.
9. Clayton, p. 7.

10. *OB*, p. 25.

11. Leonard F. Wheat, *Paul Tillich's Dialectical Humanism: Unmasking the God Above God* (Baltimore: Johns Hopkins Press, 1970), pp. 271–75.

12. Bulman, pp. 166, 173, 181–86.

13. David Kelsey, *The Fabric of Paul Tillich's Theology* (New Haven: Yale University Press, 1967), p. 195.

14. Ibid., p. 196.

15. Alan Richardson, *History Sacred and Profane* (London: SCM Press, 1964), pp. 129–31.

16. Kelsey, pp. 195–96.

17. McKelway, *Systematic Theology of Paul Tillich*, p. 258.

18. Cf. Ronald H. Nash, *The Word of God and Mind of Man* (Grand Rapids: Zondervan Publishing House, 1982), pp. 40–41, 131–32.

19. Thatcher, pp. 148–53.

20. Cushman, pp. 179–81; *ST*, II:161, 149–50.

21. Osborne, pp. 170–71, 176–77; *ST*, II:149.

22. McKelway, p. 216.

23. Donald G. Bloesch, *The Ground of Certainty: Toward an Evangelical Theology of Revelation* (Grand Rapids: William B. Eerdmans, 1971), p. 152.

24. Carl F. H. Henry, *God, Revelation and Authority*, 6 vols. (Waco: Word Books, 1976, 1979, 1982, 1983), 2(1976):282.

25. Dale Moody, *The Word of Truth: A Summary of Christian Doctrine Based on Biblical Revelation* (Grand Rapids: William B. Eerdmans, 1981), p. 31.

26. Thatcher, pp. 132–38.

27. Osborne, p. 203.

28. Eric Rust, *Salvation History: A Biblical Interpretation* (Richmond: John Knox Press, 1962), p. 127.

29. Moody, p. 304.

30. Braaten, *Christ and Counter-Christ*, pp. 63–64, 60–61.

31. Stumme, p. 240.

32. McKelway, p. 253.

33. Russell Aldwinckle, *Death in the Secular City* (Grand Rapids: William B. Eerdmans Publishing Co., 1972), p. 93; *ST*, III:419.

34. Nels F. S. Ferré, "Tillich's View of the Church," in Kegley and Bretall (1952), p. 263.

35. Aldwinckle, pp. 96–97, 99–100.

36. David E. Roberts, "Tillich's Doctrine of Man," in Kegley and Bretall (1952), p. 129.

37. Aldwinckle, pp. 118–19.

38. Thompson, pp. 16, 17, 21.

39. Thompson, pp. 6, 14–15.

40. Eric Rust, *Positive Religion in a Revolutionary Time* (Philadelphia: Westminster Press, 1970), p. 83.

41. Thompson, p. 26.

42. Ibid., pp. 26, 215; see H. D. Laswell, R. D. Casey and E. L. Smith, *Propaganda, Communication and Public Opinion 1935* (Princeton: Princeton University Press, 1946).

43. Ibid., pp. 27, 211.

44. Ibid., pp. 11, 12.

45. Ibid., pp. ix.

46. Bulman, pp. 195–96.

47. Paul Lehmann, "Review of Tillich's *The Protestant Era*," *Union Theological Seminary Quarterly Review* 4 (1949), quoted by Bulman, p. 196.

48. Clayton, p. 14; Ratschow, p. 34.

49. Thompson, pp. 14–15; *ST*, I:6.

50. Wayne G. Johnson, *Theological Method in Luther and Tillich* (Washington, D.C.: University Press of America, 1981).

51. James Luther Adams, "Tillich's Interpretation of History," in Kegley (1982), p. 344.

52. Thompson, p. 21.

53. Langdon Gilkey, "Tillich: The Master of Mediation," in Kegley (1982), p. 58.

54. Stone, pp. 154–56.

55. Ibid., pp. 143–44.

56. Clayton, pp. 4–6, *ST*, III:4.

57. Stone, p. 133.

58. John MacQuarrie, "Discussion: Tillich's Systematic Theology, vol. III," *Union Theological Seminary Quarterly Review* XIX (1964):349.

59. Thompson, p. 213; Ratschow, p. 34.

APPENDIX: SPECIAL TOPICS

1. Ratschow, pp. 23–24.

2. *PE*, pp. 200–205.

3. Ratschow, p. 23.

4. *PE*, pp. 32–51.

5. Stumme, pp. 31–32.

6. Pauck and Pauck, p. 59.

7. Hopper, pp. 62–63.

8. Stone, p. 52.

9. Stumme, pp. 27, 48.

10. Ibid., pp. 46, 67; Stone, p. 62.

11. Stone, pp. 61–62, 71, 78, 79.

12. *IH*, 77–122; Stone, p. 60. Cf. also "The Demonic Principles in Tillich's Doctrine of God" by H. Frederick Reisz, Jr., in *Theonomy and Autonomy: Studies in Paul Tillich's Engagement with Modern Culture*, ed. by John Carey (Macon, GA: Mercer University Press, 1984).

13. Bulman, p. 93.

14. Paul Tillich, *What Is Religion?* ed. by James Luther Adams (New York: Harper and Row, 1969), pp. 74–75, 115.

15. James Luther Adams, *Paul Tillich's Philosophy of Culture, Science and Religion*, (New York: Harper & Row, 1965), p. 61.

16. Brown, pp. 32–33.

17. *PE*, pp. 56, 57, 46; *ST*, I:148.

18. *PE*, pp. 46–47.

19. *P*, p. 26; Modras, p. 134.

20. Bulman, p. 211; Clayton, p. 198.

21. *RS*, p. 53.

22. Adams, p. 80; *RS*, p. 57; "Existentialist Aspects of Modern Art," p. 142.

23. Adams, pp. 81–83, 101–103, 106.

24. H. Tillich, *From Time to Time*, pp. 124–25.

25. *RS*, pp. 92–93.

26. Adams, pp. 95, 111; *RS*, p. 55.

27. "Existentialist Aspects of Modern Art," pp. 133–34, 144.

28. Paul Tillich, "Contemporary Protestant Architecture," in *Modern Church Architecture*, ed. by Albert Christ-Janer and Mary Mix Foley (New York: McGraw-Hill Book Co., Inc., 1962), pp. 122–23.

29. Paul Tillich and Theodore Green, "The Nature of Religious Art," in *Symbols and Society*, ed. by Lyman Bryson et al. (New York: Harper and Brothers, 1955), pp. 283–84.

30. *TC*, p. 48.
31. "Contemporary Protestant Architecture," pp. 123–24.
32. Paul Tillich, "Theology and Symbolism," in *Religious Symbolism*, ed. by F. Ernest Johnson (New York: Harper Brothers, 1955), p. 116.
33. "Contemporary Protestant Architecture," p. 125.
34. Adams, pp. 104–105, 107–10.
35. *PE*, p. 66.
36. Adams, p. 92.
37. Adams, pp. 93–94, 110–11.
38. "Existentialist Aspects of Modern Art," pp. 138–40.
39. Adams, pp. 68, 78.
40. Clayton, pp. 198–99.
41. Adams, p. 94.
42. *TC*, 43ff.
43. Adams, pp. 67–68.
44. Clayton, pp. 200–201.
45. *PE*, p. 67.
46. Adams, p. 112.
47. *PE*, 66–82; Clayton, p. 202.
48. Bulman, pp. 106–107.
49. *PE*, p. 76.
50. Bulman, p. 108.
51. *What Is Religion?* p. 78.

Selected Bibliography

The second edition of *The Theology of Paul Tillich*, edited by Charles W. Kegley (New York: Pilgrim Press, 1982), includes every known publication (except for book reviews) of Paul Tillich. *Religion and Culture: Essays in Honor of Paul Tillich*, edited by Walter Leibrecht (New York: Harper & Row, 1959), contains a list of Tillich's published writings from 1910 until 1958 including book reviews and prefaces. *Paul Tillich: A Comprehensive Bibliography and Keyword Index of Primary and Secondary Writings in English* (Metuchen, NJ and London: The Scarecrow Press, Inc., 1983) contains the writings of Tillich in English and dissertations, reviews, articles, and books about or related to Tillich in English. A bibliography of periodical literature on Paul Tillich (1972–1982) can be obtained from the Department of Religion, Florida State University, Tallahassee, Florida.

I. PRINCIPAL WORKS OF PAUL TILLICH USED IN THIS STUDY

A. Books

Biblical Religion and the Search for Ultimate Reality. Chicago: University of Chicago Press, 1955.

Christianity and the Encounter of the World Religions. New York: Columbia University Press, 1963.

The Construction of the History of Religion in Schelling's Positive Philosophy: Its Presuppositions and Principles. Lewisburg, PA: Bucknell University Press, 1974.

The Courage to Be. New Haven: Yale University Press, 1952.

Dynamics of Faith. New York: Harper & Row, 1957.

The Eternal Now. New York: Charles Scribner's Sons, 1963.

The Future of Religions. Edited by Jerald C. Brauer. New York: Harper & Row, 1966.

A History of Christian Thought: From Its Judaic and Hellenistic Origins to Existentialism. Edited by Carl E. Braaten. New York: Simon and Schuster, 1967.

The Interpretation of History. Translated by N. A. Rasetski and Elsa L. Talmey. New York: Charles Scribner's Sons, 1936.

Love, Power and Justice. New York: Oxford University Press, 1954.

Morality and Beyond. New York: Charles Scribner's Sons, 1963.

My Search for Absolutes. New York: Simon and Schuster, 1967.

My Travel Diary—1936: Between Two Worlds. Edited and with an introduction by Jerald C. Brauer. Translated by Maria Pelikan. New York: Harper & Row, 1970.

Mysticism and Guilt-Consciousness in Schelling's Philosophical Development. Translated by Victor Nuovo. Lewisburg, PA: Bucknell University Press, 1974.

The New Being. New York: Charles Scribner's Sons, 1955.

On the Boundary: An Autobiographical Sketch. New York: Charles Scribner's Sons, 1966.

Political Expectation. Edited with an introduction by James Luther Adams. New York: Harper & Row, 1971.

The Protestant Era. Translated by James Luther Adams. Chicago: University of Chicago Press, 1948.

The Religious Situation. Translated by H. Richard Niebuhr. New York: Meridian Books, 1956.

The Shaking of the Foundations. New York: Charles Scribner's Sons, 1948.

The Socialist Decision. Translated by Franklin Sherman. New York: Harper & Row, 1977.

Systematic Theology. 3 vols. Chicago: University of Chicago Press, 1951, 1957, 1963.

Theology of Culture. Edited by Robert C. Kimball. New York: Oxford University Press, 1959, 1965.

Ultimate Concern: Tillich in Dialogue. Edited by D. MacKenzie Brown. New York: Evanston, 1956.

What Is Religion? Edited and with an introduction by James Luther Adams. New York: Harper & Row, 1969.

B. Articles

"Contemporary Protestant Architecture." *Modern Church Architecture.* Edited by Albert Christ-Janer and Mary Mix Foley. New York: McGraw-Hill Co., Inc., 1962. pp. 122–25.

"Existentialist Aspects of Modern Art." *Christianity and the Existentialists.* Edited by Carl Michalson. New York: Charles Scribner's Sons, 1956. pp. 128–47.

"Interrogation of Paul Tillich," conducted by William I. Reese. *Philosophical Interrogations.* Edited by Sydney Rome and Beatrice Rome. New York: Holt, Rinehart and Winston, 1964. pp. 355–409.

"The Jewish Question: Christian and German Problem." *Jewish Social Studies* 33 (1971).

"Kairos." *A Handbook of Christian Theology*. Edited by Marvin Halverson and Arthur A. Cohen. New York: Meridian Books, 1958. pp. 193–97.

"The Kingdom of God and History." *The Kingdom of God and History*. Edited by H. B. Wood et al. Chicago: Willett, Clark, 1938. pp. 107–41.

"The Meaning and Justification of Religious Symbols." *Religious Experience and Truth*. Edited by Sydney Hook. New York: New York University Press, 1961. pp. 3–11.

"Missions and World History." *The Theology of Christian Mission*. Edited by Gerald H. Anderson. New York: McGraw & Hill, 1961. pp. 281–89.

"Nation of Time, Nation of Space." *Land Reborn* 8 (April–May 1957):4–5.

"The Nature of Religious Art," with Theodore M. Greene. *Symbols and Society*. Edited by Lyman Bryson et al. New York: Harper Brothers, 1955.

"The Religious Symbol." *Journal of Liberal Religion* 2 (Summer 1940):13–33.

"Symbols of Eternal Life." *Harvard Divinity Bulletin* 26 (April 1962):1–10.

"Theology and Symbolism." *Religious Symbolism*. Edited by F. Ernest Johnson. New York: Harper Brothers, 1955. pp. 107–16.

"Tillich-to-Thomas Mann Letter (23 May 1943)." *The Intellectual Legacy of Paul Tillich*. Edited by James R. Lyons. Detroit: Wayne State University Press, 1969. pp. 101–107.

II. PRINCIPAL WORKS ABOUT PAUL TILLICH USED IN THIS STUDY

A. Books

Adams, James Luther. *Paul Tillich's Philosophy of Culture, Science and Religion*. New York: Harper & Row, 1965.

Armbruster, C. J. *The Vision of Paul Tillich*. New York: Sheed and Ward, 1967.

Braaten, Carl E. *Christ and Counter-Christ*. Philadelphia: Fortress Press, 1972.

_____. *The Flaming Center: A Theology of the Christian Mission*. Philadelphia: Fortress Press, 1977.

_____. *The Future of God: The Revolutionary Dynamics of Hope*. New York: Harper & Row, 1969.

Bulman, Raymond F. *A Blueprint for Humanity: Paul Tillich's Theology of Culture*. East Brunswick, NJ: Associated University Presses, 1981.

Carey, John J., ed. *Kairos and Logos: Studies in the Roots and Implications of Tillich's Theology*. Cambridge, MA: NAPTS, 1978.

Carey, John J., ed. *Theonomy and Autonomy: Studies in Paul Tillich's Engagements with Modern Culture*. Macon, GA: Mercer University Press, 1984.

_____. *Tillich Studies: 1975*. Tallahassee, FL: NAPTS, 1975.

Clayton, John Powell. *The Concept of Correlation: Paul Tillich and the Possibility of a Mediating Theology*. Berlin: Walter de Gruyter, 1980.

Dourley, J. P. *Paul Tillich and Bonaventure*. Leiden: E. J. Brill, 1975.

Ferré, Nels F. S. et al. *Paul Tillich: Retrospect and Future*. Nashville: Abingdon, 1966.

Hamilton, Kenneth. *The System and the Gospel: A Critique of Paul Tillich*. New York: Macmillan, 1963.

Hammond, Guyton B. *Man in Estrangement: A Comparison of the Thought of Paul Tillich and Erich Fromm*. Nashville: Vanderbilt University Press, 1965.

————. The Power of Self-Transcendence: An Introduction *to the Philosophical Theology of Paul Tillich.* St. Louis: Bethany Press, 1966.

Hopper, David. *Tillich: A Theological Portrait.* New York: J. B. Lippincott, Co., 1968.

Johnson, Wayne. *Theological Method in Luther and Tillich.* Washington, D.C.: University Press of America, 1981.

Keefe, Donald J. *Thomism and the Ontological Theology of Paul Tillich: A Comparison of Systems.* Leiden: E. J. Brill, 1971.

Kegley, Charles W. and Bretall, Robert W., eds. *The Theology of Paul Tillich.* New York: Macmillan, 1952, 1961, 1964; New York: Pilgrim Press, 1982.

Kelsey, David. *The Fabric of Paul Tillich's Theology.* New Haven: Yale University Press, 1967.

Killen, R. Allan. *The Ontological Theology of Paul Tillich.* Kampen: J. H. Kok, 1956.

Leibrecht, Walter. *Religion and Culture: Essays in Honor of Paul Tillich.* New York: Harper & Brothers, 1959.

Lyons, James R., ed. *The Intellectual Legacy of Paul Tillich.* Detroit: Wayne State Press, 1969.

Macleod, Allistair. *Tillich: An Essay on the Role of Ontology in His Philosophical Theology.* London: Allen & Unwin, 1973.

Mahan, Wayne W. *Tillich's System.* San Antonio, TX: Trinity University Press, 1974.

Martin, Bernard. *The Existentialist Theology of Paul Tillich.* New York: Bookman Associates, 1963.

May, Rollo. *Paulus: Reminiscences of a Friendship.* New York: Harper & Row, 1973.

McKelway, Alexander J. *The Systematic Theology of Paul Tillich: A Review and Analysis.* Richmond, VA: John Knox Press, 1964.

Modras, Ronald E. *Paul Tillich's Theology of the Church.* Detroit: Wayne State University Press, 1976.

O'Meara, Thomas A. and Weisser, C. D., eds. *Paul Tillich in Catholic Thought.* Dubuque, Iowa: Priory Press, 1964.

Osborne, Kenan B. *New Being: A Study of the Relationship Between Conditioned and Unconditioned Being According to Paul Tillich.* The Hague: Martinus Nijhoff, 1969.

Pauck, Wilhelm and Pauck, Marion. *Paul Tillich: His Life and Thought.* New York: Harper & Row, 1976.

Ratschow, Carl Heinz. Paul Tillich. Translated by Robert P. Scharlemann. Iowa City, IO: NAPTS, 1980.

Ross, Robert. *The Non-Existence of God: Linguistic Paradox in Tillich's Thought.* New York: Edwin Mellen Press, 1978.

Rowe, W. L. *Religious Symbols and God: A Philosophical Study of Tillich's Theology.* Chicago: University of Chicago Press, 1968.

Scharlemann, Robert P. *Reflection and Doubt in the Thought of Paul Tillich.* New Haven: Yale University Press, 1969.

Schrader, Robert W. *The Nature of Theological Argument: A Study of Paul Tillich.* Harvard Dissertations in Religion. Missoula, MT: Scholars Press, 1975.

Stone, Ronald H. *Paul Tillich's Radical Social Thought.* Atlanta: John Knox Press, 1980.

Stumme, John R. *Socialism in Theological Perspective: A Study of Paul Tillich, 1918–1933.* American Academy of Religion Dissertation Series, no. 21. Missoula, MT: Scholars Press, 1978.

Tait, Leslie Gordon. *The Promise of Paul Tillich.* New York: J. B. Lippincott, 1971.

Tavard, George H. *Paul Tillich and the Christian Message.* New York: Charles Scribner's Sons, 1962.

Thatcher, Adrian. *The Ontology of Paul Tillich.* Oxford: Oxford University Press, 1978.

Thomas, John Heywood. *Paul Tillich.* Richmond: John Knox Press, 1966.

―――. *Paul Tillich: An Appraisal.* Philadelphia: Westminster Press, 1963.

Thompson, Ian E. *Being and Meaning: Paul Tillich's Theory of Meaning, Truth and Logic.* Edinburgh: Edinburgh University Press, 1981.

Tillich, Hannah. *From Place to Place.* New York: Stein and Day, 1976.

―――. *From Time to Time.* New York: Stein and Day, 1973.

Unhjem, Arne. *Dynamics of Doubt: A Preface to Tillich.* Philadelphia: Fortress Press, 1966.

Wheat, Leonard F. *Paul Tillich's Dialectical Humanism: Unmasking the God above God.* Baltimore: Johns Hopkins Press, 1970.

B. Articles

Carey, John J. "Morality and Beyond: Tillich's Ethics in Life and Death." *Tillich Studies: 1975.* Edited by John J. Carey. Tallahassee: NAPTS, 1975.

Cushman, Robert E. "The Christology of Paul Tillich." *The Heritage of Christian Thought.* Edited by Robert E. Cushman and Egil Grislis. New York: Harper & Row, 1965.

Dillenberger, John. "Paul Tillich: Theologian of Culture." *Paul Tillich: Retrospect and Future.* Nashville: Abingdon, 1966.

Fisher, James V. "The Politicizing of Paul Tillich: The First Phase." *Tillich Studies: 1975.* Edited by John J. Carey. Tallahassee: NAPTS, 1975.

Hiltner, Seward. "Tillich the Person: A Review Article." *Theology Today* XXX (1974):382–88.

Pauck, Wilhelm. "To Be or Not to Be: Paul Tillich on the Meaning of Life." *The American Academy of Arts and Sciences Bulletin* XXXIII (November 1979):9–25.

Wright, Elliott. "Paul Tillich as Hero: An Interview with Rollo May." *Christian Century* 91 (15 May 1974):530–33.

III. PRINCIPAL GENERAL WORKS OF REFERENCE USED IN THIS STUDY

Driver, Tom F. *Patterns of Grace: Human Experience as Word of God.* San Francisco: Harper & Row, 1977.

Gay, Peter. *Weimar Culture: The Outsider As Insider.* New York: Harper & Row, 1970.

Gilkey, Langdon. *Maker of Heaven and Earth: The Christian Doctrine of Creation in the Light of Modern Knowledge.* Garden City, NY: Doubleday Anchor, 1965.

Proudfoot, Wayne. *God and the Self.* Cranbury, NJ: Associated University Presses, Inc., 1976.

Richardson, Alan. *History Sacred and Profane.* London: SCM Press, 1964.

Rust, Eric. *Positive Religion in a Revolutionary Time.* Philadelphia: Westminster Press, 1970.

Tracy, David. *Blessed Rage for Order: The New Pluralism in Theology.* New York: Seabury Press, 1975.

Index of Principal Persons

Index of Principal Subjects